Benjamin Tabart's Juvenile Library

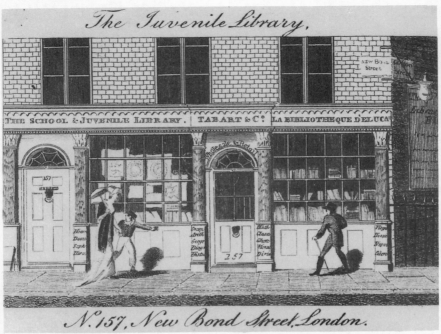

A view of the shop, from *Visits to the Juvenile Library* by Eliza Fenwick, 43(1).
Sotheby's

Inside the shop, from *A visit to London* by Elizabeth Kilner, 94(2)

Benjamin Tabart's shop in Bond Street

Benjamin Tabart's Juvenile Library

A bibliography of books for children
published, written, edited and sold by
Mr. Tabart, 1801–1820

MARJORIE MOON

1990
St Paul's Bibliographies
Winchester · Hampshire
Omnigraphics
Penobscot Building · Detroit

First published in Great Britain 1990
by St Paul's Bibliographies
1 Step Terrace, Winchester SO22 5BW
and in the United States by Omnigraphics
Penobscot Building, Detroit

Also by Marjorie Moon

The children's books of Mary (Belson) Elliott: a bibliography

John Harris's Books for Youth 1801–1843: a check-list

British Library Cataloguing in Publication Data
Moon, Marjorie
Benjamin Tabart's juvenile library: a bibliography
of books for children published, written, edited
and sold by Mr Tabart 1801–1820
1. Children's stories in English. Tabart, Benjamin
Bibliographies
I. Title   II. Alderson, Brian W.
016.8237

ISBN 0–906795–89–3

Library of Congress Card No. 90–53250

Typeset by Nene Phototypesetters Ltd, Northampton
Printed by Henry Ling Ltd, The Dorset Press, Dorchester
on Long Life paper ∞
and bound at Green Street Bindery, Oxford.

Contents

Erratum Page 127. Second paragraph: for Riley's read Ryland's

Illustrations

Where no source is shown, the illustration is taken from a book in the compiler's collection. Mr Alderson and Messrs Sotheby's are thanked warmly for their kindness in providing other illustrations.

Preface

Among the early-nineteenth-century publishers of children's books there are few who offer a more attractive field for research than Benjamin Tabart; but my enthusiasm has been curbed by the constant intrusion of Sir Richard Phillips into the landscape. I have found that many of the booklists headed 'Published by Tabart and Co.' are composed, largely and disappointingly, of Phillips's titles; so, in order to keep that fair field of literary flowers which was Mr. Tabart's charming contribution to the lighter side of children's literature from being overgrown by Greek lexicons and Latin grammars, dictionaries and history books and other useful works of reference and learning, I have assumed an unscholarly right of selection.

Certainly Tabart's name does appear, in some capacity, on the title-pages of a good number of educational works; and every one of these, to the best of my knowledge, is included in Part I of this bibliography. But there were many others with which he seems to have had no personal connection but which he did advertise, and most of these have been left out unless there seemed to be some good reason for admitting them.

One of the arguments for inclusion has been the mention of certain titles in Eliza Fenwick's *Visits to the Juvenile Library* and Elizabeth Kilner's *A visit to London*; another has been Tabart's more-frequent-than-usual advertising of a title – especially if it was an entertaining book, like Bingley's *Animal Biography*. However, these dubious titles are not included in the main bibliography but are relegated to Part II. (Perhaps, as time goes by, editions of some of them may even be found which do, in fact, carry Tabart's name on their title-pages.) This flexibility of treatment is intended to give a survey of the resources of a children's bookshop at the beginning of the last century, where agreeable food for the imagination was available as well as more solid nourishment for the mind.

Another irregularity is found in the numbering of editions, particularly those of the booklets in the Tales for the Nursery series. 'New edition' must sometimes be understood to mean 'a new edition of an old tale'; but I cannot offer any plausible explanation of the inconsequential numbering of some of the editions, particularly those of *Cinderella*.

The following notes will explain how the books are described:

Listing Items are listed alphabetically, under authors where known. Anonymous books are placed under the first word of the titles excepting 'A' or 'The'. In the Index books are listed under both title and author.

Numbering of entries Items are numbered consecutively for easy reference, showing the main integer, followed by a subsidiary number in round brackets, (1) denoting the first and main entry and (2) and after marking later printings. This does not mean that (1) is the first edition: it means that this entry is the earliest recorded for the purpose of this bibliography. Nor does (5) necessarily mean the 5th edition but only that it is the fifth subdivision.

Bibliographical descriptions   The text of the title-page is given in full, except in a few instances where indicated, using original spelling and punctuation but not original typography.

Then come details of the size of the title-leaf (height before width); the printer's name and address, unless included in the title; the number of pages; details of the illustrations, if any; and the style of binding.

Locations of copies are preceded by a square bracket and their abbreviations are listed and explained on p. xiv. The names of private owners are not shown in the descriptions because so often private collections change hands, but the collectors who have kindly helped me with information are named and acknowledged on p. xi.

Other information   After the bibliographical details come notes about such matters as entries at Stationers' Hall, American reprints and other points not mentioned above. Where it seems desirable or interesting, these are followed by a summary or indication of the material in the book. And here is an opportunity to explain my sometimes lengthy and often opinionated remarks, which may seem to exceed the requirements of a bibliography.

Many of the books described are very rare and not easily accessible to students of early children's literature. As I have had the advantage of handling and reading a good many of them, I have tried to make the entries form a brief survey of the sort of books which were on sale in a children's bookshop in the first two decades of the nineteenth century. The period was not often distinguished by imaginative or exciting stories and most of the instructive works made little attempt to arouse a child's interest, so that, when I have come across books that were written with a real feeling for the child-reader's enjoyment, I have perhaps given them more praise than they would receive had they been published today. Even so, the best of Tabart's books shine among the majority of their dull, moralistic and factual contemporaries.

Finally come notices from contemporary periodicals and from *The juvenile review*, which was not a periodical but an examination, published in 1817, of books for children. It was compiled by an admirer of Mrs. Trimmer's *Guardian of education* but, unlike that highly critical magazine, it only set out to discuss *approved* books, and so lacks the interesting acerbity of the earlier publication. It was reprinted in 1982 by Toronto Public Library.

Winchester, 1990   MARJORIE MOON

Acknowledgements

A bibliography is, in appearance, a dry, inhuman compilation of titles, dates and specifications and, to the uninitiated, the work of collecting this information might seem to be equally soulless; but one of the great pleasures of bibliographical research is the very genuine kindness and assistance which one's enquiries elicit.

The libraries and institutions which I have listed below have taken great pains to answer my queries and I am most grateful to them; yet a bibliography of this kind, whose components are widely scattered, could never be successful were it not also for the generous help given by private collectors (and here I would emphasise the value of consulting as many of them as possible, because a rare, even unique, book may be found in a small collection).

Private sources

So I thank most sincerely the following collectors and correspondents: first, Mr Brian Alderson, who has contributed an essay (Appendix D) summarizing his researches into the peculiarities in the engraved illustrations to two of Tabart's picture-and-verse books; and who, throughout my preparation of this bibliography, has given me much help and kindly advice; and Mrs Iona Opie, who, among other kindnesses, allowed me to study her Tabart books before the collection went to the Bodleian Library. To Miss Margaret Weedon I am very grateful, not only for the information she gave me about her own Tabart holdings, but also for doing some research for me in the Bodleian when I was unable to go there myself.

I also give warmest thanks to Mr Lawrence Darton, who has generously supplied me with a great many details about Tabart's titles which were later acquired by his publishing ancestors; to Mr R. D. A. Newbury, who gave me useful information about books in his collection; and to Mrs Valerie Alderson for her help in research. I am very grateful to Dr L. G. E. Bell, to Mr Lloyd E. Cotsen and his librarian, Mrs Andrea Immel, and to Miss M. P. Pollard. I have had valuable and much-appreciated assistance from Mrs G. Cockshut (Gillian Avery), Mr Peter Stockham, Mr Stuart Brenner, Mr Eric Quayle, Mr Frederick R. Gardner, Mrs Barbara Muir, Dr T. D. Hobbs of Trinity College Library, Cambridge, Mr Wilbur Smith (formerly of the University of California Research Library, Los Angeles), Mr K. N. Bloch, Sister April O'Leary and Miss Judith St John, the late Head of the Osborne Collection in Toronto. I also wish to thank Mr William St Clair for information concerning William and Mary Jane Godwin.

Last, but very far from least in my debt of gratitude, I was delighted when, late in the preparation of this bibliography, I made fortunate contact with

Miss Jane Evans, who was exploring the history of her mother's ancestors, the Tabart family. I am deeply grateful to Jane for so generously sharing with me the results of her painstaking researches, which have given the breath of life to Benjamin Tabart, hitherto regarded as 'a shadowy figure' or 'a projection of Richard Phillips'. Jane is descended from Francis Gerard Tabart's eldest daughter who eloped to Gretna Green in 1830.

Libraries and institutions consulted, personally or by mail, to whom my thanks are due:

American Antiquarian Society, Worcester, Mass., USA

Baldwin Library *see* Florida

Bath Reference Library and Mrs M. Joyce

Birmingham Reference Library and Ms Niky Rathbone

Bodleian Library, Oxford, and Mr Clive Hurst; the John Johnson Library, and the Opie Collection; with special acknowledgement for permission to quote from Tabart's catalogue.

British Columbia University Library, Vancouver, Canada, and Professor Sheila A. Egoff

British Library, London, and the staff members who have been so helpful over the years

California, University of, Research Library, and Mr James Davis for much kind help

Cambridge University Library and Mr B. Jenkins

Christ Church College Library, Canterbury, Kent

Columbia University, Butler Library, New York, and Mr Rudolph Ellen-bogen

Columbia University Teachers College, New York, and Mr David M. Ment

Connecticut Historical Society, Hartford, USA

Devon County Library, Exeter

Eton College Library, Windsor, Berkshire

Florida, University of, Libraries, Gainesville, USA, and the late Dr Ruth Baldwin for much kind help and information, including the text of William Godwin's Preface to his *Bible Stories*

Froebel Institute College, Roehampton, and Miss Felicity Lander

Guildhall Library, London

Harris Public Library, Preston (Spencer Collection) and Miss Mena Williams

Hockliffe Collection, Bedford College of Higher Education, and Miss Sauls-bury and Mr John Crompton

Hove Central Library, Sussex

Hull, University of (Brynmor Jones Library) and Mr R. F. Smeaton

Huntington Library, San Marino, California, USA

Leeds University Library and Mr J. R. V. Johnson

Leicester University School of Education Library, and Mr Roy Kirk

Lilly Library, Indiana University, Bloomington, USA, and Mr Joel Silver

Liverpool University School of Education Library and Mr J. E. Vaughan

Melbourne University Library, Australia, and Miss Mary Lugton

Miami University Library, Oxford, Ohio, USA, and Mrs Frances D. McClure

National Library of Scotland, Edinburgh, and Mr John Morris

Newcastle upon Tyne School of Education Library

Norfolk Museums Service, Norwich, and Mr John Renton

North Yorkshire County Library, Harrogate, and Ms Margaret Schofield and Mr P. C. Daw

Nottingham University Library and Ms M. L. Clarke

Osborne Collection *see* Toronto Public Library

Pennsylvania, University of, Philadelphia, USA, and Mr Stephen Lehmann

Philadelphia Free Library and Ms Karen Lightner and Mr Walter A. Frankel

Pierpont Morgan Library, New York, and Ms Janice Matthiesen, Ms Anna Lou Ashby and Mr Felix Oyens

Reading University Library and Mr Michael Bott

Ross County Historical Society (the McKell Collection) and Mr Brian Hackett

St Bride Printing Library, London, and Mrs Louise Craven

Somerset County Library, Bridgwater, and Mr Paul Smith

Sotheby's, New Bond Street, London, and especially to Mr Michael Heseltine

Southern Mississippi University (de Grummond Collection), Hattiesburg, USA, and Mr John Kelly

Theatre Museum *see* Victoria and Albert Museum

Toronto Public Library (the Osborne Collection) and Mrs Margaret Maloney and Ms Dana Tenny; I am especially grateful to the Library for permission to quote from Lady Fenn's letter

Victoria and Albert Museum Library, and Miss Anne Hobbs; also the Renier Collection and Mrs Tessa Chester; and the Theatre Museum and Mrs Rhiannon Finamore

Wayne State University Libraries, Detroit, USA

Westminster City Libraries, London

Yale University Library, New Haven, USA, and Ms Melissa C. Flannery

Abbreviations and symbols

denoting locations of books and sources of information

Baldwin	Baldwin Library, University of Florida, Gainesville, USA
Ball	Originally in the collection of Miss Elisabeth Ball, now dispersed, and this item not located
Bath	Reference Library, Bath
Birm.	Reference Library, Birmingham
BL	British Library, London
Bod.	Bodleian Library, Oxford
Bod J	John Johnson Collection in the Bodleian Library, Oxford
CBY	Exhibition catalogue, 'Children's books of yesterday' National Book League, Wandsworth, 1946
Cheltm	St Mary's College, Cheltenham
Columbia U	Rare Book and MS Library, Columbia University, New York, USA
CUL	University Library, Cambridge
De Grummond	University of Southern Mississippi Library, Hattiesburg, USA
ECB	English Catalogue of Books
Exeter	County Library, Exeter
FCB	A.W. Tuer, *Pages and pictures from forgotten children's books*, Leadenhall Press, 1898–9
Froebel	Froebel Institute College, Roehampton
Gum.	Catalogue of Gumuchian & Cie, *Les livres de l'enfance* (reprint), Holland Press, London, 1967
Hirsch	Catalogue of Daniel Hirsch, Hopewell Junction, USA
Hobbyhorse	Catalogue of Hobbyhorse Books, Inc., Ho-Ho-Kus, USA
Hockliffe	Hockliffe Collection, College of Higher Education, Bedford
Holtom	Catalogue of C. Holtom, Bristol
Huntington	Huntington Library, San Marino, USA
Leics U	University Library, Leicester
Lilly	Lilly Library, Indiana University, Bloomington, USA
Liv U	School of Education Library, Liverpool
McKell	McKell Collection, Ross County Historical Society, Chillicothe, USA
Melb.	University of Melbourne, Parkville, Australia
Miami	Miami University Library, Oxford, USA

MLA	Monthly Literary Advertiser, London
Morgan	Catalogue (1976) of exhibition, 1911, by F. C. Morgan, Malvern Public Library
Muir	Percy Muir, *English children's books*, Batsford, 1954
NLS	National Library of Scotland, Edinburgh
Norwich	Bridewell Museum, Norwich
Nottm U	University of Nottingham, Briggs Collection
NYCL	North Yorkshire County Library, Harrogate
OFCB	A. W. Tuer, *Stories from old-fashioned children's books*, Leadenhall Press, 1899–1900
Opie	Opie Collection, Bodleian Library, Oxford
Osborne	Osborne Collection, Toronto Public Library, Canada
Phila.	Free Library of Philadelphia, Philadelphia, USA
PML	Pierpont Morgan Library, New York, USA
Reading U	University of Reading Library, Whiteknights, Reading
Renier	Renier Collection, Bethnal Green Museum, London
S	Sotheby's catalogue(s), London
Som.	Somerset County Library, Bridgwater
Spencer	Spencer Collection, Harris Public Library, Preston
Sunderland	Sunderland Public Libraries, Sunderland
TCCU	Teachers' College, Columbia University, New York, USA
UBC	University of British Columbia, Vancouver, Canada
UCLA	University of California, Los Angeles, USA
V & A	The Library, Victoria & Albert Museum, London
Wandsworth	Wandsworth Public Libraries, London
Wayne	Catalogue of Eloise Ramsey Collection, Wayne State University Library, Detroit, USA
Welch	d'Alte A. Welch, *A bibliography of American children's books*, American Antiquarian Society, 1972
Whitehouse	F. R. B. Whitehouse, *Table games of Georgian and Victorian days*, London, 1951
Yale U	Yale University Library, New Haven, USA

Don Locke: *A fantasy of reason*, Routledge & Kegan Paul, 1980
Iona and Peter Opie: *The classic fairy tales*, Oxford University Press, 1974
————: *The Oxford dictionary of nursery rhymes*, Clarendon Press, Oxford, 1951
  et seq.
S. Roscoe: *John Newbery and his successors 1740–1814*, Five Owls Press Ltd, 1973
William St Clair: *The Godwins and the Shelleys*, Faber & Faber, 1989
George Speaight: *Juvenile drama*, Macdonald, 1946
W. B. Todd: *A directory of printers, 1800–1840*, Printing Historical Society,
  London, 1972
Die verkehrte Welt – The topsy-turvy world: catalogue of exhibition by the Goethe
  Institute, Amsterdam, etc., 1985
A. F. Wedd: *The fate of the Fenwicks*, Methuen, 1927

Abbreviations used in describing books

advt(s)	advertisement(s)
bd(s)	board(s)
bk, bklist	book, booklist
c.	*circa* (about)
cat.	catalogue
cm.	centimetre(s)
coll.	collection
edn	edition
eng., engvd	engraving, engraved
fp	full-page
FP, FPP	frontispiece(s)
g	gilt or gold
h/c	hand-coloured
illusn	illustration
imp.	imperfect
impt	imprint
inc.	including
MS	manuscript
n.d.	no date
p., pp.	page(s)
pl., pls	plate(s)
pr	printed
prelims	preliminary pages
pubd	published
q.v.	which see
r.	recto
sgd	signed
sp. spp.	spine(s)
TP, TPP	title-page(s)
U.	University
v., vv.	verso(s)
wct	woodcut
wmk	watermark
wrp(s)	wrapper(s)
×2	denotes 2 subjects on one plate

Introduction

At the beginning of the nineteenth century, when the professions of publisher and bookseller were so closely related that the two callings were often combined in one business, Benjamin Tabart opened his Juvenile Library (or children's bookshop) at No.157, New Bond Street and, at the same time, made a modest entry into the publishing world of children's literature when his imprint appeared on the title-pages of a few books.

Very little is known of his life prior to 1801. The Tabarts were of Huguenot descent. A Daniel Tabart, jeweller (1706–1775), whose ancestors left France and settled in England in 1687, had a son, Benjamin, born in 1732 in Savoy Spring Gardens. Benjamin predeceased his father, leaving two children, Benjamin and Elizabeth. Daniel, by his will, left these grandchildren substantial bequests which they could not inherit until they reached twenty-five years of age (and presumably they were younger than this when he died). His executors were John Gerard and Peter Kirk.

A Benjamin Tabart, born c. 1767–68 and later to be the publisher, married Susannah Vivares, who had been baptized in 1759 at St. Anne's, Soho. She was the daughter of Francis Vivares, a print-seller, and Susannah, née Parker. Two separate family trees in the Huguenot Library at University College, London, do not explicitly show that Benjamin, grandson of Daniel, was the same person as Benjamin, husband of Susannah, but it seems highly probable. Their eldest son was named Francis Gerard, Francis being his mother's father's name and Gerard, the name of Daniel Tabart's executor and guardian of the two grandchildren. Another son was called George Peter, possibly after Peter Kirk.

Benjamin and Susannah must have been well off because they were able to order a Wedgwood Queensware dinner service monogrammed with their initials, 'BST', of which a single plate survives in the Brisbane home of one of their descendants. The monogram, as ordered by a 'Mrs Tabert', is listed in the Crest Order Book in the Wedgwood Museum, Stoke-on-Trent, in Staffordshire.

They had eight children, of whom four were baptized, like their mother, at St Anne's, Soho. The eldest, a girl, died young; next came Francis Gerard (1789–1856) who, in c. 1805, went into the Navy as a purser on the *Doterel*. This was a financially hazardous and invidious job since the purser was accountable for the value of the ship's victuals and also had to buy with his own money necessary articles for which he was recouped by the ship and individual men.* The *Doterel* was on convoy duty and took part in the Peninsular War but Francis's naval career was short, as he left the Navy

---

*For a detailed account of pursery see *The wooden world An anatomy of the Georgian Navy* by N. A. M. Rodger, Collins, 1986; Fontana, 1988.

in 1811. His occupation for the next few years is not known for certain but 'F. G. Tabart' published *A collection of simple stories* (n.d.) from 12, Clifford Street so he may have been working with his father for a while; and then, between 1827 and 1830, he was listed in directories as a bookseller.

Francis married Elizabeth Dulot in 1808 but she died in childbirth in 1812, leaving a daughter. In 1817 he married his second wife, Emma Lewes (1799–1877), and two of their children were baptized at Uley in Gloucestershire, where Francis was a 'clothier' between 1819 and 1824. Then in 1830 he, his wife, his sister and five children (but not his eldest daughter, who eloped to Gretna Green in that same year) embarked for Tasmania and established themselves there. A log cabin at Eastern Marshes, near Oatlands, is still preserved, built by Francis to house his family (which eventually included five more children), but later he was able to build a stone house nearby which he called 'Fonthill', with the interesting feature of an interior stone staircase.

Benjamin Tabart died in Lambeth at the age of 65 and was buried at St. Mary's, Paddington, on 16 April 1833. Five years later, Susannah, his indomitable widow, at the age of seventy-nine, also emigrated to Tasmania, accompanied by a servant, to join her son and his family. She died in Hobart in 1839. There are now about one hundred and fifty descendants of Francis Gerard – and, so, of Benjamin – Tabart in Australia.

To go back to the early days of Benjamin Tabart and his Juvenile Library: he started his bookselling career with a flourish since, as the father of several children, he was sufficiently self-confident and experienced to produce a quite remarkable catalogue, dated 1801, listing 586 educational books that were on sale in his shop as well as a good selection of lighter reading for the nursery. The titles in this catalogue were not all, of course, his own publications. In fact, the list provides a careful survey of contemporary educational books in print for progressive age groups, and its value and interest are much enhanced by the reasoned, knowledgeable introductions which head each of the sections (see Appendix C).

He is obviously conscious of the dryness of many school books, for he writes: 'It is in writing down to the exact level of the capacity of young people, that the Authors of Books of Education have been the least successful.' He also regrets 'that we possess very few books, in which RELIGIOUS TRUTH is skilfully simplified to the Capacity of Children of between FIVE and EIGHT Years of Age' and he calls upon 'persons of taste, piety, and literary ability' to produce suitable religious books for the young; and, in discussing children of eight years, he appreciates that 'Imagination will be to them, in no small degree, vivid and expansive'.

Indeed, Tabart might almost have been aware of the forceful opinions that William Godwin would express a year later in his preface to *Bible stories* (see Appendix B), published by Richard Phillips and sold by B. Tabart in 1802. This important preface roused Mrs Trimmer's displeasure when the author deplored modern children's books as too rational and matter-of-fact and pleaded for 'that most essential branch of human nature the imagination' and for 'those things, which open the heart, which insensibly initiate the learner, in the relations and generous offices of society . . .'.

Many of Tabart's future publications would, indeed, produce food for the imagination. For instance, one of the first books to carry his imprint, though

2

only as part publisher with Crosby and Letterman, was Jane Porter's *The two Princes of Persia*, a book whose interest today lies less in its story than in the author's introduction, where she laments the passing away of former times and of 'the nurse's story of the tripping fairy, the witch riding her broomstick, the turban'd giant, and the sheeted ghost.'*

The time was right for an enterprising publisher to begin his career. Children needed him, for Mrs Sarah Trimmer and her admirers were endeavouring, with some success, to make children's books into a propaganda-mart of unquestioning obedience to parents, of facts and not fancies and, above all, of uncritical acceptance of her own narrow religious faith. In 1802 she started a periodical, the *Guardian of education*, for the purpose of examining, *inter alia*, contemporary children's books. Each one that came her way was minutely scrutinized for undue appeal to the imagination ('romantic nonsense'), for harmful influences inspired by Rousseau and the French Revolution (she called them 'engines of mischief which ... undermine Revealed Religion, by deifying Nature') and for such minutiae as irreverent jokes about the clergy. Even well-intentioned moral teaching was, to Mrs Trimmer, unacceptable unless it was admittedly inspired by the Bible and Christianity.

So, whether due specifically to Mrs Trimmer's fulminations or to public opinion generally, there was for children no great choice of imaginative, nor of just simply entertaining, books when Ben Tabart opened the doors of his Juvenile Library. It was in that same year – a propitious one for fact-stuffed, morally-inhibited children – that John Harris also began publishing under his own name in St Paul's Churchyard, having taken over her business from Elizabeth Newbery. He was soon to delight youngsters, and adults too, with a vivacious series of nonsensical, gaily-illustrated booklets, beginning in 1805, to a fanfare of applause, with *Old Mother Hubbard*.

But, while John Harris was a giant among children's publishers, Benjamin Tabart was more of a Tom Thumb. His output for two or three years was unremarkable, except that it included the first title by a pseudonymous writer who has only recently (in 1988) been discovered to be Elizabeth Kilner, a descendant of Mrs Mary Ann Kilner, the author who, like her sister-in-law, Dorothy Kilner, wrote some of the best-loved stories for children in the last two decades of the eighteenth century. Elizabeth Kilner's first book was *A puzzle for a curious girl* (1801–02); it is a mystery story and, though the solution is trivial, conjecture is well maintained to the end. A rival author, Elizabeth Fenwick, generously called it 'one of the best books that was ever written for children', and even Mrs Trimmer found it 'a very entertaining little book' and she praised the publisher for giving it 'good paper and type, and many engraved copper-plates'.

In addition to about thirteen titles of which Tabart was the sole, or joint publisher from 1801–02, there were others that carried his name as bookseller, nearly all being published by Richard Phillips. There was a close connection between Phillips and Tabart – what it was is not known, but Tabart may well have been a former *employé* or dependant of Phillips, that active and prolific publisher in the City of London, who perhaps decided that he needed a more fashionable outlet for his educational and instructive

_____
* See entry 134 in bibliography for a fuller extract.

3

books. Whatever the link between the two men, it was a strong one. For instance, some books published by Tabart were later published by Phillips and each advertised the other's titles in his own publications – in fact, there must have been more of Phillips's books in Tabart's Juvenile Library than of his own. Therefore, in assessing Benjamin Tabart's contribution to the history of children's publishing, it is important to consider also the career of Richard Phillips.

He was born in 1767, the son of a Leicestershire farmer, and he became a vegetarian at an early age when his favourite heifer was slaughtered. He was educated in London and afterwards returned to Leicester, where he was in turn a schoolmaster, a hosier and a stationer-cum-bookseller-cum-vendor of patent medicines. His business did very well after he acquired a printing-press; he also traded in pianos, music and prints, to which activities he added a lending library.

Phillips had a lively mind and held strong radical and republican views and his shop became a depot for advanced democratic literature, which resulted in his being sent to gaol in 1793 for eighteen months after he was found guilty of selling Tom Paine's *The rights of man*. From the prison he continued to edit the *Leicester herald*, a newspaper he had founded in 1792 in order to disseminate his unorthodox opinions.

He also fancied himself as a scientist and felt confident enough to question the theory of gravitation and in 1795 he founded the *Museum*, another periodical, this time of semi-scientific interest. However, a disastrous fire brought both these journalistic ventures to a sudden end and so, pocketing the insurance money, Phillips went off to London and set up in St Paul's Churchyard.

In 1796 he started the *Monthly magazine* and soon had a flourishing business. In 1805–06 he moved to Bridge Street, Blackfriars, where he published a great many school books and manuals written by himself and others with a variety of pseudonyms, one of the most prolific being 'the Rev. Dr. Blair'.* Other names that Phillips used were Abbé Bossut, Rev. Samuel Barrow, Rev. J. Goldsmith, M. or Margaret Pelham and Rev. C. C. Clarke.

In 1807 Phillips was elected a sheriff of London and in 1808, to the surprise of all who knew of his republican views, he was knighted. The expenses of office may have contributed to his ensuing financial embarrassment: by 1811 he was bankrupt, but a former apprentice enabled him to repurchase many of his best copyrights and he continued in business until 1823, when he retired to Brighton. He died in 1840.

Returning to Tabart's early years, it is a surprising fact that on 12 November 1803 he was declared bankrupt†; and yet in 1804, as 'Tabart and Co.', he began his most active period of publishing and confirmed his position as a leader in quality, if not in quantity, among the publishers of children's books.

One of his triumphs was *The book of trades*, a factual book but interesting, even today, with excellent plates and clear descriptions of working methods; it was most apposite to the great revolution taking place in industry. But

* See entries 12, 13 and 194–197 in bibliography for further details.
† See *The British book trades, 1731–1806; a checklist of bankrupts* by Ian Maxted, Exeter, 1985.

4

more impressive was the way in which he challenged the anti-fairy-tale brigade, those stiflers of imagination and suppressors of fantasy, by launching in 1804 his delightful series of Tales for the Nursery, with, initially, twenty-one paper-covered sixpenny booklets containing fairy stories and traditional tales, each one having three hand-coloured plates. At the same time he also published three volumes of *Tabart's collection of popular stories* edited by Mrs Mary Jane Godwin, with assistance from her husband, William.* Tabart advertised that his 'editions of the above stories consist either of new translations, or are modernized and improved versions, in chaste and correct language, embellished with beautiful engravings, from original designs made on purpose by Messrs. Craig and Corbould.'

It might be expected that, for reasons of economy, the bound volumes would be composed of the separate booklets but in fact the illustrations were quite different and, where it has been possible to compare the texts, they were not always identical. (The difficulty of comparison lies in the rarity of all these books, which has meant that the bound volumes are not often available in the places where the single titles are found.)

While collected volumes of fairy tales had occasionally been published previously, the production of the single Tales for the Nursery marked a great advance in the history of children's literature, for many of these popular stories and traditional legends had only been available up to now in chapbooks, a crude form of presentation intended for poor and simple readers. Now Benjamin Tabart produced them with all the respectability of careful printing and often with delectable illustrations, yet still as cheap ephemera, ensuring that they appealed to the pocket-money of the young gentry and the tastes of their elders.

This was no half-measure in an attack on the enemies of fairy lore and traditional legends, and it was surely a courageous undertaking for an almost-unknown publisher to dare to publish books of a style so out of contemporary favour. Either Benjamin Tabart was stirred into action by pity and sympathy for children's starved imaginations or, as a purely business-like enterprise, he noticed, and decided to fill, a yawning gap in nursery bookshelves.

Whatever his motive – and his subsequent publishing lists seem to indicate that it was at least tinged with benevolence – he was extremely successful, that is, if the numbering of editions on title-pages can be believed. In the year of first publication there were (if his title-pages speak truth) sixteen editions of *Cinderella*, eight editions of *The history of Fortunio* and of *The history of Whittington and his cat*, ten editions of *Blue Beard*, six of *Puss in Boots* and 'new' editions of many others (but, as pointed out in the Preface, 'new' may not indicate a previous Tabart edition).

Not surprisingly, Mrs Trimmer was outraged. Writing in the *Guardian of education* (vol. iv, p.74) she gave full rein to her feelings: 'These Tales are announced to the Public as *new translations*, but in what respect this term applies we are at a loss to say for on the perusal of them we recognised the identical *Mother Goose's tales*, with all their *vulgarities of expression*, which were in circulation when those who are now grandmothers, were themselves

*See note before entry 48 in bibliography headed [GODWIN, Mary Jane] *Dramas for children*.

5

children, and we doubt not but that many besides ourselves can recollect, their horrors of imagination on reading that of *Blue Beard*, and the terrific impressions it left upon their minds. .... *Cinderella* and *Little Red Riding Hood* are perhaps merely absurd.'

She also takes exception to the illustrations 'consisting of coloured prints, in which the most striking incidents in the stories are placed before the eyes of the little readers in glaring colours. ... A moment's consideration will surely be sufficient to convince people of the impropriety of putting such books as these into the hands of little children ...'.

Undeterred by, perhaps oblivious of, this criticism, Tabart continued to strew flowers on the paths of reading for children by publishing more titles in the Tales for the Nursery series, one being of historical interest because it put into print for perhaps the first time the old *History of Jack and the beanstalk* (1807). There were finally about thirty-three booklets in the series, 'Sinbad' being in two parts and 'Gulliver' in four. In 1809 the bound parts of the Popular Stories were reissued with a fourth, new volume, and in that year also were published the four volumes of a new collection of stories and poems, entitled *Tabart's moral tales*, which gave children a variety of reading matter that was not nearly so severe as the title implies. This may have pandered to the presumed taste of adult purchasers but the contents were selected for the pleasure of young readers.

In 1805 Tabart and Co. published *Songs for the nursery*, a collection of the old nursery rhymes. The first edition was not illustrated, but the edition of 1808 could be had for sixpence without prints, for one-and-six with plain prints or for two shillings and sixpence with coloured prints. Nine years later the book was excoriated by the author of *The juvenile review*, who was an admirer of the now deceased Mrs Trimmer. 'A very foolish book', she wrote, 'intitled "Songs for the Nursery", has we lament to say, obtained a place in the infant library, and thus the very means by which benevolent principles might have been implanted, have been perverted to the very worst of purposes, that of filling the infant mind with false ideas. What, for instance, can be more ridiculous than the idea of "a dish running after a spoon", or the moon being *in a fit*? But we will quit this unpleasant subject ...'. However, the book's popularity was not affected and by 1818 the copyright had been taken over by William Darton, Junior, who continued to reissue the title for many years; and its importance today in preserving in print the traditional rhymes which had been handed down for so long by word of mouth is underlined by the frequency with which it is quoted as a source in Iona and Peter Opie's *The Oxford dictionary of nursery rhymes*.

Benjamin Tabart was now openly on the side of children *versus* moralists and he added several more titles to his list of amusing, attractively-illustrated and usually nonsensical booklets, including *A true history of a little old woman, who found a silver penny* (1806), with its four-fold panorama, and *The adventures of Grimalkin* (1808), which recounts the sad disasters that befell Dame Trot's cat's eldest son; also the more sophisticated *Memoirs of the little man and the little maid* (1807). *The true history of a little boy who cheated himself*, whose charming plates and simple verses lightly point a moral, came out in 1809. Also among Tabart's more frivolous productions were the harlequinades which he published between 1807 and 1810; and he was associated with some imitations of William Roscoe's lilting, imaginative poem, *The butterfly's ball*, *and the grasshopper's feast*, which had created such a furore in 1807. Tabart published one of these imitations himself, *The tyger's theatre* (1808), with verses written by S. J. Arnold but with a frontispiece which was the remarkable work of a child of nine.

Though only a minor publisher so far as quantity was concerned, almost from the opening of his business Tabart attracted some of the best contemporary writers for children. Among the most important were the already-mentioned William Godwin and his wife, and Dorothy Kilner and her niece, Elizabeth Kilner, the latter following the family practice of concealing her identity under the unguessable initials 'S. W.'. When Mrs Elizabeth Fenwick became one of his authors a real catch had swum into his net. Her urge to write was inspired by the sheer necessity of providing for her two children since her disreputable husband failed to do so; but from this necessity sprang, not a hack, but a composer of interesting tales like her dog story, *The life of Carlo* (1804), which were intended primarily to entertain and please their readers.

One established children's author proposed a book to Tabart which was never, apparently, completed. This was Lady Fenn who in the previous century had produced so many instructive works intended to make learning pleasant. There is a long letter extant (in the Osborne Collection, Toronto), unfortunately undated, addressed to Mr. Tabart, Bookseller, New Bond Street, which discusses her willingness to supply 'innocent amusement for children introducing some instruction', apparently to take the form of 'Hints', and she tells Mr Tabart: 'You are welcome to do the Hints on your own account', which must mean that he, alone, was to be the publisher. Lady Fenn is already considering the method of producing this work and says, 'I must insist on good paper – to say truth your books are generally such – I do not like wire-woven or hot-pressed paper for any thing – but of a good quality and colour'. She adds: 'When you print the Hints Mrs. Frere will be so good as to correct the press if you do it whilst she is in Town. I shall wish to have several copies to distribute sending you a list of friends to whom I would give them – for you to pack & direct – & some I should have sent to me.' Her final sentence reads: 'I am very glad that you have destroyed any improper books.'

This letter also praises 'the frontispiece to Little Red Riding Hood' which 'I remarked as being so pretty that I could not refrain from buying the book – little children should have no terrifying stories & still less cuts.' She may have meant *The history of Little Red Riding Hood, in verse*, published jointly by B. Tabart and J. Harris in 1807 which does, indeed, have an unusual and pretty frontispiece. If this is so, then the allusion may help to date the letter.

In 1809 and 1810 Tabart published three books by the unknown artist and writer, 'R. R.'* These have polished, softly-coloured illustrations of comely children demonstrating the alphabet and other elementary learning skills. It was also in 1810 that Ann and Jane Taylor contributed one of his most distinguished titles – a handsomely produced retelling of *The world turned upside down* (published by Riley, among others, in the 18th century) with the title *Signor Topsy-Turvy's wonderful magic lantern*. The anarchistic theme of this long-popular work reflected a revolt in the 18th century against the rule of

---

*See note preceding 138 in bibliography for his possible identity.

reason and, in the early 19th, against the strait-jacket of repressed childhood. The idea of rôles reversed could be, and was, developed in this book to extremes; but perhaps children did enjoy pictures showing a large man hooked by a monstrous fish, a cook, skewered and trussed, being roasted by a hare, a horse driving a groom between the shafts of a chaise or two fat farmers being driven in a plough by their masters, the oxen: 'The moral let anyone find who is able; If none should occur, let us see if this suits – That some *men* behave little better than *brutes*.'

Benjamin Tabart had no hesitation in following the current practice of puffing his own titles in his publications. In *A tour through England* (1804) the supposed letter-writer visits Tabart's Juvenile Library and buys 'some of his delightful books'; in Elizabeth Kilner's *A visit to London* (1805) a family from the provinces spends a happy time in the Juvenile Library, buying liberally from Mr Tabart himself. The accompanying illustration shows the interior of the shop with a young-looking, dapper gentleman (Benjamin?) bowing politely behind the counter. But really blatant, indeed ridiculous advertising is found in Mrs Fenwick's *Visits to the Juvenile Library* (1805), which reads more like a catalogue than a story. Not only are the books themselves listed, praised and bought in quantities, but the shop itself is described in glowing terms: '... the neat arrangement of an immense quantity of books, handsomely bound in red or green leather, and lettered on the back with gold letters, together with globes, maps, and little ornamented book-cases, of various sizes, finely painted and varnished, have a pleasing effect to the eye. Besides, the library is generally full of well dressed ladies, accompanied with blooming boys and girls, who are eagerly hunting for books of knowledge, or looking at the pictures of entertaining stories; so that I think this bookseller's shop may with strict propriety be called, *a very pretty place*.'

Pretty it might be, but it was also business-like. Some of Tabart's trading practices are revealed in his advertisements. For instance, an announcement in the advertisement pages in the above-mentioned book, *A tour through England*, describing the bookshop as 'The only Establishment of the kind in Great Britain', offers 'upon purchases or orders to the amount of two pounds or upwards a discount of one shilling in the pound .... to those families who do Tabart and Co. the favour to pay ready money; but on account of the smallness and low price of the articles in which they deal, they earnestly hope that the nobility and gentry, who honour their shop with their patronage, will take into consideration the inconvenience and loss which would result from opening accounts of less than two pounds in amount.'

In Aikin's *Poetry for children* (1801) Richard Phillips lists some of his own titles (also to be had of Thomas Hurst and Benjamin Tabart) with 'a handsome allowance to schools' and 'guarantees the bookselling Trade from Loss by exchanging either of the aforementioned Books, in a clean and perfect State for any other of them.'

More inducements are offered by Tabart himself to Country Booksellers in advertisements in 1804 and in 1806, advising them that they 'may be supplied with assortments of ten, fifteen, or twenty pounds value, at six months credit, and any article deemed unsaleable may be exchanged at any time, for others in the list.' At the same time he announced that 'Schools are also supplied with copy-books, Cyphering-books, Ruled Paper for Merchants' Accounts, Slates, Quills, Pencils, &c. on the lowest terms' and 'Great

Variety of New Globes, Dissected Maps, Geographical, Historical, and other Games.' He also encouraged purchasers to buy his books at the rate of 13 books to the dozen, or the 25th book free.

In 1805 a different venture was advertised in the third edition of Lucy Aikin's 'Poetry': 'Messrs. *Tabart* and Co. have opened a Register-book for the Insertion of the Names of Families and Schools who may be in want of Tutors, Governesses, Assistants, and Teachers; and also, for the reception of the Names of Tutors, Governesses, Assistants, and Teachers wanting situations, free of expence, excepting that of postage.' No further announcements of this kind have been seen so this undertaking may not have been successful.

Another short-lived enterprise lasted from October 1808 to September 1809 when he published 12 monthly parts of an ambitious periodical for young people – the *Juvenile miscellany* – but the high cost of production prevented its continuation.

During all the years up to and including 1810 Tabart was active and productive, but in 1810 he was again declared bankrupt* and the case dragged on for three years. In 1811 he published no new titles at all and very few, whether new or reprints, thereafter. His sudden eclipse may also have been connected with Richard Phillips's bankruptcy; but, whereas Sir Richard was able to resume his publishing career for some years until his retirement, Tabart's dwindled gradually to a quiet ending.

He left his original premises in 1812 and moved to 12, Clifford Street but his occupancy of that address was brief and dishonourable, as across the Rate Book of Clifford Street South in the parish of St. James's, Piccadilly, is written 'ABSCONDED'. In 1816 his address (from imprints) was Conduit Street and then 85, Piccadilly, 'opposite the Green Park' (he gave the latter address again in 1818); in 1817 he was at 165, New Bond Street, and in 1818 and 1819 at 39, New Bond Street.

It seems likely that at these addresses he continued to sell books, if not often to publish them, and he did undertake some literary and editorial work. Phillips published several volumes of fairy tales under slightly different titles whose title-pages showed they were edited by Benjamin Tabart; and John Souter published *The national spelling book* by B. Tabart in 1818. In *c.*1817 there appeared some parts of *Tabart's school magazine* but its title-page and imprint have not been seen and it does not appear to have survived for long. Between 2 August 1814 and 22 May 1815 Tabart received a regular weekly payment of £1.11.6 from Longmans, the publishers, but the cash record (in Reading University Library) does not state what services he rendered in return.

Many of his titles were bought by William Darton, Longmans, and John Souter (who was established in No.1, Paternoster Row in about 1814 and a few years later moved to the Juvenile and School Library, No.73 St. Paul's Churchyard). Even in 1837 some of Tabart's Tales for the Nursery were being sold at threepence plain by T. Hughes of Ludgate Hill; but Benjamin Tabart's name has not been seen on a new title-page since Richard Phillips published *Popular fairy tales* in about 1820. A review of children's books in the *London magazine* in November of that year said that 'as dear to us as are the

---

* *London Gazette*, 16.6.1810, p.875.

recollections of our bull's-eyes and humming-tops' was this 'volume of delicious tales published by our friend Ben Tabart.' He could not have wished to be better remembered.

Part I

Alphabetical bibliography of books published, sold, written and edited by Benjamin Tabart

This part contains books which, with only a few exceptions, have some printed connection with Benjamin Tabart

1 (1) THE ADVENTURES OF ANDOLOCIA, with the purse and cap of his father Fortunatus: a tale for the nursery. A new edition. With three copperplates. London: printed for Tabart and Co. at the Juvenile and School Library, No.157, New Bond-street; and to be had of all dealers in books. Price sixpence. 1804.

12.4×7.6 cm. Pr by R. Taylor and Co., Black-Horse-court. Pp.32. H/c FP+2 other h/c pls dated Sep. 1804. Yellow pr stiff-paper covers, front shows 'Tabart's improved edition of Andolocia: with coloured plates. Price sixpence.' On back, advt of 'interesting little books . . .'.
[UCLA; PML

Advt on v. of TP. Plates engraved after designs by Craig. New edition entered at Stationers' Hall by R. Phillips on 5.10.04, so this is probably the first edition. 1st page of the story carries a puff of Tabart's edition of Fortunatus (see 61, *The history of Fortunatus*).

Andolocia sets out on a long journey armed with the purse of his father, Fortunatus, which will always provide him with ten gold coins, and with the cap which will transport him anywhere he wishes to go to. During his travels he falls in love with the King of England's daughter, Agrippina, who steals the two magic objects; but with cunning he takes them from her and, having found some equally magic apples, causes horns to grow on her head so that no one else wants to marry her. By various subterfuges he gives her the antidote and they are married and live together long and happily.

(2) Title almost as (1) but 'With three copper-plates' follows 'nursery' and is followed by 'A new edition'. Impt reads '. . . New Bond Street; and to be had of all booksellers. Price sixpence. 1806.'

11.8×7.8 cm. Pr by C. Squire, Furnival's-Inn Court. Pp.32+3pp. bklist. Pls as in (1). Pr wrps with advts on front and back. Advt on v. of TP.

2 (1) THE ADVENTURES OF GRIMALKIN, the eldest son of Dame Trot's cat. Illustrated with many engravings. London: printed for Tabart and Co., at the Juvenile and School Library, New Bond-street. 1808.

11.6×9.4 cm. Pr by E. Hemsted, Great New Street, Fetter Lane. Pp.15 [16]. 10 h/c engvd pls, 2 dated April, 1808. Pr wrps, upper cover titled 'The tragical wanderings and adventures . . .'. (See fig. 1)
[S 2.6.82/2 and /123; Gum. 250; PML, wmk 1807; Lilly; Private coll., imp.

This book does not seem to have been reprinted.

Grimalkin and a disreputable companion run away from home to see the world and even go to France 'Until the effects of the sad revolution/ Obliged them to leave that scene of confusion.' They are shipwrecked, the friend is drowned and Grimalkin is mortally hurt. He makes a late repentance and his tragic tale ends thus:

> Dame Trot put on mourning, and shed a fond tear,
> When she saw the poor CAT lie dead on his bier.
> The CATS and the KITTENS, in numbers untold,
> Came in from all quarters, the sight to behold.
> But when poor GRIMALKIN was laid in the ground,
> Their sad mewing was heard for many miles round.

3 (1) THE ADVENTURES OF VALENTINE AND ORSON. A tale for the nursery. With three copperplates. A new edition. London: printed for Tabart and Co. at the Juvenile and School Library, No.157, New Bond-street; and to be had of all booksellers. Price sixpence. 1804.

18°. Printed by R. Taylor and Co., Black-Horse-court. P.38+2pp. advts, 23 items. H/c FP+2 h/c pls. Green pr wrps, advt on lower v. of 'a great variety of interesting little books, adorned with beautiful coloured plates, similar to the present work . . .'. Advt on v. of TP; advt also on v. of lower cover.
[PML

This was one of the fairy-tales bought for the children visiting Tabart's shop in Mrs. Fenwick's *Visits to the Juvenile Library*, 1805. The plates were designed by W. M. Craig. Front cover text: 'Tabart's improved edition of Valentine and Orson: with coloured plates. Price sixpence.' See also 142.

Valentine and Orson, twin brothers, were both snatched from their mother at birth, one by a king, the other by a bear. The king brought up Valentine as a prince and the motherly bear raised Orson as a wild animal. At the age of 18 the brothers met and Orson attached himself to Valentine without knowing the relationship. They had many adventures, were reunited with their parents and each married a beautiful lady.

(2) Title as (1) but 'copper-plates' . . . 1807.

12×8 cm. Pr by J. Diggens, St. Ann's Lane. Pp.38+2pp. advts, 24 items. 3 h/c plates, one dated Apr 11 1804 and another signed 'Tomlinson scpt'. Yellow pr wrps, advt on lower v.; advt also on v. of TP.
[Private coll. ex S 18.6.87/425

4 (1) AIKIN, Lucy. Poetry for children. Consisting of short pieces, to be committed to memory. Selected by Lucy Aikin. London: printed for R. Phillips, No.71, St. Paul's; and sold by B. Tabart, No.157, New-Bond-street; Taylor and Wilks, Printers, Chancery-lane. 1801. [Price half-a-crown.]

He set off one Night when all were in Bed.
London, Published by Tabart & Cº. April, 1808.

1   Plate from *The adventures of Grimalkin*, 2(1). *Sotheby's*

FRONTISPIECE.

Miss C. Spencer Del.ᵗ   *London, Published by Tabart & Cº. New Bond Street April, 1808.*   *I. Nolan, Sculp.*

2   Folding frontispiece of *The tyger's theatre* by S. J. Arnold, 8(2), drawn by a girl of nine

13

13.6×8.6 cm. Pp.xii+158+10pp. advts of Phillips's bks sold by Benjamin Tabart. Marbled bds, red roan sp g. No illusns.
[UCLA; Opie; Gum. 276; Renier; Private coll.; Nottm U.

Listed in the *English catalogue of books*, Oct. 1801.

The book contains 177 poems, some signed 'Original' which, says an advertisement, are by Lucy Aikin. The printer's imprint at the end is Wilks and Taylor. None of the Phillips/Tabart editions seems to have had any illustrations.

In her preface, dated 1801 from Stoke Newington, Miss Aikin discusses the prevailing disapproval of stories about 'dragons and fairies, giants and witches' and the substitution of 'mere prose and simple fact'; and she questions whether these 'novel-like tales' may not do more injury to the mind of youth 'than the fairy fiction of the last generation, which only wandered over the region of shadows'. But she believes that 'poetry has many advantages for children over both these classes of writing. The magic of rhyme is felt in the very cradle ... By the aid of verse, a store of beautiful imagery and glowing sentiment may be gathered up ... which, in riper years ... may soothe the soul to calmness, rouse it to honourable exertion, or fire it with virtuous indignation.'

Lucy's aunt, Mrs. Barbauld held an opposite opinion, and in her preface to *Hymns in prose* she said that 'it may well be doubted whether poetry ought to be lowered to the capacities of children, or whether they should not rather be kept from reading verse till they are able to relish good verse.'

This was one of the books mentioned in E. Kilner's *A visit to London* and Mrs. Fenwick puffed it in her *Visits to the Juvenile Library*.

Reviews: 'This selection has been made with judgment from some of the best authors, and the Book is particularly valuable on account of the scarcity of collections of poetry fit for young people.' *Guardian of education*, vol. 1, p.307. 'This little book contains short pieces of poetry, selected from some of the best English writers, on subjects suitable to children; some original pieces of considerable merit are occasionally introduced.' *The juvenile review*, 1817. 'The volume of poetry is very well selected.' The *Critical review*, vol. xxxiv, 1802, p.111.

(2) Title as (1) to ... Aikin. Second edition with additions and corrections. London: printed for Richard Phillips, No.71, St. Paul's Church-yard; and sold by B. Tabart, No.157, New-Bond-street. Taylor and Wilks, Printers, Chancery-lane. 1803. Price half-a-crown.

13.6×8.2 cm. Pp.xii+168 inc. 7 (or more?) pp. advts of Phillips's bks. Marbled bds, red roan sp g.
[BL; Private coll.; S 12.10.81/85

The preface is dated as in 1801 edition.

(3) Title as (1) to ... Aikin. Third edition, with additions and corrections. London: printed for R. Phillips, No.71, St. Paul's Church-yard; and sold by B. Tabart, No.157, New-Bond-street. Taylor and Co. Printers, Black-Horse Court. 1805. Price two shillings.

13.4×8.3 cm. Pp.xii+168 inc. 6pp. bklist. Leather sp.
[Baldwin; Gum. 277; S 21.4.77/2060–1

(4) Poetry for children: consisting of short pieces to be committed to memory. Selected by Lucy Aikin. Fourth edition: with additions and corrections. London: printed for R. Phillips, No.6, Bridge-street; and sold by Tabart and Co. No.157, New Bond-street. Squire, Printer, Furnival's-Inn-court. 1806.
[Price two shillings.]

13.3×8.5 cm. Pp.xxi+161 [162]+6pp. advts of Tabart's bks. Marbled bds, red roan sp g.
[Bod.

The preface is as in (1). There have been additions and omissions since the 1st edition, making a total of 178 poems.

(5) Title as (4) (excepting 'fifth edition,') to ... sold by B. Tabart, No. 157, New Bond-street. J. Adlard, Printer, Duke-street, Smithfield. 1808. [Price two shillings.]

13.2×7.8 cm. Pp.xii+161+6pp. advts of Phillips's bks. Marbled bds, ¾ leather g.
[Opie; Baldwin; Private coll.; NLS

On July 26 1814 Longmans paid B. Tabart (not Phillips) £1.14.0 for 25 copies of Aikin's *Poetry* and subsequent editions were published by them. (From the Longman archives at Reading University Library.)

5 (1) ALADDIN; or The wonderful lamp. A tale of the nursery. With three copperplates. London: printed for Tabart and Co. Juvenile and School Library, No.157, New Bond Street; and to be had of all dealers in books. Price sixpence. 1805.

12.1×7.1 cm. Pr by Shury, Berwick Street, Soho. Pp.36. H/c FP headed 'Aladin', dated July 1805, +2 h/c pls, one dated as FP, the other dated July 11 1804. Dark ochre pr wrps, advt on lower v.
[PML, wmk 1803; UCLA, bound with others.

v. of TP blank. Entered at Stationers' Hall by R. Phillips on 19.8.05.

This is a splendid, well-illustrated retelling of the colourful and fantastic story.

(2) Title as (1) to ... copper-plates. London: printed for B. Tabart, at the Juvenile and School Library, No.157, New Bond Street; and to be had of all booksellers. Price sixpence. 1808.

11.7×7.8 cm. Pr by J. Diggens, St. Ann's Lane. Pp.35 [36]. Advt on v. of TP. Advt on p.[36] of 4 titles. H/c FP dated July 1805+2 other h/c pls, one dated as FP. Pr yellow stiff-paper covers, advts on front and lower v.
[Osborne

6 (1) ALAMON TIPPENNY; a wonderful ancient tradition of a little family who lived in a vinegar cruet.

Advtd in 1808, 1s. plain, 1s.6d. coloured; not traced.

7 (1) ALI BABA; or, The forty thieves. A tale for the nursery. With three copperplates. London, printed for Tabart and Co. Juvenile and School Library, No.157, New Bond Street, and to be had of all dealers in books. Price sixpence. 1805.

12.1×7 cm. Pr by D. N. Shury, Berwick Street. Pp.33+3pp. bklist, which includes 26 titles of Tales for the Nursery. H/c FP+2 other h/c pls, one dated 15 May 1805. Stiff yellow pr wrps, advts on lower v.
[UCLA; Wayne; PML, wmk 1804

Advt on v. of TP. Entered at Stationers' Hall by R. Phillips on 6.8.05. Welch 27 gives '1804', which is unlikely, also 1805 and 1807. T. Hughes advtd this title as one of 'Tabart's Editions' in *A new and original book of forfeits* [1837], price 3d. with plain engravings.

The excellent plates are beautifully coloured. This book was one of the fairy tales bought at Mr. Tabart's shop for the indulged children in Mrs. Fenwick's *Visits to the Juvenile Library*.

(2) ALI BABA; or The forty thieves. A tale for the nursery. With three copper-plates. A new edition. London: printed for Tabart and Co. at the Juvenile and School Library, 157, New Bond-street, and to be had of all booksellers. Price sixpence. 1807.

11.5×7.7 cm. Pr by J. Diggens, St. Ann's Lane. Pp.33+3pp. bklist starting on v. of p.33. Advt on v. of TP. H/c FP dated 15 May 1805+2 other h/c pls, one dated as FP. Light orange-coloured stiff-paper pr covers, advts on front and lower v.
[Osborne; McKell

8 (1) [ARNOLD, S. J.] The tyger's theatre; London: printed for B. Tabart, and Co. at the Juvenile Library, No.157, New Bond Street. [1808]

12.3×9.6 cm. Pr by E. Hemsted, Great New-street, Fetter Lane. Pp.[viii]+[9]–31 [32]. P.[32] = Moral. Folding h/c FP engvd by I. Molan after Miss C. Spencer, April, 1808, +5 other h/c pls, no impts. Yellow or light brown wrps dated 1808, advt on lower v.
[BL, bound with others; Opie, bound with others; Lilly

The dedication to Miss Caroline Spencer is signed 'S. J. Arnold' 'in acknowledgment of having suggested the following trifle; in tribute to the dawning talents of an early and uncommon genius, evinced by the frontispiece of this little book, invented and drawn at nine years of age; and above all, in admiration of the captivating vivacity of a most amiable disposition.'

The preface is addressed to 'The Publisher' and signed 'J.S. Dec. 22, 1807', explaining how the book came to be written; the frontispiece was drawn by a little girl of nine and Mr. Arnold (who was evidently staying in the house) was asked to 'write some poetry properly adapted to it. – On the ensuing evening ... the following lines were produced, and read, to the infinite amusement of the whole Society.'

S. J. Arnold wrote libretti for comic operas, melodramatic romantic plays, musical farces, etc, so that composing the verses to accompany Caroline's drawing was no hard task.

The poem begins with reminiscences of *The butterfly's ball*, *The peacock 'At home'* and *The lion's masquerade*, which all made the tiger envious and, growling 'By my whiskers I'll not be laid thus on the shelf', he decided to 'give such a Party, shall make the world stare'. It was agreed that the party should include amateur theatricals. When the cast was being assembled the tiger sent a greyhound 'To fetch Roscius Carlo (his Hero) from Drury – ' [see 39, E. Fenwick's *The life of Carlo*].

The date of the performance was fixed for St. Thomas's Day and a footnote informs that this was 'The day on which these verses were written, and on which the birthday of Mr. Spencer, Lady Elizabeth Spencer, and their eldest son was celebrated'. The invitations were sent by the Two-Penny Post and the poet compares the excitement and agitation the animals felt 'As when first at Winton – (his feelings we guess on) A Scholar goes trembling to say a hard lesson! – ' and a footnote explains that 'Mr. Spencer's eldest Son is at Winchester School.'

Alas, the entertainment never got under way, for the Lion attacked the Tyger, and soon all were embroiled. The poem ends with the Moral: 'What in ENVY begins, oft in TRAGEDY ends.'

(2) Title and details as (1) except as follows: Pr salmon-col'd stiff-paper covers; on front: 'The Tyger's Theatre. Illustrated with engravings. London: Published by J. Souter, School Library, 73, St. Paul's Church Yard. 1823. Price 6d. plain, and 1s. coloured.' Also, the preface is sgd 'John Spencer' and dated Dec. 22, 1807, from Wheatfield House. Dedication as (1) to Miss Caroline Spencer. (See fig. 2)
[Private coll.

9 (1) BEAUTY AND THE BEAST: a tale for the nursery. With three copperplates. A new edition. London: Printed for Tabart and Co. at the Juvenile and School Library, No.157, New Bond-street; and to be had of all dealers in books. Price sixpence. 1804.

12.2×7.8 cm. Pr by Taylor and Co., Black Horse Court. Pp.36. H/c FP+2 h/c pls all dated July 11 1804. Yellow or green pr wrps, on front 'Tabart's improved edition of Beauty and the Beast: with coloured plates. Price sixpence.' On lower v. advt of Tabart's Library and of 'interesting little books adorned with beautiful coloured plates, similar to the present Work; ...'. Advt on v. of TP.
[V & A; PML; Lilly

The plates are engraved after designs by Craig. T. Hughes advertised this title as one of 'Tabart's Editions' in *A new and original book of forfeits* [1837], price 3d. with plain engravings.

'Beauty and the Beast' was one of the stories in Mme Leprince de Beaumont's *Magasin des enfans*, 1756, which was published in an English translation in 1759 with the title *Magasin des enfans: or, The young misses magazine*. ... The plot of Tabart's 'tale for the nursery' closely follows the events in Mme de Beaumont's story but the text has been completely rewritten: the language has occasionally been 'modernised' and the content is slightly abridged, without omitting anything of moment. The rewriting is not always an improvement on the older form – for instance, these are the verses written in letters of gold which de Beaumont's Beauty read:

> Welcome Beauty, banish fear,
> You are queen and mistress here:
> Speak your wishes, speak your will,
> Swift obedience meets them still.

And here are Tabart's:

> Beauteous lady, dry your tears,
> Here's no cause for sighs or fears;
> Command as freely as you may,
> Compliance still shall mark your sway.

(2) Title as (1) to ... nursery. With three copper-plates. A new edition. London: printed for Tabart and Co. at the Juvenile and School Library, No.157, New Bond Street; and to be had of all booksellers. Price sixpence. 1806.

12.1×7.1 cm. Pr by Squire, Furnival's-Inn-court. Pp.36. H/c FP dated July 11 1804+1 (only) h/c pl dated as FP. Advt on v. of TP.
[UCLA, imp. and bound with others.

10 (1) [BERTHOLET, G.] Leçons choisies dans la morale, l'histoire, et la biographie, à l'usage des écoles et de la jeunesse; par Mademoiselle G.B. Dédiées à ses élèves. A Londres: chez B. Tabart et Co. à la bibliothèque de la jeunesse, New Bond Street; et chez les autres libraires respectables. 1808.

13.5×8.6 cm. Pr by R. Juigné, 17, Margaret Street, Cavendish-square. Pp.xii+125+1p. list of subscribers, repeated on p.[vi] of prelims. No illusns. Marbled bds, green roan sp g.
[UCLA; Bod.

'A mes écoliers' is signed 'G. Berthelot [*sic*], Feuvrier (*sic*), 1808.' The book was advertised in E. Fenwick's *Infantine stories*, 1810, as 'par Mademoiselle Berthelot', the same spelling as above; but there seems little doubt that this is the same writer as the author of *Soirées d'automne* (11), where the author's name is given on the title-page as Bertholet.

Lessons from the Bible are mingled with very simple lessons in morals and history, all in easy French.

11 (1) BERTHOLET, G. Soirées d'automne; ou, Le vice puni, et la vertu recompensée; à l'instruction de la jeunesse, et pour l'usage des écoles. Par Mademoiselle G. Bertholet. Se vend chez C. Knight, rue due Château, à Windsor; B. Dulau and Co. Soho Square, Mr. Tabart, Bond-street, Mr. Boosey, No.4, Broad-street, Royal Exchange, et Messrs. Longman and Co. Paternoster Row, à Londres. 1810.

17.4×9.9 cm. Pr by C. Knight, rue du Château, à Windsor. ½-title. Pp.v [vii]+339. No illusns. Leather, g back and sides.
[UCLA; BL; Birm.

This is an extended story based on the Bible history of Jacob, Joseph and Joseph's brothers. Pp.[i]–v = Liste des souscriptions, including many noble and distinguished names.

Review: The *British critic*, v. 36, p.426: 'We do not pretend to know who Mademoiselle G. Bertholet may be, but this we know, that the publication to which she has prefixed her name, is the performance of M. Bitaubé, by no means an undistinguished French writer. It was published by Bitaubé, as it ought to have been here, with the title of the History of Joseph, and there is a splendid and elegant English version of it, by a writer of reputation among us. The name of Bitaubé no where appears in the preliminary dialogue, which however is introduced by a long list of royal and noble subscribers. The motive certainly requires some explanation; which it behoves Mademoiselle G.B. to give, for the publication carries at present on the face of it, the appearance of a most unjustifiable literary fraud.'

BLAIR, Rev. David   This is a pseudonym of Sir Richard Phillips or of his assistants. One book, at least, with this name on its title-page is known to be the work of another writer – see 36, *The class book* under FENWICK.

12 (1) BLAIR, Rev. David. The first catechism for children. Listed in the *English catalogue of books*, 1807, and entered at Stationers' Hall by R. Phillips on 28.9.07. No copy of this edition located.

(2) BLAIR, Rev. David. The first catechism for children containing common things necessary to be known at an early age. By the Rev. David Blair author of the Class Book, Reading Exercises Grammar of Philosophy etc, etc. London Printed for Richard Phillips; sold by B. Tabart, New Bond Street; Champante and Whitrow, Jewry Street; Wilson and Spence, York; H. Mozley, Gainsborough; and all other booksellers. J. Adlard, Printer, Duke Street. 1809. (Price nine pence)

14.2×8.8 cm. Pp.72. No illusns. Brown paper bds, green paper sp. and corners.
[Melb

Tabart advertised this book in 1808 quoting the price as 9d, or 13 to the dozen, with the full allowance to schools.

The preface is dated from Islington, Oct. 1807. Its last paragraph recommends parents and tutors to consult 'the Author's Reading Exercises, for the earliest classes (a supplement to Mavor's Spelling Book) or his Class Book or 365 Lessons, books which he has reason to believe are now in the hands of all intelligent Schoolmasters and Governesses.' [But for real authorship of *The class book* see this title under 36, FENWICK.]

The poems entitled 'My father', 'My mother', 'My brother', 'My sister', are present on pp.64–72. For the author of these verses see note to (6) below.

This 'charming little book' was bought by the visitors to Tabart's Juvenile Library in E. Kilner's *A visit to London*, 1808.

(3) ... The first, or Mother's catechism. Richard Phillips, 1810. Calf-backed boards.
[S 19.2.73/100

No further details are known about this edition.

(4) ... *Cover-text*: The first or Mother's catechism, containing common things necessary to be known at an early age. By the Rev. David Blair, author of The Class Book, Universal Preceptor, Models of Letters, Reading Exercises, Grammar of Philosophy, &c. &c. Twenty-first edition. London: Printed for William Darton, 58, Holborn Hill; and sold by Darton, Harvey, and Co., Gracechurch Street; B. Tabart, Clifford Street; Champante and Whitrow, Jewry Street; Wilson and Sons, York; H. Mozley, Gainsborough, and all other booksellers. J. Adlard, Printer, 23, Bartholomew-close. 1812. (Price ninepence.)

Title-page reads as cover text to ... And sold by Darton, Harvey and Co. Gracechurch-street;- C. Law, Ave Maria-lane;- Longman, Hurst, and Co., Sherwood, Neely, and Jones; Gale, Curtis, and Co., and Cradock and Joy, Paternoster-row;- Champante and Whitrow, Jewry-street, Aldgate;- John Harris, Corner of St. Paul's Church-yard;- Wilson and Sons, York;- Henry Mosley, Gainsborough;- and all other booksellers. J. Adlard, Printer, 23, Bartholomew-close. 1813.

13.8×8.6 cm. Pp.72. No illusns. Brick-red stiff-paper pr covers (see text above). Lower cover v. carries list of 8 titles, all pubd by Tabart.
[Private coll.

(5) Title as (4) to ... &c. Twenty-second edition. London: Printed for William Darton, 58, Holborn-hill; ... Bartholomew Close. 1813.

12.8×7.5 cm. Pp.68. No illusns.
[BL, rebound

(6) ... The first, or, Mother's catechism; containing common things necessary to be known by children at an early age. By the Rev. David Blair, author of 'The Class Book,' 'Universal Preceptor,' 'Models of Letters,' 'Reading Exercises,' &c. &c. A new edition, revised by the author, with an added chapter on the accidents of children.

London: printed for Sir R. Phillips and Co.; sold by Cumming, Dublin; Stirling and Slade, Edinburgh; Mozley, Derby; and all other booksellers. 1821.

13.6×8 cm. Pr by Shackell and Arrowsmith, Johnson's-court, Fleet-street. Pp.70 [71]. Wood-engs in text.
[BL, bound with others

Pp.52–59 contain the four poems listed in (2). Here, the author says that they are 'the production of Mr. Lynch, an ingenious Friend of the Author's' (see note headed LYNCH, W. R.). In view of the frequent attribution to Mary Elliott of all poems with these titles, it may be useful to record the first verse of each of Mr. Lynch's poems:

1. Who call'd me first his little boy,
   His source of hope and future joy;
   And bade me not those hopes destroy?   My Father.

2. When first my eyes beheld the light,
   Who said those little eyes were bright,
   And that I was her soul's delight?   My Mother.

3. Who shar'd with me our parent's love,
   And, when my tender limbs could move,
   Would all my infant ways approve?   My Brother.

4. Who was it when we both were young
   First prais'd me with her artless tongue,
   And on my neck delighted hung?   My Sister.

Pp.60–71 contain short, but telling, cautions about 'Tumbling down stairs', 'Riding a wild horse', 'Climbing trees' and so on, vividly illustrated with explicit woodcuts.

This edition was entered by R. Phillips at Stationers' Hall on 5.10.21, giving Phillips's address as New Bridge Street.

13 (1) BLAIR, Rev. David. Reading exercises, for the use of schools; being a sequel to Mavor's Spelling-book, and an introduction to The Class Book, Speaker, Reader, and Pleasing Instructor. By the Rev. David Blair. Author of The Class Book, &c. &c. London: printed for Richard Phillips, No.6, Bridge Street, Blackfriars. Sold also by Tabart and Co. 157, New Bond Street; Champante and Whitrow, Jewry Street; Wilson and Spence, York; H. Mozley, Gainsborough; and by all booksellers and stationers; (price half-a-crown bound) with full and liberal allowance to schools. 1806.

16.8×10.6 cm. Pr by W. Marchant, Greville Street, Holborn. Pp.237 [240]. 56 text wcts, some after Bewick. Sheep.
[Norwich

This title was entered at Stationers' Hall by R. Phillips on 1.8.06. It was one of the books mentioned in E. Kilner's *A visit to London*, 1808. The Editor's advertisement is dated 'D. B. Islington July 1, 1806.'

(2) New edition entered by R. Phillips at Stationers' Hall on 4.1.09.

Longmans entered the 10th edition on 29.12.14.

THE BOOK OF ENGLISH TRADES: see Appendix A, 16(8) and (9).

14 (1) THE BOOK OF GAMES; or, A history of the juvenile sports practised at the Kingston Academy. Illustrated with twenty-four copper plates. London: printed by J. Adlard, Duke-street, Smithfield, for Tabart and Co. at the Juvenile and School Library, No.157, New Bond-street; and to be had of all booksellers. 1805. [Price 3s.6d. half-bound.]

13.4×8 cm. Pp.[iv]+156+16pp. list of Phillips's bks in some copies. Engvd FP+23 other pls, some dated, variously, in 1804 or 1805. Marbled bds, ¾ black roan or red sheep; or plain yellow bds, red roan sp g. (See fig. 3)
[Osborne; Opie, 23 col'd pls and 'Cricket' plain; Private colls; UCLA; McKell; S 13.3.72/136, 19.2.73/102, 2.6.88/235, etc.

The coloured version was priced at 5s. This title was entered at Stationers' Hall by R. Phillips on 7.2.05. It was reprinted in America in 1811 by Johnson & Warner, Philadelphia. Welch 109.

The full-page plates are carefully drawn and show in detail children's activities indoors and out. Some of the boys' games are trap-ball, fives, flying a kite, archery, trundle-hoop, cricket, marbles and foot-ball. Girls are shown playing at ball, on a see-saw, blind-man's-buff, hunt the slipper, helping a small child on a rocking-horse, and skipping. Each game is fully described in conversations and there is a thread of narrative connecting them. Altogether, a book to bring great pleasure to its readers. It was one of the titles selected by the visitors to Mr. Tabart's shop in Eliza Fenwick's *Visits to the Juvenile Library*.

Review: The *Guardian of education*, vol. iv, p.301, disapproved: 'What will the heads of Schools, both public and private, say to an Author who has thus thrown temptation in the way of their Scholars, to employ that time in studying the games which are designed for recreation only, when they ought to be learning their tasks or writing their exercises! ... The prints, for the most part, are as good as they need be in children's books (where the price is moderate), and the designs are far better than the engravings. By themselves, or with the History only without the Rules this Set of Prints would be an acceptable present to children, as the subjects are familiar and pleasing ... endeavours have been used throughout the story which connects the history of the games, to make the Work *instructive*, by the occasional intermixture of moral reflection.'

(2) THE BOOK OF GAMES; or, A history of juvenile sports, practised at a considerable academy near London. Illustrated by twenty-four copper plates. London: printed for Tabart & Co. at the Juvenile and School Library, No.157, New Bond-street; and to be had of all booksellers: by B. McMillan, Bow Street, Covent Garden. 1810. [Price 3s.6d. half-bound.]

13.7×8.5 cm. Pp.[iv]+168+8pp. Phillips's bklist in some copies. Pls as in (1). Marbled bds, green or red roan sp.
[BL, rebound; UCLA; Baldwin; V & A; Gum. 804; S 27.7.84/876; McKell; Private coll., h/c, with 'Price 3s.6d.' altered in MS to 'Price 5s. col.']

(3) Title as (2) to ... London: printed for Richard Phillips, No.7, Bridge-street, Blackfriars; and to be had of all booksellers; by J. Gillet, Crown-court, Fleet-street. 1812. [Price 3s.6d. half-bound.]

13.3×8.9 cm. Pp.[iv]+168+8pp. advts. Pls pubd by Tabart & Co., some dated July 13 or Nov. 5, 1804. Marbled bds, green roan sp g.
[Hockliffe; BL (destroyed); UCLA; Private coll.; S 26.7.84/500

(4) Another edition with the same TP but with pls dated Dec. 24 1818 pubd by W. Darton. Marbled bds, red roan sp.
[PML, wmk 1811; UCLA; Osborne

15 (1) THE BOOK OF THE RANKS AND DIGNITIES OF BRITISH SOCIETY. Chiefly intended for the instruction of young persons. With twenty-four coloured engravings. Dedicated (by permission) to Her Royal Highness the Princess Elizabeth. London, printed for Tabart & Co. at the Juvenile and School Library, 157, New Bond-street, by William Heney, Banner-street. Price seven shillings, coloured. [1805]

15.4×9.4 cm. Pp.[iii]+119 [120]+36pp. Phillips's bklist pr by Roden and Lewis, Paternoster-row. H/c FP dated June 4, 1805, +23 h/c pls dated June 1 or June 4, 1805. Yellow paper over bds, red roan sp g.
[Osborne; BL; UCLA; de Grummond; Miami; Gum. 3593; S 20.4.71/337, 9.7.76/284, 24.11.77/378, 23.5.83/66; Private coll. imp.

The dedication is dated Nov. 1805 from London and reads: 'To Her Royal Highness the Princess Elizabeth, whose taste for the fine arts, whose accomplishments in literature, whose affability and benevolence, do honour to her exalted station, and afford a model for imitation to *every rank of her own sex*, this work is humbly dedicated, by the author.'

Gum.'s copy had 24 h/c pls+one plain, that of a court dress. BL's and UCLA's copies have 24 h/c pls *including* the court dress. In some copies, at least, the red of the cheeks has not been blackened as in (2).

Although this book was first published in 1805, its authorship is often ascribed to Charles Lamb on the strength of a remark made in a letter dated Jan. 2 1810 to Thomas Manning:

> I have published a little book for children on titles of honour; and to give them some idea of the difference of rank and gradual rising, I have made a little scale, supposing myself to receive the following various accessions of dignity from the King, who is the fountain of honour – As at first, 1, Mr C. Lamb; 2, C. Lamb, Esq.; 3, Sir C. Lamb, Bart.; 4, Baron Lamb, of Stamford: 5, Viscount Lamb; 6, Earl Lamb; 7, Marquis Lamb; 8, Duke Lamb. It would look like quibbling to carry it on farther, and especially as it is not necessary for children to go beyond the ordinary titles of sub-regal dignity in our own country; otherwise I have sometimes in my dreams imagined myself still advancing, as 9th, King Lamb; 10th, Emperor Lamb; 11th, Pope Innocent; higher than which is nothing upon earth. Everyman's Library edition of the *Letters*, vol. i, p.295.

It will be seen from Lamb's own account of the content of his book that it bears no resemblance to *The book of the ranks and dignities* ..., which is a dull, instructive work, with not a glint in its writing of the sparkle that illumines Lamb's style. However, the plates are handsome.

(2) A BOOK EXPLAINING THE RANKS AND DIGNITIES OF BRITISH SOCIETY. Intended chiefly for the instruction of young persons. With twenty-four coloured engravings. Dedicated (by permission) to Her Royal Highness the Princess Elizabeth. London: printed for Tabart and Co. at the Juvenile and School Library, 157, New Bond-street, by Heney & Haddon 12, Tabernacle-walk. Price seven shillings, coloured. 1809.

14.6×9.1 cm. Pp.[iii]+136 [137]+(in some copies) 2pp. list of Phillips's school books. Plates as in (1). Marbled or brown-paper bds, red roan sp g. (See fig. 4)

3 'Cricket' in *The book of games*, 14.
Original water-colour drawing,
Sotheby's

A Lady in a Court Dress.
Pub. by Tabart & Cᵒ June 4 1805 Bond Strᵗ

4 Plate from *A book explaining the
ranks and dignities of British
society*, 15(2)

Calico Printer.
Pub. by Tabart & Cᵒ 157 New Bond Street Jan. 1805.

5 Plate from *The book of trades*,
part III, 16(2), Appendix A

THE BARBER !!
C. Knight sculp
see Page 124
London : Pub. Febᵞ 1809, by B. Tabart, & Cᵒ

6 Plate from *Learning better
than house and land* by
J. Carey, 17(2)

[BL; Baldwin; UCLA; de Grummond; Private colls, one with 4 pp. advts; Bod J; Gum. 3594; S many lots inc. 23.5.83/65, 27.7.84/876.

Dedication dated Feb. 2 1809 but text as 1805. Due to chemical change in the pigments, the red of the cheeks in the plates is usually blackened. In this edition the scarlet of the robes is brighter than in (1). In some copies there is no plate for A Knight but there are two plates for Court Dresses, making a total of 24 h/c plates.

THE BOOK OF ENGLISH TRADES: see Appendix A, 16(8) and (9).

16   THE BOOK OF TRADES: see Appendix A.

17   (1) CAREY, J. Learning better than house and land, as exemplified in the history of a squire and a cow-herd. By J. Carey, LL.D. Private teacher of the classics, French, English, and short-hand. London: printed for B. Tabart and Co. at the Juvenile Library, New Bond Street. By Turner and Harwood, St. John's Square, Clerkenwell. 1808.

13.2×8.2 cm. Pp.xii+132. FP dated Feby 1809+5 pls, same date. Marbled bds, red roan sp g.
[V & A

The story is about two boys, one, Harry Johnson – the son of 'a gentleman of noble descent' with 'an unconquerable aversion to his books', – the other, Dick Hobson, the son of the rich man's cowherd, 'careful, attentive, and diligent'. Dick taught himself to read from the Bible and from *Whittington and his cat*, 'a little penny book'. When Dick's father was dismissed because Harry's father lost his estate, he decided to emigrate to America about a month before the Squire and his son took the same course. The story follows their experiences in the New World. Dick prospered, but Harry sank lower and lower until, having become a barber, he found himself shaving the cowherd's son.

   (2) Title as (1) to ... history of Harry Johnson and Dick Hobson. By J. Carey, LL.D. A new edition. London. Printed for B. Tabart and Co. at the Juvenile Library, New Bond Street, By Ellerton and Byworth, Johnson's Court. 1810.

13.7×8.4 cm. Pp.x+[11] 12–143. Engvd FP+5 other pls all dated Feby. 1809. Brown paper-covered bds, red roan sp g. (See fig. 6)
[Opie; Private coll.

   (3) Title as (1) to ... LL.D. The third edition, revised and improved. London: printed for W. Darton, 58, Holborn-hill. (Price half-a-crown.) 1813.

13.3×8.1 cm. No printer. Pp.x+[11] 12–147+5 pp. advts. Engvd FP dated Aug. 17th 1813+5 pls. Blue bds, blue roan sp g.
[Renier; Baldwin; UCLA; BL

William Darton (with subsequent imprints) issued editions up to *c*.1866.

18   (1) THE CHILDREN IN THE WOOD: a tale for the nursery. With three copperplates. London: printed for Tabart and Co. at the

Juvenile and School Library, No.157, New Bond-street; and to be had of all booksellers. Price sixpence. 1804.

12.7×7.7 cm. Pr by R. Taylor, Black Horse Court. Pp.28+4pp. 3 h/c pls dated July 1804. Stiff ochre wrps, advts on lower v. Advt on v. of TP.
[PML, wmk 1804

Plates engraved after designs by Craig. This title was entered at Stationers' Hall by R. Phillips on 20.7.04. T. Hughes advertised it in his list of 'Tabart's Editions' of children's threepenny books, with plain engravings, in *A new and original book of forfeits* [1837].

(2) An edition of 1807 listed in CBY 398, also S 2.7.74/426 and 11.10.79/303. 'B. Tabart, 1807.' Engvd h/c FP+2 h/c pls. Pr wrps.

19 (1) THE CHILD'S SECOND BOOK, containing a variety of new and instructive lessons, in easy and familiar language, principally designed for the use of preparatory schools. To which are added moral tales, calculated to impress on the tender mind sentiments of virtue. Sixth edition. London; printed and sold by Watts and Bridgewaters, Queen-street, Grosvenor-square; sold also, by Tabart, Bond Street, price 4d. in paper covers; 6d. bound. Entered at Stationers Hall. [Can be dated 1802 or earlier – see *The child's third book*, below.]

14×8.7 cm. Pp.36+1p. advts of *The child's third book* and *The new and pleasing game of Multiplication*. Wct FP with 4 lines verse beneath and 14 wct headpieces to poems and stories. Embossed rust-colour paper wrps with pattern in white, floral design with title in elliptic frame on front; on back 'a Nice Book for a good little GIRL.'
[Liv U

The bold, rather crude, almost medieval and most comprehensive frontispiece depicts a village green, with cottages, one large house in its walled garden with a gate, the church, a stream, a road, and boys playing cricket, riding a wooden horse, bowling a hoop, flying a kite, driving a horse and cart and engaged in other busy-nesses. Underneath the picture, in letterpress, are printed the lines: 'Upon the Green, each Holliday,/ Little Boys may skip and play;/ Merrily, from morn till night,/ Themselves, with harmless sports delight./

The long f is used in the text. The page facing last page of text carries an advertisement of *The child's third book*, 'now published, and may be had where this was bought ... (price 4d. – bound 6d.)' So, although Tabart's name does not appear on the title-page of the 'Third book', he evidently sold it.

The 1st to 5th editions have not been traced. Since 'The author's farewell address' in *The child's third book* (see below) is dated 1802, the 'Second Book' was probably published before that year.

20 (1) THE CHILD'S THIRD BOOK, containing moral tales, in verse and prose, on subjects peculiarly interesting to children in general. Interspersed with spelling, selected from the different tales, familiarly explained. With other lessons calculated to correct many vulgar errors, children are liable to, both in speaking and writing. Second

25

edition. London. Printed and sold by Watts and Bridgewater, Queen-street, Grosvenor-square; sold also, by Wilmott and Hill, High-street, Borough. Price 4d. in paper covers; 6d. bound. Entered at Stationer's Hall.

14×8.8 cm. Pp.[36]+1p. advt of *The multiplication cards*, price 1s.6d. per pack. Wct FP, no text. A poem entitled 'The author's farewell address' on p.[36] is sgd 'E.B.' and dated Sep. 1st, 1802. Black embossed paper wrps, on front, in shaped frame, titled in white 'CHILD'S Third Book'; on back, 'A NEW BOOK FOR A GOOD GIRL.'
[Liv U

Tabart's name is not mentioned, but see end of note to 'Second book', showing that Tabart sold this edition. The long f is used in the text.

   (2) Title as (1) to ... prose; on subjects ... writing. Third edition. London. Printed and sold by Watts and Bridgewater, Queen-street, Grosvenor-square; sold also, by Howard and Evans, 42, Long-lane, West Smithfield. Price four-pence. Entered at Stationer's Hall.

13.7×8.7 cm. Pp.34 [36] (possibly [37]). Wct FP as (1) and text wcts. Author's farewell address as in (1). Front cover as (1), back cover not seen.
[Private coll., imp.

21 (1) THE CHILD'S TRUE FRIEND. An edition of 1806, with 5 engravings. was entered at Stationers' Hall by R. Phillips on 12.6.06 but has not been traced.

   (2) THE CHILD'S TRUE FRIEND. A series of examples for the proper behaviour of children. With five beautiful engravings. London: printed for Tabart and Co. at the Juvenile and School Library, New Bond-street; and to be had of all booksellers. 1808.

13.2×8.5 cm. Pr by W. Marchant, 3, Greville-street, Holborn. Pp.108. FP dated June 4, 1806, +4 other pls same date. Marbled bds, red roan sp g. with pr label.
[V & A; Phila., Bod J

Reprinted in America in 1811 by Johnson & Warner, No.147, Market-street, Philadelphia. Welch 199.

The book contains five nice little tales, each with a moral precept at the head. The illustrations, by William Mulready, are full of feeling, with a charming frontispiece.

   (3) Title as (2) except date, 1809.

13.6×8.5 cm. Pr by W. Marchant, 3, Greville-street, Holborn. Pp.108+36pp. Phillips's bklist. FP dated June 4 1806+only 2 other engs in copy seen. Marbled bds, green roan sp g.
[Osborne

22 (1) COCKLE, Mary. The fishes grand gala. A companion to the 'Peacock At Home,' &c. &c. By Mrs. Cockle, author of The Juvenile Journal, &c. Part I [Part II]. *Thus the humble at all times will copy the*

great,/ In matters of pleasure, as matters of state./ London: printed for
C. Chapple, Pall Mall; B. Tabart, New Bond-street; J. Harris, St.
Paul's Church-yard; Darton and Harvey, Gracechurch-street; and all
other booksellers. 1808.

13.1×9.6 cm. Part I pr by Reynell, 21, Piccadilly; Part II pr by H. Reynell,
Piccadilly. Pp. 16, 16. Part I has plain or h/c engvd FP 'Published Jany. 1808 by
C. Chapple Pall Mall & B. Tabart New Bond St.' +5 other plain or h/c pls. Pp.15
and 16 = Notes. Part II has plain or h/c FP, n.d., +5 plain or h/c pls, one dated Feby
1808. Pp.12–16 = Notes. Yellow pictorial stiff-paper covers with bklists on lower v.
Part I carries Chapple's titles; Part II, Tabart's. Price on front covers 1s.6d. coloured;
or, 1s. plain.
[BL, rebound; Osborne; CUL; UCLA; Renier; CBY 353; UBC; Lilly; Opie; 2 private
colls; S 27.7.84/885 etc.

The plates are after W. Mulready. In Part I two plates have no imprint and three
have Tabart before Chapple; in Part II only the last plate has an imprint, with
Tabart first.

This book was reprinted in America in 1809 by Benjamin C. Busby, Philadelphia.

23 (1) COCKLE, Mary. The juvenile journal; or, Tales of truth.
Dedicated, by permission, to Lady Eden. By Mrs. Cockle. [3 lines
prose: 'See page 33'.] London: printed by J. G. Barnard, 57,
Snow-hill, for C. Chapple, 66, Pall-Mall; J. Harris, corner of St.
Paul's Church-yard and B. Tabart, 157, New Bond-street. 1807.

19×10.7 cm. Pp.iv+143 [144]. Stipple-engvd FP dated Jany 1807 by C. Chapple.
Marbled bds, brown leather sp. or brown paper over bds, dark green paper sp.
[Osborne; UBC; Exeter; UCLA; Baldwin; Miami

The dedication is dated Jan. 1 1807. The 2nd edition was published by Chapple.

This is an improving story about a spoilt girl whose parents engage a cultivated lady
as governess for her. This lady keeps a daily record of the child's doings, which she
allows her to read; it forms a cohesive account in which the girl's gradual
improvement in behaviour and education can be followed; and it includes a number
of tales and anecdotes.

Review: The juvenile review, 1817, called it 'a very entertaining and useful little work ...
in every respect suited to children, by whom it will doubtless be read with pleasure
and advantage'.

24 (1) COCKLE, Mary. The three gifts; or, The history of young
farmer Gubbins. By Mrs. Cockle, author of The Fishes' Grand Gala,
Juvenile Journal, &c. Embellished with six excellent engravings, from
original designs, by a Lady of Distinction. London: printed for
C. Chapple, Pall Mall; B. Tabart, Bond Street; and may be had at
every Juvenile Library in the Kingdom. 1809. Price 1s. plain; 1s.6d.
coloured.

12.7×10 cm. Pr by Reynell, Sons, and Wales, 21, Piccadilly. Pp.15. Last p. dated March 1, 1809. H/c folding FP bound in facing 1st p. of text dated June 1, 1809; +5 other h/c folding pls. Yellow stiff-paper pr covers, text on front same as TP. Bklist on lower v. with impt 'H. Reynell, 21, Piccadilly'.
[Birm., Ball

The story (in rather elaborate verse) is about a young farmer who was handsome but stupid and longed for 'A House – a Wife – one darling Boy'. His wishes are granted by a fairy but alas, within two years his farm is failing, his wife is a scold, and 'His darling boy – a very *devil*'. In a clap of thunder the fairy returns and points out, with evident self-righteous relish, that she knew when she gave him the gifts that woe 'from each granted wish would flow' and that 'life's best blessing is – CONTENT.' And so the poem ends. The illustrations are far more attractive.

This title was sometimes advertised as 'being a companion to the Three Wishes, by Mrs. Dorset', published by M. J. Godwin as *Think before you speak*, 1809.

A COLLECTION OF SIMPLE STORIES: see 153(2).

25 (1) [DALLAWAY, R. C.] Observations on the most important subjects of education: containing many useful hints to mothers, but chiefly intended for private governesses. 'We must, while young, elevate the heart above sensible objects, and fill the soul with sacred truths, before the world has engrossed its capacity.' – Saurin. London: printed for W. Richardson, Greenwich; and sold by Darton, Harvey, & Darton, Gracechurch-street; White, Cockrane, and Co. Fleet-street; J. Harris, St. Paul's Church-yard; and Tabart and Co. Juvenile Library, 12, Clifford-street, Bond-street, London. 1812.

17.4×9.8 cm. Pr by Darton, Harvey, and Co. Gracechurch-street Pp.x+126 [128] (i.e. 226 [228]), errata on r. of last leaf. ½ calf, spine g.
[UCLA, rebound; Ximenes, New York, cat. 78

(2) Title as (1) to ... governesses, by R. C. Dallaway; author of the 'Servant's Monitor'. [3 lines prose – Saurin.] The second edition, revised and corrected. Greenwich: printed and sold by E. Delahoy; sold also by Darton, Harvey, and Darton, Gracechurch Street; Longman and Co. Paternoster Row, and Dickenson, New Bond Street; and by Lomax, Lichfield, and Upham, Bath. 1818.

18.8×10.3 cm. Pp.xi [xii]+228. Marbled bds, black paper sp (? original). Impt on p.228 reads: Eliz. Delahoy, (Albion Press,) Greenwich.
[BL; Osborne; Yale U.

The book is largely concerned with religious teaching but the contents also include The Advantages of Good Temper, The Regulation of the Temper, Conversation and Reading, Education of Boys and Advice to Young Women unexpectedly reduced from affluence to a dependent situation. [This note is based on the 2nd edition.]

26 (1) [D'AULNOY, Marie Catherine la Mothe, Countess] The history of Fortunio, and his famous companions. With three copper-plates. Third edition. London: printed for Tabart and Co. at the

Juvenile and School Library, No.157, New Bond-street; and to be had of all booksellers. Price sixpence. 1804.

13×8 cm. Pr by R. Taylor, Black-Horse-court. Pp.35 [36]. 3 h/c pls dated July 1804. Pr buff stiff-paper wrps, advt on lower v. Advt also on v. of TP.
[PML

The 1st and 2nd editions have not been seen.

The plates are engraved after Craig. The story is an English version of Mme d'Aulnoy's *Belle-Belle, ou, Le Chevalier Fortune.*

Entered at Stationers' Hall by R. Phillips on 27.7.04. Tabart's address as given at the head of the booklist on p.[36] is 'Corner of Grafton-street, New Bond-street'.

The *London magazine*, in an article headed 'The literature of the nursery', no. XI, Nov. 1820, vol. ii, recalled the pleasure of reading old nursery tales; 'for really there is more pleasure to us in the names of past delights, than in most of the realities by which we are surrounded. Fortunio, and her band of seven, with their expressive titles, should never be forgotten. Master Strongback, who thought he had not deserved salt to his broth, unless he had carried wood enough before breakfast to load a couple of waggons; sharp-sighted Master Marksman, who used to bind up his eyes when he shot at partridges, lest he should kill more than he wished; quick-hearing Master Fine Ear, to whom the world was a whispering gallery; Master Grugeon, whose stomach was capable of carrying 'six inside;' Thirsty Tippler, Thunder-throated Boisterer, – and Lightfoot who tied his legs when he went to hunt, that he might not outrun his game! It is in this tale that we find the following magnificent description of an ogre: 'Galifron is a giant as high as a steeple; he devours men as an ape eats nuts; when he goes into the country he carries cannons in his pockets to use as pistols!'

> Fa, fe, fi, fo, fum!
> I smell the blood of an Englishman!
> Be he alive! or be he dead,
> I'll grind his bones to make me bread!

'What is well worthy of admiration in the above is the accuracy with which the giant disposes his vowels: but the horrible intimation of these mysterious monosyllables will never in after life, leave tingling on the ears of those who have heard them pronounced with becoming solemnity in their infancy.'

(2) Title and date as (1) except for 'Eighth edition'.

12.5×7.8 cm. Pr by R. Taylor, Black-Horse-court. Pp.35 [p.36 = advts]. H/c FP dated July 1804+2 pls same date. Pink pr stiff-paper covers, text on front: 'Tabart's improved edition of Fortunio: with coloured plates. Price sixpence.' On lower v. advt of Tabart's Juvenile and School Library.
[Private coll.

Advertisement on v. of TP.

27 (1) [D'AULNOY, Marie Catherine la Mothe, Countess] The history of the White Cat. With three copperplates. London: printed for Tabart and Co. at the Juvenile and School Library, No.157, New Bond-street; and to be had of all booksellers. Price sixpence. 1804.

12×7 cm. Pr by Taylor, Black Horse Court. Pp.40. H/c FP+2 other pls dated July 1804, engvd after designs by W. M. Craig. Pr green wrps, advt on lower v. (See fig. 7)

[UCLA, bound with others; private coll. in marbled paper wrps, perhaps not original; PML; S 14.3.72/457, bound with others.

Entered at Stationers' Hall by R. Phillips on 27.7.04. The cover text includes 'Tabart's improved edition'. The plates are engraved after W. M. Craig.

This is an English version of 'La Chatte Blanche', Mme d'Aulnoy's story about a wandering prince who comes upon a magnificent palace. The door opens – he enters – and is splendidly entertained by a beautiful white cat and her feline retinue. In her delightful company time flies. After several remarkable adventures, when they have become deeply attached to each other, the cat begs the prince to cut off her head and tail. He is horrified, but obeys, whereupon the cat is changed into a lovely princess, freed from an evil spell.

Such a bald précis in no way reflects the charm of this imaginative, romantic story, memorable for the tiny, barking dog in an acorn – the magic, disembodied hands that serve the prince – the feast where 'a fricassée of the fattest mice obtainable' repels the prince until he is offered 'certain dishes ... in which there was not a single morsel of either rat or mouse' – and the mystery of a small white cat endowed with human attributes and culture.

The *London magazine*, no. XI, Nov. 1820, vol. ii, in an article headed 'The literature of the nursery', recalled that 'our greatest favourite, if we recollect rightly, was the description of the feats of the White Cat ... This we consider still as a truly elegant tale.'

(2) New edition (not traced) dated 1806, with 3 h/c pls and pr wrps.
[S 17.10.75/1261

(3) Title as (1) to ... copper-plates. A new edition. London: printed for B. Tabart, at the Juvenile and School Library, No.157, New Bond Street; and to be had of all booksellers. Price sixpence. 1808.

12.1×7.7 cm. Pr by J. Diggens, St. Ann's Lane. Pp.36. H/c FP dated July 1804+2 other h/c pls, same date. Pr yellow stiff-paper covers, advts on front and lower v. Advt on v. of TP.
[Osborne

28 (1) DEFOE, Daniel. The life and adventures of Robinson Crusoe, originally written by Daniel Defoe. Revised for the use of young persons, and illustrated with sixteen copper plates. London: printed for Tabart & Co. at the Juvenile and School Library, No.157, New Bond-street, and to be had of all booksellers. Price 4s.6d. half bound, with the plates plain, or 7s. with the plates coloured. Heney, Printer, 23, Banner-street.

14.9×9 cm. Pp.iv+244, (p.[245] = list of pls)+3pp. bklist beginning on v. of p.[245]. FP dated June 4 1805+15 pls dated variously June 4 1805 and Aug. 1805. Marbled bds, red roan sp g.
[Opie; Osborne; Baldwin; Miami

The Advertisement is dated 1805, from London.

(2) Title as (1) to ... copper plates. A new edition, corrected and improved. London: printed for C. Cradock and W. Joy, 32, Paternoster-row, J. Harris; Charles Law; Darton, Harvey, and Darton; W. Darton,•Holborn Hill; and Champante and Whitrow, Jewry Street, by E. Blackader, Took's Court, Chancery Lane. 1813.

The White Cat persuading the Prince to cut off her head.

London Published July 1804 by Tabart & Cº

7   Frontispiece of *The history of the White Cat* by Mme d'Aulnoy, 27(1)

8   Illustration by William Mulready for *The lion's masquerade*, 31(1)

14.5×9.5 cm. Pp.iv+242 (p.[243] = list of plates), p.[244] blank, pp.[245]–[248] = bklist. 16 pls pubd by Tabart & Co., dated variously June 4 1805 and Augt 1805. Buff paper bds, red roan sp g.
[Renier; private coll.; S 21.10.74/685

29 (1) [DEFOE, Daniel] Robinson Crusoe [Harlequinade]. Sold by B. Tabart & Co. June 1, 1809.
[Private coll.

30 (1) THE DOG OF KNOWLEDGE; or, Memoirs of Bob, the spotted terrier: supposed to be written by himself. – I am a friend to Dogs,/ For they are honest creatures. Otway. By the author of Dick the little Poney. [Vignette of spotted terrier as in Harris's edn, 1801.] London: printed for Tabart and Co. at the Juvenile and School Library, New Bond-street. 1809.

13.8×8.6 cm. Pr by W. Marchant, 3, Greville-street, Holborn. Pp.[iv]+140+(in some copies) 7pp. bklist inc. 30 titles of Tales for the Nursery. No FP seen. Wood-engvd TP vignette signed Lee. Marbled bds, red roan sp g.
[Baldwin; Gum. 2235; private coll., 2 copies, one with dark blue roan sp; UCLA; Melb.

First published by J. Harris in 1801 with an excellent frontispiece showing Bob trying to drag a cottage woman to rescue his master, who had fallen into a 'hideous pit'. The eventful tale ends with three short stories demonstrating the fidelity of dogs to their masters. This story's popularity continued to at least about 1840, when it was advertised by Belch.

Review: Writing in the *Guardian of Education*, vol. i, p.327, Mrs. Trimmer said: 'We should have ranked it among *Novels* – as such it is entitled to praise; for, though in some instances too satyrical, we think it certainly describes life and manners, for the most part, in just colours, and in animated and spirited language ... it certainly may be read by young persons in preference to the generality of novels...'

31 (1) [DORSET, Catherine Ann (Turner), attributed to]. The lion's masquerade. A sequel to The Peacock at Home. Written by a lady. Illustrated with elegant engravings. London: printed for J. Harris, successor to E. Newbery, corner of St. Paul's Church-yard; and B. Tabart, Old Bond-street. 1807.

13+10 cm. Pr by H. Bryer, Bridge-street, Blackfriars. Pp.16. Engvd FP dated 10 Dec. 1807+5 other pls by Springsguth after William Mulready, plain or h/c. Pictorial stiff-paper covers dated 1807 with Harris's advts on lower v. (See fig. 8)
[Osborne, plain; BL, bound with others; Gum. 2239–40; Opie; UCLA; Sunderland; FCB pp. 157–60; Bod.; McKell; S 25.2.76/115, 5.4.79/9, etc.; CBY 348; Baldwin; private colls

Variant covers: some copies have covers lettered 'Harris's Cabinet of Amusement and Instruction' and, in MS, 'Lion'; others have printed title omitting 'Cabinet' reference. The wrps are coloured variously blue, grey or buff.

The Publisher's (probably Harris's) note reads: 'It is unnecessary for the Publisher to say anything more of the above little Productions, than that they have been purchased with avidity, and read with satisfaction, by persons in all ranks of life; he has only to hope that the present Production will be equally acceptable.'

(2) Title as (1) to . . . Bond-street. 1808.

13×10 cm. Pr by H. Bryer, Bridge-street, Blackfriars. Pp.16. H/c or plain FP signed 'Springsguth', Dec. 1807, +5 h/c or plain unsigned pls. Plain yellow stiff-paper covers with pr label on front, 'Lion' in MS and 'One shilling coloured'; or buff pictorial stiff-paper covers, on front, picture of J. Harris's shop, on lower v. Harris's advt; or grey wrps with label.
[BL; UCLA; Baldwin; UBC; S 25.2.76/99, 27.7.84/885 and 925; private coll.]

32 (1) [ELLA, Anthony?] Visits to the Leverian Museum; containing an account of several of its principal curiosities, both of nature and art: intended for the instruction of young persons in the first principles of natural history. London: printed for Tabart and Co. at the Juvenile Library, No.157, New Bond-street. Heney, Printer, Banner-square. [1805–6]

13.6×8.7 cm. Pp.xii+163+5pp. bklist (31 titles) beginning on v. of p.163. Folding engvd FP showing the Rotunda, engvd by S. Porter, dated Nov. 12, 1805, no other illusns. Marbled bds, red roan sp g.
[UCLA; Baldwin; de Grummond; BL; rebound; S 23.5.83/18; private coll.]

The Preface is signed 'Anthony Ella' but makes no claim to authorship, though its phrasing seems to indicate that it was written by the author.

Mr. Ashton Lever, the founder of the museum (which was first situated at Alkerington, near Manchester) was nearly ruined by the cost of his undertaking and he was allowed by Parliament to dispose of it by a lottery of 36,000 tickets at one guinea each. However, he was left with about 28,000 unsold tickets which he risked buying for himself. He was unlucky, and the museum fell to a Mr. Parkinson, who built to contain it an elegant house in Albion Street, on the Surrey side of Blackfriars Bridge in London.

Admission was 1/– per person 'without any additional gratuity to the door-keeper' and it was open from 10 a.m to 5 p.m. The apartments were kept well-aired by good fires; and in all the principal rooms there were sofas for weary visitors to rest upon. The cases were labelled so that it was unnecessary to have any staff present to explain their contents (there was evidently no security hazard). The museum contained weapons, articles collected by Captain Cook, minerals, specimens of art, costumes, birds (presumably stuffed) and other objects of natural history.

This information is derived partly from the book itself and partly from *The picture of London* by John Feltham, 1806.

33 (1) L'ENFANT PRODIGUE; ou Azael et Lia. This title was advertised in 1817 as 'Conte moral. Accompagné de douze gravures. Price, 3s.' Not traced.

34 (1) ENTERTAINING INSTRUCTIONS, in a series of familiar dialogues between a parent and his children: interspersed with original fables well adapted to the capacities of youth. London: printed for

J. Hatchard, bookseller to Her Majesty, No.190, opposite Albany House, Piccadilly. 1805. [This edition has no connection with Tabart, but see (2) below.]

15.5×9.6 cm. Pr by S. Gosnell, Little Queen Street. Pp.iv+150+2pp. advts. 24 wcts in the text illustrating 24 stories. Calf, black label on sp, g.
[UCLA

One wct is signed 'Lee'. The lively, attractive illustrations and large, clear type with good margins, make this a better-designed book than its feeble contents deserve. Short, rather pointless fables are introduced by extremely polite conversations between a fond, but instructive papa and his unnaturally moral children.

(2) Title as (1) to ... youth. A new edition. By a lady. London: printed by S. Gosnell, Little Queen Street, for J. Hatchard, bookseller to Her Majesty, No.190, Piccadilly: sold also by J. Harris, St. Paul's Churchyard; Tabart and Co. New Bond Street; and Mrs. Peacock, Oxford Street. 1807. Price 2s.6d. in boards.

13.8×8.4 cm. Pp.iv+150+2pp. bklist of J. Hatchard. Dedication to the Countess Poulett dated from Roehampton, August 21st, 1807. Text wcts.
[CUL, bound with others

35 (1) THE EXILE [Harlequinade]. Sold by B. Tabart & Co. June 1st 1809. As performed at the Royal Theatres.

A folded, h/c, engvd sheet, folded size approx. 8¼×3½", with flaps, each fold and each flap with a h/c picture and verse. When lifted, the flaps reveal more scenes and verses beneath. Front cover has wood-eng. of a fat man in kneebreeches, wearing a witch's hat; lower v. has wood-eng. of a child carrying a bucket of water.
[Private coll.; listed by Muir, pp.209 and 233; CBY no.832; Speaight's *Juvenile drama*, p.110.

This title was included in an article by Harry B. Weiss on Metamorphoses and Harlequinades in *American book collector*, Aug.–Sept. 1932, pp.100–18.

The exile was a melodrama first performed in London in 1808.

36 (1) [FENWICK, Eliza (Jaco)]. The class book: or, Three hundred and sixty-five reading lessons, adapted to the use of schools; for every day in the year. Selected and arranged from the best authors. By the Rev. David Blair, A.M. London: printed for Richard Phillips, 6, Bridge-street, Blackfriars. Sold by Tabart and Co. at the Juvenile and School Library, New Bond Street; by Champante and Whitrow, Jewry Street; Wilson and Spence, York; H. Mozley, Gainsborough; M. Keene, Dublin; and by all booksellers and dealers in books. (Price five shillings bound. [*Sic*, no closing bracket.] 1806.

17.4×10.3 cm. Pr by R. Taylor & Co. Shoe-lane, Fleet Street. Pp.[iv]+500 inc. 4pp. bklist. No illusns.
[BL, rebound; Nottm U

Entered at Stationers' Hall by R. Phillips on 3.4.06 as by 'D. Blair'. Preface dated March 1806 from Islington.

Mrs. Fenwick's authorship is confirmed by a remark in a letter to her good friend, Mary Hays, *c.*1807–8: 'Law, the bookseller, is also willing to employ me. He is enamoured of the extraordinary success of that Class Book I did for Phillips, under the name of the Revd David Blair.'

One of Phillips's advertisements of this book (in which he refers to the author as a male) claims that 'elegance has been united with utility; sound and sense have been studiously combined; and eloquence has always been adapted to the purposes of instruction. In short, every one of the lessons in this Class Book, is calculated to make the young Reader both wiser and better ...'

The daily readings that the book provides are, indeed, solidly improving and instructive; but they are varied in subject and scope. Tabart advertised it for 'miscellaneous reading'; and it was one of the books bought by the visitors to his Juvenile Libary in E. Kilner's *A visit to London*, 1808.

(2) The second edition has not been traced.

(3) Title as (1) to ... year. Selected arranged and compiled from the best authors. By the Rev. David Blair, A.M. The third edition. London: printed for Richard Phillips, 6, Bridge-street, Blackfriars. Sold by Benj. Tabart, No.157, New Bond Street; by Champante and Whitrow, Jewry Street; Wilson and Spence, York; H. Mozley, Gainsborough; M. Keene, Dublin; and by all booksellers and dealers in books. (Price five shillings bound.) 1807.

17.1×10 cm. Pr by R. Taylor & Co., Shoe Lane, Fleet Street. Pp.[iv]+492. No illusns. Calf.
[BL

The third edition was entered at Stationers' Hall by R. Phillips on 15.9.07.

37 (1) FENWICK, Eliza (Jaco). Infantine stories, composed progressively, in words of one, two, & three, syllables. By E. Fenwick, author of The Life of Carlo; Mary and her Cat; Presents for good Boys and Girls, &c. Adorned with excellent engravings, by Charles Knight, Esq. London: published by Tabart and Co. at the Juvenile and School Library, New Bond-street. 1810.

13.5×8.7 cm. Pr by Galabin and Marchant, Ingram-court. Pp.iv+164+10pp. bklist. 6 pls, some dated Jany 1810. Marbled bds, red roan sp g.
[BL; UCLA; Phila.

Contents: Old Ruth; John Jones; The red and white rose; The deaf and dumb boy; Rain at home; Bad tricks; A walk to the fair; The ball dress. Part II: The play room; Lazy David; The French-man; Mary's robin red-breast.

The book was reprinted in America by Munro & Francis, and David Francis, Boston, 1818. Welch 404.

Reviews: The *Critical review*, Feb. 1815, said: 'These little stories are very inviting'; and *The Juvenile Review*, 1817, considered that 'The stories in this work are told with admirable simplicity; we must particularly notice, among others, "A walk to the fair".'

An edition was published in 1815 by Longman, Hurst, Rees, Orme, and Brown, and another in 1816, also by Longmans. John Souter published editions in *c.*1820 and *c.*1823 and a French translation was published in 1826, as shown below.

38 (1) [FENWICK, Eliza (Jaco)]. Infantine stories in French. Contes enfantines en mots d'une, deux & trois syllabes. Orné de cinq gravures. 2. ed. A Paris, chez Masson & Yonet, 1826.

Engvd FP, TP+3 pls.
[UCLA

[FENWICK, Eliza (Jaco)] The life of Carlo, the famous dog of Drury-lane Theatre.

Note Carlo was a real-life dog. In fact, he was the canine hero of *The Caravan; or, The driver and his dog*, which opened at the Theatre Royal, Drury Lane, on 5 December 1803, and the success of the play restored the dwindling fortunes of the theatre. Contemporary caricatures may be seen in the Theatre Museum in Tavistock Street, London, which show the manager of Drury Lane Theatre (R. B. Sheridan) building on this success by planning new seasons of plays featuring not only dogs, but animals of all kinds.

There is no reason to believe that Mrs. Fenwick's story of Carlo's earlier life is anything but fictitious; nor was he, at first, quite as brilliant an actor as he complacently avers on p.63 of his Life: 'Noises were made in the pit, and in many parts of the house, to see if I should be alarmed by them, but I played my part with zeal and sagacity.' In truth, at his first rehearsals he could *not* be persuaded to play his part at all. He was meant to jump from a rock into a tank of water, to seize a drowning child and to swim ashore with him, but he was distracted by the glare of the stage lights and only when the scenery was adjusted to shield the lights did he plunge into the water – but, once learnt, his act never failed. A playbill claims that it 'was received with rapturous applause, by a most brilliant and overflowing audience', and one critic said 'No actor was ever saluted with louder acclamations than this hero from Newfoundland'. The play's author, Frederic Reynolds, cleared £350 in fees.

Sources: Playbill of *Lovers' Vows*, followed by *The Caravan* ... at Theatre Museum, London; article in the *Sketch*, 19 July 1899, 'Dogs on the stage'. And thanks to Mrs Rhiannon Finamore, Assistant at the Theatre Museum.

39 (1) [FENWICK, Eliza (Jaco)]. The life of Carlo, the famous dog of Drury-lane Theatre. With his portrait, and other copper plates. London: printed by J. Wright, St. John's Square, for Tabart and Co. at the Juvenile and School Library, No.157, New Bond-steet [*sic*]; and to be had of all booksellers. 1804.
[Entered at Stationers' Hall.]

13.6×8.3 cm. Pp.ii+[3] 4–68+2pp. bklist. FP (portrait of Carlo) dated Sepr 1804+3 pls, 2 dated as FP. Pr yellow paper over bds, advt on lower v. for Tabart's Juvenile and School Library. (See fig. 10)
[CUL, bound with others; UCLA, with only 3 pls, rebound; private coll. with FP+2 dated pls.

Mrs. Fenwick's authorship is confirmed in the title of 37 above.

This book is puffed in the same author's *Visits to the Juvenile Library*. It is an interesting and eventful story, quite free from didacticism and moralising. It tells how Carlo, as a puppy, was spared from drowning by a very poor boy who shared all his food with him until at last he had to give him away. Carlo won the affection of his new family by saving a child from drowning; later on, his young master took him to sea. One unlucky day, when they were in port, the ship sailed away, leaving Carlo on land. In despair, he wandered about until he lay down under a monastery wall, where he watched poor people coming up to the gate and ringing a bell. He saw that they were given bread and meat, so he, too, learnt to ring the bell; the monks were touched and fed him on scraps. He became quite famous and was at last given a happy home in an English tavern where he was noticed by a playwright who needed a dog to perform in his play – and so the imaginary tale is brought up to reality.

Reviews: The *Critical review*, Jan. 1805, p.107, wrote favourably of this book: 'These memoirs contain the history of Carlo, prior to his coming out as an actor; and they will be found as amusing to little children, as his subsequent exploits were to those greater ones for whose entertainment Mr. Reynolds prepared them. It is hardly necessary for us to add that they are more in place here than they possibly could be on the stage of our greatest national theatre.'

The opinion of *The juvenile review*, 1817, was that 'the dog is above all other animals the peculiar favourite with children, to whom, therefore, this little book will always be interesting; it is indeed a very pleasing production, capable of affording amusement at any age.'

(2) Title as (1) to ... other copper-plates. London: printed by C. Squire. Furnival's-Inn-court, for Tabart and Co. at the Juvenile and School Library, No.157, New Bond Street; and to be had of all booksellers. 1806. [Entered at Stationer's Hall.]

13.4×9 cm. Pp.iv+70+2pp. bklist. FP dated Sepr 1804+3 other pls, same date. Pr yellow card covers, advts on front. On lower v. 'This day is published, in Lilliputian folio, price sixpence, three beautifully coloured engravings from designs by Craig, The Sleeping Beauty in the Wood, a legend for the nursery performing at this time with great applause at the Theatre-Royal, Drury-lane'. Also, list of 32 Tales for the Nursery.
[BL

(3) ... The life of the famous dog Carlo. With his portrait, and other copper plates. London: printed by W. Flint, Old Bailey, for Tabart and Co. at the Juvenile and School Library, No.157, New Bond-street; and to be had of all booksellers. 1809. [Entered at Stationers' Hall.]

13.7×8.3 cm. Pp.68+4pp. bklist. Pls as in (2). Yellow pr stiff-paper covers dated 1809; on lower v. list of 9 titles.
[Osborne; Hockliffe; UCLA; S 27.2.67/1; NLS

(4) Title as (3) to ... London: printed for Richard Phillips, 7, Bridge-street, Blackfriars; and to be had of all booksellers. 1812. [Entered at Stationer's Hall.]

13.5×8.3 cm. Pr by J. Adlard, 23, Bartholomew Close. Pp.68+4pp. advts. Pls as in (2). Brown paper over bds.
[BL

40 (1) [FENWICK, Eliza (Jaco)]. Mary and her cat. In words not exceeding two syllables. London. Printed for B. Tabart & Co. Juvenile Library New Bond Street 1804. Price one shilling

13.4×8.7 cm. Pr by C. Squire, Furnival's-Inn-court. Pp.36. Pictorial engvd TP+11 text engs. Pr yellow or orange-tan stiff-paper covers dated on front 1805, showing '[Price one shilling plain, or eighteen-pence coloured.]' Lower part of top cover carries advts of *The book of trades* and *The book of ranks*; advts continue on lower v.
[UCLA; PML; Miami; private coll.; S 13.11.73/404, 8.7.76/70, 23.5.83/76

Mrs. Fenwick's authorship is confirmed in the title-text of 37 above. No copy dated 1804 on the cover as well as on the title-page has been found. As the title was entered at Stationers' Hall by R. Phillips on 5.10.04 the publishers may have put the coming year's date on the cover to make the book acceptably up-to-date not only at Christmas, 1804, but in 1805 as well. Reprinted in America in 1806 by Jacob Johnson, No.147, Market-street, Philadelphia. Welch 821.

Mary's nurse 'would tell stories to her, or sing old songs, such as she had learnt from the books sold at Mr. Ta-bart's shop, in New Bond Street, where all kinds of books that can amuse or in-struct chil-dren are to be bought.' But the later editions published by Darton changed the address of the shop to 'Mr. Darton's . . . on Holborn Hill.'

Mrs. Fenwick included this book in the list of purchases made at Tabart's shop in her *Visits to the Juvenile Library.*

Reviews: The *Guardian of education*, vol. iv, p.41, said: 'A little simple but interesting tale, invented to intice young children to read . . . We rank it with interesting and innocent books, which is all that an author can aim at in publications for infants.'

The juvenile review, 1817, wrote: 'This innocent little story we have found a universal favourite with children, both on account of its simplicity, and as being a book of more *consequence* . . . as it contains words of *two* syllables . . .'

(2) An edition titled as (1) but with covers dated 1808.

14×8.5 cm. Pr by W. Marchant, 3, Greville-street, Holborn. Pp.36. TP and pls as in (1). Yellow or buff stiff-paper wrps dated 1808, bklist on lower v.
[Hockliffe; PML

(3) An edition as (2) but pr by J. Adlard, Duke Street, Smithfield. Covers as (2).
[CUL; Spencer; Bod., imp.

(4) The possibility of an edition of 1812 is based on the imprint on the covers of the next entry but it has not been found.

(5) [An edition published by William Darton, 1814, but with covers published by Phillips]: Mary and her cat. In words not exceeding two syllables. London. Printed by William Darton Junr. Juvenile Library, No.58, Holborn Hill, 1814. Price one shilling.

14×8.7 cm. Pr by J. Adlard, Duke Street, Smithfield. Pp.36+12pp. bklist in Bod.'s copy. Engvd TP+11 engs. Pr wrps, text reads: 'Mary and her cat. A tale for good children; chiefly in words of two syllables. Adorned with beautiful engravings. London: printed for R. Phillips, No.7, New Bridge-street; and to be had of all booksellers. 1812. [Price one shilling plain, or eighteen-pence coloured.]'
[Phila.; Bod.

Darton frequently reprinted this popular story, e.g. in 1819, 1821, *c.*1824 titled 'The story of little Mary . . .', up to at least *c.*1855. In *c.*1830 he also published a version in French, translated by A. F. E. Lépée, titled *Histoire de la petite Marie et son chat.*

41 (1) [FENWICK, Eliza (Jaco)]. Presents for good boys in words of one and two syllables. London: printed for Tabart & Co. at the Juvenile & School Library, 157, New Bond Street, March 1st. 1805, and sold by all booksellers & toy shops in the Empire. Price one shilling.

13.3×7.8 cm. Pr by W. Marchant, 3, Greville-street, Holborn. Pp.36. H/c engvd pictorial TP+11 h/c oblong engs in text, one dated 1805. Pr yellow stiff-paper covers, on front advts for *The London primer* and Dr. Mavor's *English spelling book.*
[Opie; Osborne

This title was entered by R. Phillips at Stationers' Hall on 15.3.05. It was re-issued in Philadelphia, USA, with Tabart's title-page but with the cover-imprint of H. Conrad & E. Parsons, N. E. Corner of Fourth and Chestnut Streets, 1805; on its p.36 the colophon is: W. Marchant, Printer, 3, Greville-street, Holborn.
[Phila; Welch 1057.

Eliza Fenwick's authorship is shown on the title-page of her *Infantine stories*.

This very pretty book was one of the purchases made by children in *Visits to the Juvenile Library* by the same author. Mrs. Fenwick had no false modesty when it came to puffing her own books.

Reviews: Mrs. Trimmer, in the *Guardian of education*, vol. iv, objected to the price as being too high but *The juvenile review*, 1817, said of it, and of its companion for good girls: 'These little productions make us regret that the author has not condescended to increase their number; for we have met with none that are better suited to young children.'

  (2) A variant edition, as (1) but printed by Squire, Furnival's-Inn-court, Holborn. Buff wrps.
[PML

42 (1) [FENWICK, Eliza (Jaco)]. Presents for good girls. London: printed for Tabart & Co. at the Juvenile & School Library 157, New Bond Street. Price 1 shilling. [1804]

13.6×8.4 cm. Pr by Barnard and Sultzer, Water-lane, Fleet-street. Pp.vi+[3] 4–44. H/c pictorial engvd TP+11 h/c engs in text. Buff pr wrps dated 1804, advt on lower v. for Tabart & Co.'s Juvenile and School Library. (See fig. 9)
[Private coll.; S 10.12.80/52

This title was entered at Stationers' Hall by R. Phillips on 9.7.04. It was reprinted in America in at least three editions, the first by Jacob Johnson, Philadelphia, in 1806. Welch 1058. 1, 2 and 3.

Mrs. Fenwick's authorship is confirmed in the title of her *Infantine stories*, q.v. (37). She puffed this book in another of her works, *Visits to the Juvenile Library*; and so did E. Kilner in *A visit to London*.

An introductory message 'To parents' discusses suitable material for little children's books and says: 'It has been much the practice of late to exclude dolls from among the toys of female children, from the supposition that dolls render them trifling and inactive. A boy is promised manhood and he delights in whips, horses, guns, and drums, because he notices such things to be among the pleasures or occupations of men; and why should not the little girl, with her doll in her arms, imitate the gentle and affectionate duties of her mother? The writer of the following pages has frequently observed the care of the doll to be the foundation of habits of regularity and industry, without in the least preventing girls from joining, as much as was useful and necessary, in the more active exercises of their brothers.'

The text consists of conversations in very simple language about five presents; (1) 'A large wax doll for Lu-cy'; (2) 'A bed for Lu-cy's doll'; (3) 'A din-ner ta-ble for Em-ma'; (4) 'A tea-table for Em-ma' and (5) 'A dres-sing ta-ble for Lu-cy's doll'. 'Gift the Sixth' is a story.

Reviews: *The juvenile review*: 'This book is in the same style as Mary and her Cat, and is apparently written by the same author.' The *Guardian of education*, vol. iv, p.143: 'We conceive this little book to have been the production of the same amusing pen as

NUMBER I.

GIFT THE FIRST,

A large Wax Doll for Lu-cy.

THIS doll has black eyes, brown hair, red cheeks, red lips, and a white neck. It smiles; and you may see two of its white teeth, and its red gums. It looks

as if it could speak, but we know a doll can-not speak. It has a white frock, like Lu-cy's frock. It has gloves on its hands, and red shoes on its feet; and a straw hat hangs on its arm. Ma-ma sends this doll to Lu-cy, for Lu-cy is five years old, and can now take care of a wax doll, and will not let it fall on the ground to break its nose and spoil its face, nor hold it near the fire, as the fire would melt its face, and neck, and hands. Lu-cy will be fond of her doll, and will play with it, and nurse it as ma-ma does the ba-by. Nor will Lu-cy tear and spoil the cloathes of her doll, like a rude girl; but she will take care of the doll's frocks; and when

A 3

9 From *Presents for good girls* by Eliza Fenwick, 42(1). *Brian Alderson*

[Mary and her cat]. We agree with the writer in approving of *dolls* and other toys of what may be called a *domestic nature*, as exciting a taste for feminine employments.'

(2) Title as (1) but can be dated 1806.

13.7×8 cm. Pr by Marchant, 3, Greville-street, Holborn. Pp.vi+[3] 4–44. H/c pictorial engvd TP+11 h/c engs in text. Rose-coloured pr wrps dated 1806.
[PML; Birm., lacking covers but otherwise as above; NLS

43 (1) [FENWICK, Eliza (Jaco)]. Visits to the Juvenile Library; or, Knowledge proved to be the source of happiness. By E. F. author of The Life of Carlo. London: printed by Barnard and Sultzer, Water-lane, Fleet-street, for Tabart and Co. at the Juvenile and School Library, No.157, New Bond-street, and to be had of all booksellers. 1805. [Entered at Stationers' Hall.]

13.6×8.6 cm. Pp.107+16 or 36pp. bklist. Engvd FP (depicting the outside of Tabart's shop, a smart-looking but smallish exterior, with well-dressed people looking in the window)+5 other pls, 3 of them dated July 1805. Two show views of the shop's interior. Marbled bds, red roan sp g. (see frontispiece)
[Opie; CUL; UCLA; Phila.; S 22.10.74/918, 23.5.83/41, etc.; TCCU

This appears to be the only edition, a comment on its lack of appeal, though the story is written in an interesting way. The book must surely have proved a disappointment to young readers since it is really a large-scale advertisement for Tabart's publications. (Mrs. Fenwick's glowing description of the shop will be found in the Introduction to this bibliography.) The list of titles bought or discussed in this story is too long to be quoted in full; but it is noticeable that it chiefly comprises Tabart's most interesting and entertaining books, unlike the much more improving choices of the children in Elizabeth Kilner's *A visit to London*. Between the two visits Mr. Tabart must have sold most of his stock.

Mrs. Fenwick also managed to squeeze in a romantic little adventure among the exuberances of book-buying: on one of their visits to the bookshop the children notice a girl of 12 or 13 years of age who brings in to Mr. Tabart some pictures that he had employed her to colour. Seeing that the work is remarkably well done, he gives her another hundred and they learn that she is helping to support her sick 'mother'. Readers of tales of this period will not be surprised to discover that the girl proves to be the long-lost daughter of the estimable lady who frequents Tabart's shop.

44 (1) THE FORCE OF EXAMPLE. London: published by B. Tabart & Co. at the Juvenile & School Library, New Bond Street. 1810.

12×9.6 cm. Pp.8. H/c engvd TP vignette+8 h/c pls, one dated Jany 1 1810 and another, Nov. 1 1810. Plain dark green or brown stiff-paper covers.
[Opie; Lilly; UCLA

Told in verse, this is an improving story about keeping oneself occupied. A little boy learns this useful lesson from birds, bees, animals, etc.

It was reprinted in America by William Charles, Philadelphia, in 1819. Welch 418.

Review: The juvenile review includes this among titles which 'contain little pieces of childish poetry, some of which are very pretty.'

45 (1) THE FRENCH AND ENGLISH PRIMMER, or An easy vocabulary of twelve hundred common words, for the use of children. London: printed for Richard Phillips, 6, Bridge-street, Blackfriars; and to be had of B. Tabart, No.157, New Bond-street; and of all booksellers. Price ninepence. J. Adlard, Printer, Duke-street, West Smithfield.

13×10 cm. Pp.64. No illusns. Pr yellow wrps, advts for French lesson-bks on front and back.
[BL; V & A, imp.

This title was entered at Stationers' Hall by R. Phillips on 14.9.04.

The book is well and clearly printed, with good spacing and a well-chosen selection of words. In E. Fenwick's *Visits to the Juvenile Library* it is given to a girl about to learn French, but as compensation she also receives *Songs for the nursery*.

46 (1) GENLIS, Stephanie Félicité Ducrest de Saint-Aubin, comtesse de. The Palace of Truth. A moral tale. With engravings. Translated from the French of Madame la Comtesse de Genlis. London: printed for B. Tabart, at the Juvenile Library, New Bond Street. 1817. Price 2s.6d. bound.

13.9×8.2 cm. Pr by G. Sidney, Northumberland Street, Strand. Pp.[iv]+160+2pp. advts. H/c FP+3 h/c pls. Red marbled bds (rebacked), g title on front.
[Bod.

Elegant, prettily-coloured engravings illustrate stories written in the mannered, artificial mode.

The Preface claims, perhaps extravagantly, that 'It has been agreed by Divines, Philosophers, and Critics, that this story of The Palace of Truth is not only the master-piece of the celebrated authoress, but that it is the most effective moral tale to be found in any language. ... It could not fail to correct the most enormous of vices, and will infallibly produce the happiest effects on the dispositions of all its readers.'

(2) In 1819 J. Souter reprinted this book with 152pp.
[Osborne.

47 (1) A GEOGRAPHICAL COMPANION TO MRS. TRIMMER'S SCRIPTURE, ANTIENT AND ENGLISH ABRIDGED HISTORIES, with prints, calculated to render the study of history more interesting to children, and to serve as an easy introduction to the knowledge of the earth. In three parts. Part 1st, agreeing with Scripture History. Part 2d, with Antient and Roman History. Part 3d, with English History. Part I [II, III]. London printed for B. Tabart, 157, New Bond-street. 1802.

15.8×8 cm. Pr by Exton, 87, Great Portland-street. Pp.xiv (+1 blank leaf)+44[49]; [iii]+29 [+1 blank leaf]; [iii]+41 [48]. Folding h/c FP map, dated Jany 20th 1802 by B. Tabart+9 other folding, h/c maps, same date. Marbled bds, black leather sp g.
[Osborne; Gum. 5627; private coll.

There is 1p. errata at end of Parts I and II in some copies but only at end of Part I in others. The long ſ is used occasionally in the Introduction and more consistently in the lessons. Each part has its own title-page followed by an approving note on one page (v. blank) signed 'Sarah Trimmer', recommending the work 'as a most desirable appendage to my Course of History for Children'. This note makes it quite clear that Mrs. Trimmer is not the author of the book and that it was written by a woman.

The author suggests that the teacher should trace the bare outlines of the maps and paste them on card to be hung up on the wall, the details to be filled in as they are encountered in the lessons.

Reviews: The *Guardian of education*, vol. i, said that 'The author has imitated the style of Mrs. Trimmer's infantine histories, so as to produce a proper coincidence with them ... it will be found by itself well calculated to facilitate the future and more comprehensive study of both history and geography.'

The juvenile review's opinion was that 'it is indeed a worthy companion to the Little Histories, by Mrs. Trimmer'. The *Critical review*, vol. xxxv, 1802, p.472, noticed the book and quoted from Mrs. Trimmer's opinion prefixed to it.

(2) Another edition with title-page also dated 1802 was published by J. Harris, Darton and Harvey, B. Crosby and Co. and J. Hatchard, using Tabart's sheets and maps.

[GODWIN, Mary Jane] Dramas for children

Note Though it is not one of Tabart's publications, the following title is recorded here to explain the attribution of the editorship of *Tabart's collection of popular stories* to Mary Jane Godwin, because it has often been ascribed to her husband, William. In a letter in the Ashley Library catalogue from William Godwin to his wife, dated 26 September 1812 from Andover, he writes: 'You well know, you cannot but remember, the surprise I felt at the perusal of your juvenile drama, so firm in character, so far from any mark of a raw and puerile genius.'

This seems to indicate fairly clearly that *Dramas ...* was Mary Jane's work; and so, by inference, was *Tabart's collection of popular stories*. However, entries in William's journal show that he helped her.

For simplicity of reference, and because Tabart's name appears in the title, this collection of stories is listed under TABART, but this is not intented to derogate from Mrs. Godwin's editorship of the volumes.

48 (1) [GODWIN, Mary Jane]. Dramas for children. Imitated from the French of L. F. Jauffret, by the Editor of Tabart's Popular Stories. London: printed for M. J. Godwin, at the Juvenile Library, No.41, Skinner Street. 1809.

16.1×8.9 cm. Pr by B. McMillan, Bow Street, Covent Garden. Pp.[vi]+[3] 4–209 (pp.[210–212] = advts). FP engvd by C. Knight dated Octr 15 1808.
[BL; Opie; Ball; UCLA; Melb.

[GODWIN, Mary Jane] (editor) Tabart's collection of popular stories – see TABART'S COLLECTION ..., 167 below.

49 (1) [GODWIN, William] Bible stories. Memorable acts of the ancient patriarchs, judges and kings: extracted from their original historians. For the use of children. By William Scolfield [pseudonym]. In two volumes. Vol. I [vol. II]. London: printed for R. Phillips, 71, St. Paul's Church-yard; sold by Benj. Tabart, No.157, New Bond-street; and by all other booksellers. Taylor and Wilks, Printers, Chancery-lane. 1802. [Price 4s. half-bound.]

13.5×8.5 cm. Pp.xvi+196; 191+4pp. contents. 5pp. advts. Vol. I has FP+4 pls; vol. II has FP+5 pls. Marbled bds, red roan sp.
[Baldwin

The true author of this book was William Godwin, as has only recently been revealed in *The Godwins and the Shelleys* by William St Clair (Faber and Faber, 1989). It was favourably mentioned – as 'Bible Histories' – in Elizabeth Kilner's *A visit to London*, 1808. It was reprinted several times in America, Welch 1167. 1–5.

Godwin was reared in the narrow religion of dissenting parents and himself became a minister. Later, when he lost his faith, he retained his admiration for the Bible and in his remarkable preface to *Bible stories* he regrets 'how much we lose for the cultivation of the youthful mind by laying aside the bible ... There are no stories in the world so exquisitely fitted to interest the youthful imagination. There is no language in which stories can be told so simple, so dignified, so natural, and so impressive, as the language in which these stories are told. The stories here selected are entirely detached from the greater mysteries of religion. I would advise that they should be read merely as historical tales of ancient times, and a selection made for the pleasure of children.'

Godwin was proud of this preface, which is a notable defence of the rights of children to use their imagination and to read books which cultivate the heart; and he asked that his literary executors should reprint it with his major works. The full text is given in Appendix B.

Review: However, the preface horrified Mrs. Trimmer. She was probably quite unaware of the true identity of 'William Scolfield' but, had she known that he was William Godwin, the famous philosopher and unbeliever, she could not have written a more scathing condemnation of the book. Its author, she declares, is not one of 'the persons we should look up to for *selections* of Scripture for the use of children', for he is not 'capable of understanding the dictates of Divine Wisdom'. 'Let us teach [our children] to shun such teachers, as those *whose mouth is an open sepulchre, who flatter with their tongues, while the poison of asps is under their lips.*'

Mrs. Trimmer further warns parents 'to examine with care every Abridgement of the Bible, every Selection from Scripture ... since the Sacred Volume itself is frequently employed by the enemies of Religion, as an engine of mischief.'

(2) Title approximately as (1) but 'A new edition'. London. Printed for R. Phillips ... 1803. [Price 4s. half-bound.]
[Smith College, Northampton, Massachusetts.

(3) ... Sacred histories; or, Insulated Bible stories: extracted from the Old and New Testament, in the words of the original, and printed in a large type for the use of children. By William Scolfield. In two volumes. Vol. I [vol. II not seen]. A new edition. London: printed for R. Phillips, 6, Bridge-street, Blackfriars; sold by Benj. Tabart, No.167 [*sic*], New Bond-street; and by all other booksellers. 1806. [Price 4s. half-bound.]

13.5×8.6 cm. Pp.xvi+197+3pp. Phillips's bklist. 8 engvd pls. ¼ roan marbled bds.
[Holtom's cat. 69/717

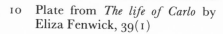

10 Plate from *The life of Carlo* by Eliza Fenwick, 39(1)

11 Plate from *The juvenile Plutarch*, 85(2)

12 One of the many plates in *Geography, on a popular plan* by the Rev. J. Goldsmith, 51(3)

It has not been possible to compare this book with *Bible stories* but it seems probable that it is a newly-titled 3rd edition of that work. The two prefaces are alike except that the preface of *Sacred histories* lacks the long final paragraph in *Bible stories* explaining the author's use of the term 'Jehovah'.

50 (1) GOLDSMITH, Rev. J. The geographical copy-book; containing the outlines of countries, to be filled up by junior students of geography. By the Rev. J. Goldsmith, author of The Grammar of Geography, of The Popular Geography with sixty plates, &c. &c. Entered at Stationer's Hall. Printed for Richard Phillips, No.6, Bridge-street, Blackfriars: sold by Tabart and Co. at the Juvenile Library. Price three shillings.

19.8×24.4 cm. (oblong). Pr by Lewis and Hamblin, Paternoster-row. 2pp. Advt signed 'J. Goldsmith', dated November 1806, from London, repeated in Part II. Part I has 2 folding maps dated Nov. 7 1806+13 fp maps, same date. Part II has 2 folding plans dated Novr 1806 signed 'J. C. Russell junr sculpt' or 'del et sculp.' +13 plans all marked out, ready to be filled in with maps. Yellow stiff-paper pr covers with title as above, no TPP. advts on lower vv.
[Private coll.

Parts I and II were entered at Stationers' Hall by Richard Phillips on 10.11.06. Listed in MLA, April 1807, 3s. each. See also 149, *The school atlas*.

In 1820 Phillips advertised that 'Without these copy-books, geography cannot be studied with success or effect; and by their use more may be learnt in a month than without them in a year.'

(2?) ... THE GEOGRAPHICAL COPY-BOOK. Richard Phillips.

15 engvd pls pr in outline. S's suggested date *c*.1808.
[S 19.4.88/1184

(3?) A copy of Part II, wmk 1810, listed in Blackwell's (of Oxford) 'Children's literature' catalogue, Sept. 1988, item 47, without front wrapper, containing 15 engvd outline maps, 2 folding, dated Nov. 1806, landscape 8vo.

51 (1) GOLDSMITH, Rev. J. Geography, on a popular plan, for the use of schools, and young persons. Illustrated with sixty copper-plates. By the Rev. J. Goldsmith, Vicar of Dunnington, and formerly of Trinity College, Cambridge. [7 lines verse. Cowper.] A new edition. London: printed for R. Phillips, No.6, Bridge Street, Black-friars, by T. Gillet, Salisbury-square. And sold by B. Tabart, No.157, New Bond-street; Wilson and Spence, York; H. Mozley, Gains-borough; E. Balfour, Edinburgh; and J. Archer, Dublin. 1805. Price half-a-guinea, bound and lettered.

16.5×9.3 cm. Pp.xii+647 [648]. Pls dated 1805, some with 2 subjects. 8 maps called for in List of Plates; copy seen lacked 4 maps but had 4 folding maps.
[UCLA, rebound

Osborne notes 1st edition 1802.

In E. Kilner's *A visit to London* this was one of the books bought for the children. It is a handsome and very fully illustrated book. The plates are vivid, full of interest and variety and well executed, and could provide much entertainment in leisure as well as in school hours.

Review: In the *Critical review*, Feb. 1804, p.236, the reviewer complains that 'the real geographical information is included within, comparatively, a few pages, which are filled by judicious selections from the authors of travels who have described the manners of different nations, illustrated with plates. This collection is pleasing; but it is very remotely connected with geography as a science: it is an appendage, rather than a part of the subject. . . . The maps are greatly superior to those of any preceding elementary work.'

(2) Title as (1) to . . . plan, illustrated with sixty copper-plates, for the use of schools, and young persons: being a sequel to the Grammar of Geography. By the Rev. J. Goldsmith. [7 lines verse, Cowper.] A new edition. London: printed for Richard Phillips, No.6, Bridge Street, Blackfriars, and sold by Tabart & Co. at the Juvenile and School Library, No.157, New Bond-street; Wilson and Spence, York; H. Mozley, Gainsborough; and Martin Keene, Dublin. 1806. Price half-a-guinea in boards, or 12s. bound & lettered.

17.3×9.8 cm. Pr by T. Gillet, Salisbury-square. Pp.xii+645+3pp. Phillips's bklist starting on v. of p.645. Folding FP map of the world, 'J. C. Russell junr. delt et sculpt', dated 1807, +9 other folding maps and pls+45 full-p. pls. Calf, title label, sp g. [Osborne; private coll.

The 'Contents' lists 57 engvd plates including maps. The volume seen had 55, including 10 folding. The 'sixty' mentioned in the title were perhaps not strictly adhered to and the placing of the illustrations in this volume does not follow the 'Contents' pagination exactly.

(3) Title as (2) to . . . plan, designed for the use of schools, and young persons: illustrated with sixty copper-plates. By the Rev. J. Goldsmith. Author of Grammar of Geography, of the Geographical Copy-Books. &c. &c. [7 lines verse. Cowper.] Fifth edition. London: printed for Richard Phillips, No.6, Bridge-street, Blackfriars; and sold by Tabart and Co. at the Juvenile and School Library, No.157, New Bond-street; Wilson and Spence, York; H. Mozley, Gainsborough; Stoddart and Craggs, Hull; and Martin Keene, Dublin. 1808. [Price 14s. bound and lettered.] J. G. Barnard, Printer, Snow-hill.

17.2×9.6 cm. Pp.xii+656+2pp. bklist. Folding map FP of the two hemispheres dated 1808+6 other folding maps, n.d. or 1808, +2 folding diagrams, Linear Geography 1805 and Globular Method of Constructing Maps, 1808; +2pp. diagrams: Construction of Maps, Decr 1 1808, Explanation of artificial Globe 1808; +46 engvd fp pls+one fp pl x 2. Pls dated 1806 or n.d. Calf, red label on sp. (See fig. 12) [Private coll.

The 7th edition, 1815, was published by Longmans with Phillips's folding plate dated May 1, 1809. It was entered at Stationers' Hall by Longmans on 2.8.15. The 8th edition, printed for Longman, Hurst, Rees, Orme, and Brown in 1818 still used Phillips's folding plate but other plates were dated 1815.

52 No entry.

[GOLDSMITH, Rev. J. ?] The school atlas, or Key to the Geographical copy-books. Authorship is uncertain. Listed anonymously under 149 below.

53 (1) GRIG, Dorothy. The darling's delight; or Mother's melodies.

Advertised in 1817 as 'consisting of simple ballads, and popular stanzas, composed by the English Poets, from Merlin to the present Laureat, with some Originals.' Price 9d. Not traced.

The author (pseudonymous?) is described as 'Chief Nurse to the Princes and Princesses of the Court of Lilliput.'

54 (1) GUNNING, Elizabeth (afterwards Plunkett). Family stories; or, Evenings at my Grandmother's; intended for young persons, of eight years old. By Miss Gunning, author of The Packet, &c. &c. In two vols. Vol. I [II]. London: printed for B. Tabart, 157, New Bond-street. Exton, Typ. Great Portland-street. 1802.

16.4×8.9 cm. Pp.151; 184. No illusns. Calf, sps g with red labels, also g.
[BL

A collection of stern tales about the misdeeds of naughty children and the more-or-less lurid cautionary stories told by their grandmother to illustrate the faults.

Review: The *Critical review*, vol. xxxv, 1802, p.473: 'These family stories are amusing enough; but the language is, in general, above the comprehension of a child of eight years old.'

55 (1) GUNNING, Elizabeth (afterwards Plunkett). Family stories; or, Evenings at my Great Aunt's. Intended for young persons of ten years old. By a lady. In two volumes. Vol. I. London: printed for B. Tabart, 157, New Bond-street, by Exton, Great Portland-street. 1802.

15×9.2 cm. Pp.122 [123]. No illusns. Marbled bds, red roan sp g.
[UCLA, vol. I only

The prologue refers to 'Those who have condescended to peruse the tales of my poor old Grandmother . . .' – see 54 above. The great-aunt and teller of these new stories took over the care of the young family when the grandmother died. Vol. I contains three longish-short stories with suitable morals. Vol. II has not been located.

56 (1) GUNNING, Elizabeth (afterwards Plunkett). Family stories; or The rural breakfasts of my uncle. Intended for young persons of twelve or fourteen years old. By a lady. 2 vols. bound. Tabart. 1802. Noticed by the *Critical review*, vol. xxxix, p.117. It has not been traced.

57 (1) GUNNING, Elizabeth (afterwards Plunkett). A sequel to Family Stories; or, Evenings at my Grandmother's; intended for young persons of eight years old. By Miss Gunning, author of The

Packet, &c. &c. London: printed for B. Tabart, 157, New Bond-street, by Exton, Great Portland-street. 1802.

16.5×9.5 cm. Pp.145 [p.147 = Tabart's impt]. No illusns. Calf, red label, g, on sp, or marbled bds, red roan sp g.
[BL; Osborne

These fantastic, unnaturally exaggerated stories, told by a fearsome grandmother, are meant to frighten children into good behaviour or meek acceptance of unhappy circumstances.

HARLEQUINADES – see [DEFOE, D.] *Robinson Crusoe*, 29; THE EXILE, 35; MOTHER GOOSE, 112; PARNELL'S HERMIT, 117; [PERRAULT, C.] *Hop o' my thumb*, 127; POLISH TYRANT, 133; ROBIN HOOD, 144.

58 (1) HISTORICAL DIALOGUES FOR 1806 AND 1807. Tabart advertised these in 1807 at 4s. each, but they have not been found. It is, therefore, not known whether he actually published them.

59 (1) THE HISTORY OF DISCOVERIES AND INVENTIONS, chiefly intended for the entertainment and instruction of young persons; being a sequel to The Book of Trades. London: printed for Tabart and Co. No.157, New Bond-street; and to be had of all dealers in books. 1808. T. Gillet, Crown-court.

13.6×8.3 cm. Pp.viii+[9] 10–144. No illusns. Marbled bds, red roan sp.
[BL, rebound; Baldwin; UCLA; PML; Private colls; S 9.6.75/651 and 27.7.84/859/ 876; Renier; Bath

Includes a great variety of inventions – paper, use of sea coal, discovery of gunpowder, printing, parish registers, the microscope, the spinning jenny, etc.

60 (1) THE HISTORY OF DOMESTIC QUADRUPEDS, with entertaining anecdotes: adorned with plates. [3 lines verse.] London: printed for Tabart and Co. at the Juvenile and School Library, 157, New Bond-street; and to be had of all booksellers. 1804. [Price half-a-crown.] Marchant, Printer, Greville-street, Holborn.

15.3×9.5 cm. Pp.viii+[9] 10–135+9pp. bklist beginning on v. of p.135. Engvd FP, 3 subjects, dated Aug. 7 1804+8 pls, 2 or 3 subjects on each, same date. Calf, g sides and back.
[BL; Bod.

Dedicated to Her Royal Highness Charlotte, Princess of Wales, June 1, 1804. On v. of dedication advt of *A tour through England*.

Entered at Stationers' Hall by R. Phillips on 16.8.04. 214 below is by the same author.

(2) THE HISTORY OF DOMESTIC QUADRUPEDS; interspersed with entertaining anecdotes: and illustrated with plates. A new edition. [3 lines verse.] London: printed by W. McDowall, Pemberton Row, Gough Square, for Tabart and Co. at the Juvenile and School Library, New Bond-street; and to be had of all the booksellers. 1808. Price half-a-crown.

13.9×8.6 cm. Pp.viii+137+4pp. or 7pp. bklist. FP+8 pls as in (1), plain or h/c; or different FP – 'A horse' – dated Aug. 11 1804. Marbled bds, green roan sp g.
[BL; UCLA; PML; Miami; CUL

Dedicated to Miss Emily Phillips, June 1, 1808. V. of dedication leaf carries advt for 2 titles.

(3) Title as (2) to ... London: printed for Richard Phillips, Bridge-street. And to be had of all booksellers. 1811. (Price three shillings.)

13.9×8.4 cm. Pr by James Gillet, Charles-street, Hatton Garden. Pp.viii+[9] 10–143 inc. 6pp. bklist. FP of a horse+8 pls with 2 or 3 subjects, some 'Published by Tabart & Co. Aug 7 1804'. Marbled bds, red roan sp g.
[BL; Baldwin

Dedicated to Miss Emily Phillips, June 1, 1811.

61 (1) THE HISTORY OF FORTUNATUS. With three copperplates. London: printed for Tabart and Co. at the Juvenile and School Library, No.157, New Bond-street; and to be had of all booksellers. Price sixpence. 1804.

12×7 cm. Pr by R. Taylor and Co., Black-Horse Court. Pp.36. Pls dated July 1804. Pink pr paper covers.
[Lilly, bound with others; PML

R. Phillips entered this title at Stationers' Hall on 20.7.04. The plates are engraved after designs by Craig. The text is abridged from the same story in *Tabart's collection of popular stories*.

Fortunatus, raised in great poverty, set out on an adventurous journey to seek his fortune. He acquired, by gift, a magic purse which would always contain 10 pieces of gold; and, by trickery, a magic hat which would transport him wherever he wished to go. And so lived in riches and contentment with a loving wife and two sons, one of whom was Andolocia, whose adventures are told in another little book in this series of Tales for the Nursery.

(2) Title as (1) but 'New edition' follows 'copperplates.'

12×7 cm. Pr by R. Taylor and Co., Black Horse Court. Pp.36. H/c FP and 2 pls as in (1). Pr paper wrps titled: 'Tabart's Improved Edition of Fortunatus, with coloured plates. Price sixpence.' Advt on lower v.; advt also on v. of TP.
[Lilly; UCLA, bound with others

(3) Title as (1) to ... copper-plates. A new edition. London: printed for Tabart & Co. at the Juvenile and School Library, No.157, New Bond Street; and to be had of all booksellers. Price sixpence. 1806.

12.1×7.8 cm. Pr by Squire, Furnivals-Inn-court. Pp.35 [36]. H/c FP+2 h/c pls as in (1). Light brown pr covers, advts on front and on lower v. P.[36] = bklist, 4 numbered items.
[Private coll.; S 16.10.75/1181

62 (1) THE HISTORY OF GOODY TWO-SHOES, and The adventures of Tommy Two-Shoes. With three copper plates. A new edition. London: printed for Tabart and Co. at the Juvenile and School Library, No.157, New Bond-street; and to be had of all dealers in books. Price sixpence. 1804.

12.2×8 cm. Pr by R. Taylor & Co. Black-Horse-court. Pp.35 with advt on v. of p.35 and on v. of TP. H/c engvd FP+2 pls, all dated Sep. 1804. Pale green or yellow pr stiff-paper wrps, advt on lower v.
[Hockliffe; PML, wmk 1801; S 14.3.72/457

The plates are engraved after designs by W. M. Craig.

The second part of the story tells how Tommy's ship was wrecked and only he survived. He swam to the African shore where he was seized by a party of 'Indians'. They would have eaten him but they were so impressed by his ticking watch that they came to revere him. However, he began to long for home and, accompanied by a faithful lion which both fed and protected him, he set out to walk across the deserts of Africa, finding on the way a buried chest full of gold. Towards the end of the journey, to his great sorrow, the lion died. At last he came to the sea and beheld an English ship; he carried his wealth on board and they set sail, arriving in England in time to attend his sister's wedding.

(2) New edition dated 1806. Engvd FP+2 h/c pls. Pr wrps. No further details known.
[S 16.10.75/1216

63 (1) THE HISTORY OF JACK AND THE BEAN-STALK. Printed from the original manuscript, never before published. London: printed for B. Tabart, at the Juvenile and School Library, No.157, New Bond Street. 1807.

12×7.7 cm. Pr by C. Squire, Furnival's-Inn-court. Pp.34 [36] inc. 2½pp. bklist. H/c FP+2 h/c pls, no dates seen. Plain blue card covers; or pr yellow covers, title at top, advts below.
[Hockliffe, lacking part of bklist; Opie, lacking a plate; PML

The illustrations are admirable for the simplicity of design and skill of the drawing. Like all in this series, the colouring is exceptionally good. The story is told in forceful, uncomplicated English. It had never appeared in print before this edition (so far as is yet known and as is claimed in Tabart's title) except for a fantastic and highly-coloured version included in *Round about our coal-fire: or Christmas entertainments*, in its edition of *c.*1734, about Jack Spriggins and the enchanted bean. John Harris also published an edition in 1807; it was a different version, in rhyme, titled *The history of Mother Twaddle, and the marvellous atchievments of her son Jack*, by B.A.T.

64 (1) THE HISTORY OF JACK THE GIANT-KILLER. With three copper-plates. A new edition. London: printed for Tabart and Co. at the Juvenile and School Library, No.157, New Bond-street; and to be had of all booksellers. Price sixpence. 1804.

18°. Printed by R. Taylor and Co., Black-Horse-court. Pp.36. H/c FP+3 h/c pls. Advt

on v. of TP. Pr green wrps, advt on lower v. of 'a great variety of interesting little books, adorned with beautiful coloured plates, similar to the present work . . .'.
[PML

The plates were designed by Craig. R. Phillips entered 'a new edition' at Stationers' Hall on 14.9.04. This book was one of the fairy-tales bought from Mr. Tabart in Mrs. Fenwick's *Visits to the Juvenile Library*, 1805.

(2) An edition dated 1806 was catalogued by Sotheby's, 13.3.72/6, but no copy has been traced.

65 (1) THE HISTORY OF ROBIN HOOD. With three copperplates. London: printed for Tabart and Co. at the Juvenile and School Library, No.157, New Bond-street; and to be had of all dealers in books. Price sixpence. 1804.

12.4×8.2 cm. Pr by R. Taylor & Co. Black-Horse-court. Pp.[3] 4–40. H/c engvd FP+2 other h/c pls all dated Aug. 1804. Mauve or pale green pr wrps. On front: 'Tabart's improved edition of Robin Hood: with coloured plates. Price sixpence.' On lower v.: advts of 'a great variety of interesting little books adorned with beautiful coloured plates, similar to the present work; all of which may be had of every bookseller'. Advt on v. of TP.
[Renier; PML; private coll.

Entered at Stationers' Hall by R. Phillips on 14.9.04. The plates are engraved after designs by Craig.

The book opens with an account of England in Robin Hood's day, describing particularly the state of the poor, and the whole story is told in vigorous, unpedantic English.

(2) Title as (1) to . . . copper-plates. A new edition. London: printed for Tabart and Co. at the Juvenile and School Library, No.157, New Bond-street, and to be had of all booksellers. Price sixpence. 1806.

12.4×7.9 cm. Pr by C. Squire, Furnival's-Inn-court, Holborn. Pp.36. H/c FP+2 other pls dated Aug. 1804. Pr deep yellow stiff-paper covers, advts on front and back.
[CUL, imp.; Osborne; S 13.11.73/374

Advertisement on v. of TP. Misprint on p.22: 'vension', 5th line from bottom.

THE HISTORY OF SEVENTY-FOUR BRITISH BIRDS. Advertised in 1808 – coloured engravings of the birds, their nests and eggs. Price 5s. ½-bound. This title has not been found but is almost certainly *The history of British Birds*, q.v. in Part 2, 214A.

66 (1) THE HISTORY OF TOM THUMB: a tale for the nursery. A new edition. With three copperplates. London: printed for Tabart and Co. at the Juvenile and School Library, No.157, New Bond-street; and to be had of all dealers in books. Price sixpence. 1804.

12.8×7.5 cm. Pp.32. Pr by Taylor and Co., Black Horse Court. H/c FP+2 other h/c pls dated Sep 14 1804. Pr yellow or green stiff-paper wrps, advts on lower v.
[BL, rebound; PML; Miami; Renier

New edition entered at Stationers' Hall by R. Phillips on 5.10.04. The plates are engraved after designs by Craig. Advertisement of Tabart's Library on v. of TP. The story is told in prose, with verses interpolated.

T. Hughes advertised this book in his list of 'Tabart's editions', with plain engravings, 3d, in *A new and original book of forfeits* [1837].

The *London magazine*, No.11, Nov. 1820, vol. ii, in an article headed 'The literature of the nursery', said of this noble character, 'The glory of his life, and the sorrow of his death, are yet fresh in the recollections of all who are likely to read this article.'

(2) Title as (1) to ... nursery. With three copper-plates. A new edition. London: printed for Tabart and Co. at the Juvenile and School Library, No.157, New Bond Street; and to be had of all booksellers. Price sixpence. 1806.

11.9×7.7 cm. Pr by Squire, Furnival's-Inn-court. Pp.34+2pp. bklist. H/c FP+2 h/c pls dated Sep 14 1804. Plain blue card covers.
[Hockliffe

67 (1) THE HISTORY OF WHITTINGTON AND HIS CAT. The 1st edition has not been traced.

(2) THE HISTORY OF WHITTINGTON AND HIS CAT. With three copper plates. Second edition. London: printed for Tabart and Co. at the Juvenile and School Library, No.157, New Bond-street; and to be had of all booksellers. Price sixpence. 1804.

12×7 cm. Pr by R. Taylor, Black Horse Court. Pp.36. H/c FP+2 other pls dated July 1804.
[UCLA, bound with others.

2nd edition entered at Stationers' Hall by R. Phillips on 16.7.04. The plates are engraved after designs by W. M. Craig. Advertisement on v. of TP. T. Hughes advertised this title in his list of 'Tabart's editions', with plain engravings, price 3d, in *A new and original book of forfeits* [1837].

The story is told in excellently simple but effective prose and accompanied by three pretty engravings. It is a model story-book for young children of a style unfortunately not too common in those days.

(3) and (4) The 3rd and 4th editions have not been traced.

(5) Title as (2) except 'copperplates' and 'Fifth edition'.

12.5×7.7 cm. Pr by R. Taylor, Black Horse Court. Pp.36. FP+2 h/c pls dated July 1804. Pink pr wrps, advt of Tabart's Juvenile and School Library on lower v.
[Private coll.

(6) and (7) The 6th and 7th editions have not been traced.

(8) Title as (2) except 'Eighth edition'.

12.6×7.5 cm. Pr by R. Taylor, Black Horse Court. Pp.36. 3 h/c pls as in (2). Stiff blue pr wrps.
[PML, wmk 1804.

It should be noted that (2), (5) and (8) are all dated 1804.

(9) The 9th edition has not been traced.

(10) Title as (2) except ... copper-plates. Tenth edition ... 1806.

12×8 cm. Pr by C. Squire, Furnival's-Inn-court. Pp.35 [36]. H/c engvd FP+2 other h/c engs dated July 1804. Light brown pr stiff-paper covers. Bklist on lower v.
[Exeter

68 (1) HOOLE, Barbara (Wreaks) afterwards Hofland. La fête de la rose; or, The dramatic flowers. A holiday present for young people. By Mrs. B. Hoole. Sheffield: printed by J. Montgomery, Iris-Office; for Longman, Hurst, Rees, and Orme, London. 1809.

11.9×10.8 cm. Pp.22. No illusns seen.
[Private coll., lacking covers

This 1st edition has no connection with Tabart, but see (2). It did not apparently have a frontispiece nor an author's Advertisement. The printer was James Montgomery, the poet, and proprietor of the *Sheffield Iris* newspaper.

This is an amusing imitation of Roscoe's *The butterfly's ball* (1807), as acknowledged in the opening lines, though far removed in treatment, for the flowers were not content with a feast but performed a tragedy on the lawn, followed by a pantomine, before which a blackbird provided the interlude by singing 'Rule Britannia'. At last came the banquet but, 'Alas! though the Queen had provided a treat,/ Yet she could not prevail on one Floweret to eat;/ But, they all were agreed, as the day had been warm,/ In drinking a little there could be no harm;/ ... So the Gardener dispensed 'rich Nectarian draughts ... all o'er the table', which 'The guests freely drank, while to drink they were able' and went home rejoicing.

Review: The *British critic*, vol. 34, p.69; 'We have read these verses with singular pleasure, and young people in their holidays, may be delightfully amused by them. A walk in the garden, with this book in the hand, will be a very interesting entertainment.'

(2) Title as (1) to ... rose: or, The dramatic flowers. A holiday present, for young people. Second edition. By Mrs. B. Hoole. Knaresbrough: printed by Hargrove and Sons, for Longman, Hurst, Rees, and Orme, Paternoster-row; sold by Tabart and Co., London; Hargrove and Sons, Knaresbrough and Harrogate; Wilson and Son, and Todd and Sons, York; and all other booksellers. 1810.

13.7×12.9 cm. Pp.24. 2 small text engs, no FP. Blue pictorial stiff-paper covers.
[Private coll.

In her Advertisement on p.[3] the author, encouraged by 'the very liberal and flattering manner, in which this little poem is mentioned, by The British Critic, for August, 1809' hopes it will 'weave a chaplet for the brow of youth,' and will 'offer a banquet to the hand of innocence; and thus, strew a thornless rose, on the path of opening life.' In the copy seen the word 'banquet' has been changed in MS to 'bouquet' – see note to (3).

(3) Title as (2) to ... people. Third edition. By Mrs. B. Hoole. Knaresbrough: printed by Hargrove and Sons, for Longman, Hurst, Rees, and Orme, Paternoster-row; sold by Tabart and Co., London; Hargrove and Sons, Knaresbrough and Harrogate; Wilson and Son, and Todd and Sons, York; and all other booksellers. 1810.

13.4×12.2 cm. Pp.24. H/c engved FP+2 small plain engs in text. Brown pictorial stiff-paper covers dated 1810 and showing 'Price one shilling'.
[Osborne; CBY 362; Baldwin

The author's Advertisement is almost as in (2) with the word 'banquet' changed to 'bouquet'.

69 (1) [HOOLE, Barbara (Wreaks) afterwards Hofland] Tales, in verse, for the use of children, of both sexes, designed for a Midsummer present. Knaresbrough; printed by Hargrove and Sons; for Longman, Hurst, Rees, and Orme, Paternoster-row; sold by Tabart and Co., London; Hargrove and Sons, Knaresbrough and Harrogate; Wilson and Son, and Todd and Sons, York; and all other booksellers. 1810.

13.6×11.3 cm. Pp.24. No illusns. Tan pictorial wrps, upper titled: 'Tales, in verse, for the use of children of both sexes'; lower: 'A Midsummer present, for children.' (At foot) Hargroves, Knaresbrough.
[Lilly

70 (1) IRVING, David. The elements of English composition. Containing practical instructions for writing the English language with perspicuity and elegance; and designed, in the progress of education, to succeed to the study of English grammar, and of the Latin and Greek classics. By David Irving, A.M. London: printed for R. Phillips, St. Paul's Church-yard: by T. Gillet, Salisbury-square. Sold by T. Hurst, H. D. Symonds, J. Wallis, and West and Hughes, Paternoster Row; Crosby and Letterman, Stationer's Court; W. Trespass, St. Martin's-le-grand; Lackington, Allen, and Co. Finsbury-square; Benj. Tabart, Juvenile Library, New Bond-street; Wilson and Spence, York; E. Balfour, Edinburgh; J. Archer and H. Colbert, Dublin; E. and J. Larkin, Boston, New England: and by all other booksellers. 1801. (Price 4s.6d. bound, or 4s. in boards.)

17.2×9.6 cm. Pp.x+262+2pp. bklist. No illusns.
[BL, rebound

Review: The *Critical review*, vol. xxxiii, 1801, p.105; 'We have ... borne willing testimony to the merit of very many excellent treatises on the manner of speaking and writing our native language with propriety; but the greatest number of these productions are of too considerable a bulk to be applied to the purpose of instructing youth. In the pages before us the compiler has avoided that inconvenience, yet, nevertheless, his positions are laid down in very clear terms ...'

(2) Title as (1) to ... composition. By David Irving, LL.D. A new edition. London: printed for Richard Phillips, No.6, Bridge-street, Blackfriars; by J. Adlard, Duke-street, Smithfield. 1809. (Price 7s.6d. bound and lettered.)

19.7×11.1 cm. Pp.x+318. No illusns.
[BL, rebound

71 (1) JAUFFRET, Louis François. The little hermitage, a tale; illustrative of the arts of civilized life. By L. F. Jauffret, author of The

Travels of Rolando, &c. London: printed for Richard Phillips, No.6, Bridge-street, Blackfriars. W. Heney, Printer, Banner-square. 1805.

13.2×8.2 cm. Pp.72. Engvd FP+one other pl. Yellow pr card covers showing 'Price one shilling' and 'Published by Tabart & Co. at the Juvenile and School Library ...'. v. of lower cover carries list of bks instructive, interesting, and superior.
[BL, Gum. 3181

The little hermitage was serialized in the *Juvenile Library*, q.v. (215). The story is about three children who have decided to build a little house and are working hard but without skill. Along comes a stranger who asks for lodging and work and their father takes him on as a cowherd. The stranger soon sees that the children will never build a strong house by themselves so he shows them a simple way to go about it and in three days it is done. He goes on to instruct them in all sorts of natural history and they come to love him. At last he goes away; but he sends them from Paris a box full of the prettiest presents and books and a letter expressing both his gratitude for their kindness when he was in need and his hopes of seeing them again one day.

This is a very interesting, well-told story with sensitive descriptions of the country scene and about happy, enterprising children. It was one of the books chosen by the visitors to Mr. Tabart's bookshop in E. Fenwick's *Visits to the Juvenile Library*.

S 10.12.80/34 lists an undated edition published by Brandard, Birmingham, *c.*1805, with 3 plates.

72 (1) [JAUFFRET, Louis François] The little hermitage, with other tales. Good and Evil, The Characters, and The Gifts of Fate. London: printed for R. Phillips, No.71, St. Paul's Church-yard, sold by B. Tabart, at the Juvenile Library, New Bond Street; and by all other booksellers. Wilks and Taylor, Printers, Chancery-lane. 1801. (Price two shillings.)

13.9×8.7 cm. Pp.133. FP+one other pl. Marbled bds, leather sp.
[Baldwin; Wayne

The tales were serialized in the *Juvenile library*, q.v. This is one of the books listed in Mrs. Fenwick's *Visits to the Juvenile Library*.

Reviews: The *Critical review*, vol. xxxiv, 1802, p.111, said that this collection of stories 'elucidates many technical terms, and developes [*sic*] many branches of the science of gardening.' Writing in the *Guardian of education*, vol. i, p.119, Mrs. Trimmer detects Rousseauist influence and can see no good in a story that will 'draw children's mind's [*sic*] from regular studies, and set their imaginations at work upon impracticable schemes' and she finds it 'very improper for the perusal of boys either as a book of amusement or instruction'. She concludes caustically that 'it was originally written for the young *citizens* of France after whose model we trust Christian parents will not think it expedient to educate the children of Britain.'

The unexceptionable *moral reflections* of the second tale ('Good and Evil') 'cannot hide from the attentive reader, the design of this Tale, which is evidently to prejudice young minds against the ministers of public justice'. The third tale, 'The Characters', does not excite any acerbity, but the fourth, 'The Gifts of Fate', can only be understood by children who 'must have advanced farther in the paths of corruption, than we hope is possible for any to do in their early years, who are not brought up among the most abandoned of their species.'

(2) Title as (1) to ... hermitage, and other tales; translated from the French of L. F. Jauffret, author of The Travels of Rolando. Second edition. London: printed for R. Phillips, No.71, St. Paul's Church-yard; and sold by all booksellers. Taylor, Printer, Black-Horse-court. 1804. [Price two shillings.]

13.6×8 cm. Pp.[iv]+176 inc. 5pp. bklist. FP+one other engvd pl. Marbled bds, red roan sp g.
[Osborne; Phila.; Miami

The Advertisement states that 'To The Little Hermitage are now added The Characters, Winter, The Father and his Three Sons, The Wooden Leg, Selico, and True Courage.'

73 (1) JAUFFRET, Louis François. The travels of Rolando; containing, in a supposed tour round the world, authentic descriptions of the geography, natural history, manners, and antiquities of various countries. Translated from the French of L. F. Jauffret. In four volumes. Vol. I [II, III, IV]. London: printed for Richard Phillips, St. Paul's Church-yard; by J. Taylor, Black-Horse-court; and sold by Tabart and Co. at the Juvenile and School Library, No.157, New Bond-street; and all booksellers. 1804.

15.5×9 cm. Marbled bds, red roan sp g.

Vol. I: Pp.viii [x]+220. Folding map FP dated Feb. 20 1804+3 pls dated Feb. 14 1804.
Vol. II: Pp.[iv]+224. Folding map FP+3 pls dated Feb. 14 1804.
Vol. III: Pp.[iv]+228. 3 pls dated Feb 14 or Mar. 1 1804, drawn by Dayes, engvd by W. J. Newton.
Vol. IV: Pp.[iv]+220. 3 pls dated Mar. 1 1804, drawn by Dayes, engvd by W. J. Newton.
The maps and plates are sometimes arranged differently.
[BL, rebound; Osborne; UCLA; PML; Birm. vols I and IV; private coll.

The 'Preface by the Translator', signed 'L.A. [i.e. Lucy Aikin], Stoke Newington, Feb. 1804', describes this work as 'a series of authentic descriptions, interweaving them with a set of imaginary adventures.'

The work appeared in fortnightly numbers, with the 24th of which this translation concludes; and thereafter it was published in volumes. The excellent illustrations are full of action and interest. This was a splendid book of adventures for boys (and probably for girls too).

(2) Title as (1) to ... Phillips, Bridge Street, Blackfriars; and sold by Tabart and Co. at the Juvenile and School Library, No.157, New Bond Street; and all booksellers. 1808. [Price 14s. half-bound.]

15×9.2 cm. Pr by B. McMillan, Bow Street, Covent Garden. Pp. as in (1). Marbled bds, red roan sp g.

Vol. I: FP dated Feb. 14 1804+3 pls, 1 folding.
Vol. II: 3 pls, FP dated Feb. 14 1804.
Vol. III: 3 pls, FP dated Mar 1 1804.
Vol. IV: Pp.[iv]+220+[4]. 4 pls, one folding, FP dated Mar 1 1804, signed 'Dayes del. W. J. Newton sculp.'
[PML; Miami; Renier, vol. I; Nottm U

No edition is mentioned in the title. There is an error in pagination in vol. II: 109 as 10 .

(3) Title as (2) to ... In four volumes. Vol. I [II, III, IV]. Third edition. London: printed for Richard Phillips, sold by John Souter, No.1, Paternoster Row; and to be had of all booksellers. 1813. [Price 14s. half-bound.]

15.3×9.1 cm. Pr by G. Sidney, Northumberland Street, Strand. Pp. as in (1). Blue bds, red roan sp g. Plates:
Vol. I: FP dated Feb. 14 1804+2 pls.
Vol. II: FP dated Feb. 14 1804.
Vol. III: Folding map FP.
Vol. IV: FP+1 pl., both dated Mar. 1 1804.
[Renier; Baldwin; UCLA

Later editions were printed for Richard Phillips in 1822, 1823, 1829; an edition of 1853, illustrated by William Harvey, was published by George Routledge & Co.

74 (1) JAUFFRET, Louis François. Visits to the Menagerie, and the Botanical Garden at Paris: containing a view of natural history, for the instruction of young persons. From the French of L. F. Jaufret. Vol. I [vol. II]. London: printed for R. Phillips, No.71, St. Paul's; sold by B. Tabart, at the Juvenile Library, New Bond-street. By T. Gillet, Salisbury-square. 1801. (Price four shillings.)

13.6×8 cm. Pp.vi [viii]+123; [iv]+152 inc. 11pp. list of Phillips's bks. Folding FP in vol. I dated Oct. 17 1801 engvd by T. Owen, no other illusns. Blue marbled bds, red roan sp g.
[BL; Renier; Baldwin; private coll.

This work was serialized in the *Juvenile Library*, q.v. (215).

In E. Kilner's *A visit to London* a girl asked her mother to buy this book, but the mother replied 'I have already ordered a great many books for you, and when I have bought some for Henry and Emma, I shall have laid out as much money as I can afford at one time'. However, in Eliza Fenwick's *Visits to the Juvenile Library* this book *was* bought for one of the children.

Reviews: In the *Guardian of education*, vol. i, p.201, Mrs. Trimmer approves on the whole, though she detects a republican flavour in the account of Nature's orderliness.
The *British critic*, vol. 22, p.694: 'We recommend these little volumes for the use of children from the age of about seven to twelve years. The accounts contained in them of birds, insects, quadrupeds, and vegetables (carried off from various countries) are brief, but yet entertaining; and, in many instances, novel and instructive. ... The translator has executed his task well; and the volumes deserve, in another impression, the addition of *plates*, which are necessary to very young persons.' The *Critical review*, vol. xxxiv, 1802, p.111, considered that 'In the Visits to the Menagerie ... are some very pleasing views of animated nature.'

(2) Title as (1) to ... Menagerie, and the Botanical Garden at Paris: being an introduction to natural history and botany, for the instruction of young persons. (With four plates.) From the French of L. F. Jauffret. London: printed for R. Phillips, No.71, St. Paul's; and sold by B. Tabart, at the Juvenile Library, New Bond-street. 1804. [Price half-a-crown.]

13.5×8.5 cm. Pr by Marchant, 3, Greville-street, Holborn. Pp.x+[11] 12–247+4pp. on 2 leaves of Tabart's and Phillips's bklists. Folding FP as in (1)+3 other engvd pls, one folded at top. Marbled or brown-paper-covered bds, red roan sp g.
[UCLA; Gum. 3128; private colls, one with wmks 1803, 1805, another with wmk 1802.

Two of the three new plates have apparently been designed for other books, one being too tall and the other headed 'Frontispiece'.

(3) Title as (2) to ... persons. With four plates. From the French of L. F. Jauffret. London: printed for R. Phillips, 6, Bridge-street, Blackfriars; and sold by B. Tabart, at the Juvenile Library, New Bond-street. 1806. [Price half-a-crown.]

13.6×8.4 cm. Pr by W. Heney, 76, Fleet-street. Pp.viii+[9] 10–180+36pp. bklist of R. Phillips. Folding FP as in (1)+2 other folding pls and 1 full-p. headed 'Frontispiece'. Marbled bds, red roan sp g.
[CUL

(4) As (3) but no bklist. FP same subject but not folding, no text. Other pls as in (3). Marbled bds, green roan sp g.
[CUL

(5) ... Visits to the Menagerie and the Botanical Garden at Paris: being an introduction to natural history and botany, for the instruction of young persons. With four plates. From the French of L. F. Jauffret. London: printed for R. Phillips, 7, Bridge-street, Blackfriars; and sold by all booksellers. 1811. [Price half-a-crown.]

13.6×8.7 cm. Pr by James Gillet, Charles-street, Hatton Garden. Pp.viii+180. No FP present in Osborne's copy, 2 folding pls+1 full-p. Marbled bds, red roan sp g.
[Osborne, imp.

75 (1) [JENNER, Isaac] Fortune's football. Most humbly dedicated, by permission, to the young family of the Right Honble Lady Ann Hudson. London: printed for the author; and sold by Tabart and Co. Juvenile Library, No.157, New Bond Street. 1806.

13.5×7.8 cm. Pr by S. Gosnell, Little Queen Street. Pp.120. Engvd FP showing a man reading outside a bkshop and one other pl, a full-length portrait of a stumpy man, facing verses:

> Famed Aesop of old,
> I've often been told,
> Was short and deformed like me...

Plain brown bds, leather sp; or Dutch floral bds.
[BL; Osborne; Bod.; S 13.3.72/94 and 27.7.84/876; CUL; UCLA; PML; TCCU; FCB p.135

'To the Readers' on pp.[5]–13 is an earnest plea on behalf of reading carefully. The author advises his 'dear young friends' to pay full attention to the stops, which 'are not merely to allow breathing-time, but also to arrange each suggestion in a sentence in due order as it passes in successional review before our eyes; and that there may be time for them to affect the heart. ... Though there are no bones in a cheesecake or custard, yet if eaten in too much haste, the crumbs may occasion us such a disagreeable sensation, as its sweetness can scarcely make amends for.'

The book begins: 'My father, John Jenner, was born at Hesse Cassel in the year 1700 ...' and goes on to say that he brought the art of silver-plating from Paris to England before 1722. The author was born in 1750. By the time he was 13 he had had several serious accidents and, by mismanagement rather than accident, his legs were bowed.

A mobile chair was made specially for him so that he could move around. He became a mezzotint engraver and later obtained the friendship and patronage of Sir Joshua Reynolds.

Review: The *Guardian of education*, vol. v, p.420: '... we recommend not to the *perusal* only of our Readers, but to their *purchas*; as, at a trifling expence, they may contribute towards the comfort of an ingenious Man, who has been called upon to endure, in the course of nearly sixty years, a series of misfortunes, such as do not fall to the lot of many men; but which, under the disadvantageous circumstance of *personal deformity*, he has hitherto struggled through, with *cheerfulness* and *fortitude* ... we are particularly anxious to promote the sale of the Book ...'.

76 (1) [JOHNSON, Richard] The seven champions of Christendom: a tale for the nursery. With three copper plates. A new edition. London: printed for Tabart and Co. at the Juvenile and School Library, No.157, New Bond-street: and to be had of all dealers in books. Price sixpence. 1804.

12.8×8.2 cm. Pr by Taylor and Co. Black Horse Court. Pp.[ii]+3–44. H/c FP (caption illegible)+2 h/c pls, one dated Sept. 13 1804, the other shaved. Yellow, pale green or purple pr stiff-paper covers with advt on lower v. of Tabart's shop.
[V & A; Hockliffe; UCLA, bound with others and date on TP shaved; PML

Advertisement on v. of title-page. The plates are engraved after designs by Craig. A new edition was entered at Stationers' Hall by R. Phillips on 5.10.04. T. Hughes advertised this title in his list of 'Tabart's editions', with plain engravings, 3d, in *A new and original book of forfeits* [1837].

(2) ... The seven champions of Christendom. A tale for the nursery. With three copper-plates. [Then as (1) to ...] of all booksellers. Price sixpence. 1806.

11.8×8.2 cm. Pr by Squire, Furnival's-Inn-court. Pp.44. H/c FP dated Nov. 1804+one pl dated Sep. 14 1804 and one other n.d. Orange-coloured stiff-paper pr covers, advts on front and lower v. Advt also on v. of TP.
[Baldwin; Osborne

JOHNSON, W. R.
Note W. R. Johnson appears to be the same person as W. R. Lynch, who wrote *The world described, in easy verse* ... 'by W. R. Lynch, Esq. author of the poetical histories of England, Greece, and Rome.' The advertisements at the end of the 1820 edition of that book (which was published by Sir Richard Phillips) include an entry for itself, again showing W. R. Lynch, Esq. as the author of the 'Poetical histories'. Perhaps W. R. Johnson changed his surname to Lynch after writing the history books. *A tour through England*, 1811, in its booklist still shows them as by Johnson, but Longman's advertisement in Mavor's *The English spelling book*, 273rd edition, 1822, gives *The world described* as by Mr. T. Lynch Johnson which, if anything, increases the confusion. See also [LYNCH, Mr.] *The nursery concert* ..., 99 below.

77 (1) JOHNSON, W. R. Goldsmith's Grammar of Geography, rendered into easy verse. Describing the situation, manners, and produce of all nations. For the use of young persons. By the Rev. W. R. Johnson, author of the Poetical Histories of England, Greece, and Rome. Illustrated by notes. London: printed for B. Tabart, Juvenile

Library, New Bond Street. Sold by all booksellers; with full allowance to schools. 1809. Price 4s. half-bound.

15×9.2 cm. Pr by W. McDowall. Pp.8+208 inc. 8pp. bklist. Folding map FP pubd by Phillips, dated 1809. No other illusns. Marbled bds, red roan sp g.
[Opie

78 (1) JOHNSON, W. R. The history of England, in easy verse: from the invasion of Julius Caesar, to the beginning of the year 1806. Written for the purpose of being committed to memory by young persons of both sexes. By W. R. Johnson, A.M. London: printed for Tabart and Co. No.157, New Bond Street; and sold by all booksellers, with the full allowance to schools. 1806. J. Adlard, Printer, Duke Street, Smithfield. (Price half-a-crown.)

14.7×9.1 cm. Pp.xii+129+3pp. bklist. Folding map of England, undated, unsigned. Marbled bds, green roan sp g.
[BL; UCLA; Liv U; S 12.11.73/92 and 2.6.75/54

The work is inscribed to 'Master Richard Phillips, a young gentleman, who in his seventh year evinces a love of learning, and a dutiful and amiable disposition, such as render him an example to those of his own age, and a source of hope to his parents.' It is dated March 1806 from Richmond Hill. The Preface is dated March 16, 1806. There is no Advertisement. E. Kilner puffed this book in *A visit to London*.

(2) Title as (1) to . . . Caesar, to the close of the year 1809. Written for the purpose of being committed to memory by young persons of both sexes. By W. R. Johnson, A.M. The second edition, improved and corrected. London; printed for Tabart and Co. No.157, New Bond Street; and sold by all booksellers, with the full allowance to schools. 1810. (Price three shillings.)

15.2×8.5 cm. Pr by W. McDowall, Pemberton Row, Gough Square. Pp.viii+136 (the '6' has dropped out). Folding map of England engvd by S. I. Neele, Strand, dated June 1st 1805, pubd by R. Phillips, New Bridge Street. Brown-paper-covered bds, red roan sp g.
[BL, rebound; Osborne

The Dedication is almost as in (1) except that Master Phillips is now in his 10th year and it is dated Jan. 1810, as are the author's Advertisement and the Preface.

(3) Another 2nd edition dated 1812 was printed for R. Phillips, No. 7, Bridge Street, Blackfriars, by J. Adlard, 23, Bartholomew Close, price three shillings. The engraved map is not signed.
[UCLA

79 (1) JOHNSON, W. R. The history of Greece, in easy verse; from the earliest period, to its conquest by the Romans. Written for the purpose of being committed to memory by young persons of both sexes. By W. R. Johnson, A.M. author of the Histories of England and of Rome, in easy verse. Illustrated with a map. London: printed for B. Tabart, Juvenile Library, New Bond Street. Sold by all booksellers; with full allowance to schools. 1807. (Price half-a-crown.)

14.8×8.7 cm. ½-title. Pr by W. McDowall, Pemberton Row, Gough Square. Pp.[ix]+129 (+1 blank leaf+16pp. Phillips's advts in some copies). Folding map of Ancient Greece, pr for Richard Phillips, 6, New Bridge Street, at the beginning or end of the book. Marbled bds, red roan sp g.
[BL, rebound; private coll.

Dedicated to 'Master Alfred Phillips, a young gentleman, in his sixth year, ... by his friend and tutor, W. R. Johnson. Richmond Hill, May 1807.'

E. Kilner puffed this book in *A visit to London*.

(2) An edition dated 1811 was printed for Richard Phillips, Bridge Street, Blackfriars.
[Baldwin

80 (1) JOHNSON, W. R. The history of Rome. In easy verse. From the earliest period to the extinction of the Western Empire. Written for the purpose of being committed to memory by young persons of both sexes. By W. R. Johnson, A.M. author of The Histories of England and of Greece, in easy verse. Illustrated with a map. London: printed for B. Tabart, Juvenile Library, New Bond Street, sold by all booksellers; with full allowance to schools. 1808. Price half-a-crown.

14.6×8.6 cm. ½-title. Pr by W. McDowall, Pemberton Row, Gough Square. Pp.150+4pp. Phillips' bklist. Folding map FP of the Roman Empire, drawn and engvd by J. C. Russell junr. Marbled bds, green roan sp g.
[BL; Baldwin; Birm.; S 17.10.75/1375

The Preface is dated Nov. 5 1808 from Richmond Hill. Dedication, same date, to Master Horatio Phillips. This book was puffed in E. Kilner's *A visit to London*.

(2) An edition dated 1811 printed for Richard Phillips, Bridge Street, Blackfriars, by B. McMillan, Bow Street, Covent Garden, with a map engraved by Neele.
[BL; CUL

81 (1) JOYCE, Rev. J. A key to Joyce's Arithmetic; containing solutions and answers to all the questions in the work. To which is added, an appendix, showing the method of making mental calculations, with numerous examples. By the same author. London: printed for Richard Phillips, Bridge-street, Blackfriars; by T. Gillet, Crown-court; and sold by Tabart and Co. New Bond-street; Wilson and Co. York; Mozley, Gainsborough; Stoddart and Co. Hull; Berry, Edinburgh; Keene, Dublin; and by all other booksellers: with the full allowance to schools. 1808.

14×8.2 cm. Pp.viii+208. Calf.
[BL

Entered at Stationers' Hall by R. Phillips on 22.10.08. In the Preface, dated Oct. 4, 1808, from Camden Town, 'the author hopes the answers will be found correct ... still ... "humanum est errare"'.

(2) As (1) to ... work. To which are added, appendices, showing the method of making mental calculations, and a new mode of setting sums in the early rules of arithmetic, without trouble to the master. With numerous examples. By the same author. A new edition, carefully corrected. London: printed for Richard Phillips, Bridge-street, Blackfriars; by Gillet and Son, Crown-court; and sold by Sherwood and Co. Paternoster-row; Tabart and Co. New Bond-street; Wilson and Co. York; Mozley, Gainsborough; Stoddard and Co. Hull; Bryce and Co. and Berry, Edinburgh; Keene, and Wogan and Co. Dublin; and by all other booksellers: with the full allowance to schools. 1810. [price 3s.6d. bound.]

14×8.2 cm. Pp.viii+220+6pp. bklist.
[BL, rebound

A new edition was entered by R. Phillips at Stationers' Hall on 20.2.10.

82 (1) JOYCE, Rev. J. A system of practical arithmetic, applicable to the present state of trade, and money transactions, illustrated by numerous examples under each rule; for the use of schools. By the Rev. J. Joyce, author of Scientific Dialogues, &c. &c. Second edition. London: printed for Richard Phillips, Bridge-street, Blackfriars; and sold by Tabart and Co. New Bond-street; Wilson and Co. York; Mozley, Gainsborough; Stoddart and Co. Hull; and by all other booksellers; with the full allowance to schools. 1808. T. Gillet, Crown-court, Fleet-street.

17.1×10.1 cm. Pp.viii+256.
[BL

Entered at Stationers' Hall by R. Phillips on 11.6.08. The Preface is dated May 24, 1808, from Camden Town.

(2) As (1) to ... Joyce. A new edition, revised and corrected. London: printed for Richard Phillips, and sold by Sherwood and Co. Paternoster-row: Tabart and Co. New Bond-street; Wilson and Co. York; Mozley, Gainsborough; Stoddart and Co. Hull; Bryce and Co. and Berry, Edinburgh; Keene and Wogan and Co. Dublin; and by all other booksellers: with the full allowance to schools. 1810. [Price three shillings and sixpence bound.]

17×10 cm. Pr by T. Gillet, Crown Court, Fleet Street. Pp.v [vi]+258.
[BL, rebound

The Preface is undated. A new edition was entered by R. Phillips at Stationers' Hall on 20.2.10.

83 (1) JUVENILE FRIENDSHIP; or The holidays: a drama, in three acts. To which is subjoined The Arrogant Boy: a dramatic after-piece, in verse. Intended for the representation of children. London: printed for J. Hatchard, No.180, Piccadilly, and B. Tabart, Juvenile Library, No.157, New Bond Street. 1802.

21×12 cm. Pr by Brettell and Bastie, No.54, Great Windmill Street, Haymarket. Pp.80.
[Huntington, rebound

84 (1) THE JUVENILE MISCELLANY; or, Magazine of knowledge and entertainment, for young persons of both sexes. Illustrated with numerous engravings. London: printed for Tabart and Co. at the Juvenile Library, New Bond Strret [*sic*]. By T. Gillet, Crown-court, Fleet-street, London. 1809. [Price fifteen shillings in boards.]

21×12.4 cm. Pp.758 [760]. 23 engvd pls, 17 folding, one double-page. Tree-calf g. 2 vols in one.
[Private coll.; Miami

On p.69 only 21 plates are listed, that facing p.353 being omitted and the two plates between pp.688 and 689 being listed as a single plate.

The work was issued in 12 monthly parts from Oct. 1808 to Sept. 1809. It was intended to be an annual production but owing to lack of support this is all that was published. The publisher explains the situation thus:

> Notwithstanding the Plates given with the Work have been worth treble the cost of the respective Numbers, and the Work in other respects has been honoured with the approbation of intelligent persons, yet the encouragement has not been sufficient to warrant its continuance beyond the first envoulume.
>
> The WONDERS of the HUMAN BODY; the EXCURSIONS ROUND LONDON; and The MORNING WALKS, will be published in separate volumes, and will, doubtless, maintain, in that shape, the reputation which they have acquired in this Work.

85 (1) THE JUVENILE PLUTARCH: comtaining [*sic*] accounts of the lives of children, and of the infancy of illustrious men, who have been remarkable for their early progress in knowledge. London: printed for R. Phillips, No. 71, St. Paul's; sold by B. Tabart, at the Juvenile Library, New Bond-street. T. Gillet, Salisbury-square. 1801. (Price two shillings and sixpence.)

13.5×8.6 cm. Pp.[iii]+212 (pp.202–212 = advts). FP+3 undated pls. Brown or marbled bds, red or green roan sp g.
[BL; Osborne; S 16.3.70/34, 3.3.77/35; Baldwin; UCLA; NYCL; NLS

The long ſ is used. Osborne attributes this work to J. F. Savill. It is mentioned in E. Kilner's *A visit to London*, 1808, and Mrs. Fenwick puffed it in her *Visits to the Juvenile Library*.

It contains 13 stories; all but 'John Ross' are included in the 1806 edition, Part I. They are far removed from the milk-and-watery moral tales that were often believed to encourage juvenile emulation: the experiences of some of the young protagonists were, to say the least, highly coloured. There was Frances Maria, who was baking bread when 'a she-wolf, with five whelps, burst into the room'. She saved her brother's life but was herself killed by the furious animal. Mrs. Trimmer was not impressed and wrote: 'We trust that the Parents of this country in general will not wish their daughters to imitate the example of this heroine; nor is her story probable.' (*Guardian of education*, vol. i).

Then another biography tells how Volney Becker 'was devoured by a shark at the age of twelve years' after diving into the sea and saving his father and a little girl. As *The juvenile review*, 1817, said, 'Children delight in everything wonderful, it is not, therefore, surprising that this work is a general favourite.'

Reviews: In addition to the above, the *Critical review*, vol. xxxiv, 1802, p.111, said: 'Dispersed occasionally through these pages we meet with a number of valuable remarks, which will have a powerful effect on the moral sentiments of the young student. "Of what important is birth? What is the effect of riches? They often corrupt the morals. He who is worthy, he who is honest and wise, has no need of ancestors." Juvenile Plutarch, p.38. A more important doctrine, to such children as are intended to excel in wisdom and virtue, cannot be inculcated.'

(2) THE JUVENILE PLUTARCH: containing accounts of the lives of celebrated children, and of the infancy of persons who have been illustrious for their virtues and ['or' in Part the Second] talents. With plates. Part the First [Part the Second]. Second edition. London: printed for Tabart and Co. at the Juvenile Library, 157, New Bond Street. 1806. (Price half a crown.)

13.5×8.6 cm. Pr by Joyce Gold, Shoe Lane. Pp.[iv]+185+3pp. bklist; pp.[iii]+204. FP+3 pls; [2nd part] 4 pls by R. Phillips dated Aug. 1806. Marbled bds, green or red roan sp g. (See fig. 11)
[BL; Osborne; S 17.10.75/1428; V & A; Baldwin part II; UCLA; de Grummond; Miami; Private coll. Part I

Part the First contains 17 subjects, 12 being revised versions of biographies in (1); Part the Second contains 18. The text of the TP in Part the Second is as Part the First except 'virtues or [not 'and'] talents'. There is also no mention of 2nd edition. The printer of the second part is shown as 'Gold'.

(3) Third edition pr for R. Phillips, No.7, Bridge-street, Blackfriars; and sold by all other booksellers. By James Gillet, Crown-court, Fleet-street, 1812. Price half-a-crown. Contents as in (2), with 8pp. advts at end of Part the Second.
[BL; Baldwin, Part I; private coll. Part II; NLS, imp.

(4) Fourth edition printed in 1820 by assignment of the Assignees of Richard Phillips, by William Darton, 58, Holborn Hill. Each part has 6 plates, 4 plates in (1) have been redrawn. Price half-a-crown.
[V & A; Osborne; UCLA; private coll.

KILNER, Dorothy

Note In vol. i of the *Guardian of education* Mrs. Trimmer lists a number of Dorothy Kilner's titles and says: 'All these little volumes were produced by the pen of a lady who has kept her name concealed ever since she became an author, which we think was about the year 1780. . . . The simplicity of style in which they are written; and the lessons they furnish for the regulation of the moral conduct of early childhood, give them a decided claim to a place in the Infant Libraries, which it is now the fashion to form, and we hope they will regain their original station in preference to some books of inferior merit, which have of late occupied their places.'

86 (1) [KILNER, Dorothy] Dialogues for good children. By M. Pelham, author of 'Tom Brown's first going to school', &c. &c. Adorned with many cuts, price 1s. Advertised by Tabart in 1804–6; and Mrs. Fenwick puffed this title in *Visits to the Juvenile Library*; but it has not been traced. It is probably *New dialogues for the amusement of good children*, see 89 below.

87 (1) [KILNER, Dorothy] First going to school; or The story of Tom Brown, and his sisters. By M. Pelham, author of The Village

School, Perambulation of a Mouse, First Principles of Religion, Miscellaneous Thoughts, &c. London: printed for Tabart and Co. at the Juvenile and School Library, 157, New Bond Street, by Barnard and Sultzer, Water Lane, Fleet Street. 1804.

13.1×8 cm. Pp.126 inc. 7pp. Tabart's advts. H/c FP dated Nov. 5 1804+5 pls, one dated Oct. 25 1804, 2 as FP, 2 n.d. Marbled bds, red roan sp g.
[Osborne; S 18.6.87/416

R. Phillips entered this title at Stationers' Hall on 12.11.04. Mrs. Fenwick puffed it in *Visits to the Juvenile Library* and so did E. Kilner in *A visit to London*, 1808.

This is a human, amusing and realistic story about a little boy's expectations of, and experiences at, his first school. The children talk and play and tease one another as children do, even today. The illustrations are delightful and are excellently drawn.

Review: The *Guardian of education*, vol. iv, p.412: 'We shall say of this book that a little boy of our acquaintance has read it through with pleasure, and therefore we consider that other little boys will do the same ...'

(2) Title as (1), excepting colon after 'school') to ... sisters. A new edition. By M. Pelham, author of The Village School, Perambulation of a Mouse, First Principles of Religion, Miscellaneous Thoughts, &c. London: printed by C. Squire, Furnival's-Inn-court, for Tabart and Co. at the Juvenile and School Library, No.157, New Bond Street; and to be had of all booksellers. 1806. [Price two shillings.]

13.5×8.4 cm. Pp.119+7pp. bklist containing 46 numb'd items+1p. on *The sleeping beauty*. FP+5 pls, 3 dated Nov. 5 1804, one dated Aug. 25 1804 and 2 n.d. Marbled bds, red or green roan sp.
[Baldwin; private colls; Bod J has FP+3 pls dated 1804 and 2 pls dated Oct. 25 1804

(3) Title as (2) to ... printed by W. Flint, Old Bailey, for Tabart and Co. at the Juvenile and School Library, No.157, New Bond Street; and to be had of all booksellers. 1809. [Price two shillings.]

13.5×8.3 cm. Pp.108+35 [36] pp. bklist of Sir Richard Phillips, pr by W. Lewis, Paternoster-row, in some copies. 6 pls dated October 25 and Nov. 5 1804. Marbled bds, green roan sp.
[Osborne, rebound; PML

88 (1) [KILNER, Dorothy?] Jingles; or, Original rhymes for children. By M. Pelham. London: printed for Tabart and Co. at the Juvenile and School Library, 157, New Bond-street; by W. Heney, 76, Fleet-street. 1806. Price six-pence without plates, one shilling with plates, and eighteen-pence with the plates coloured.

12.9×10.2 cm. Pp.[iv]+[5] 6–60+4pp. advts. 12 plain (or coloured) pls dated Augt 1806, pr on both sides of 6 leaves. Pr yellow card wrps showing 'Price ninepence'. Advts on front and back, the back cover headed 'The Sleeping Beauty. This day is published, in Lilliputian folio ...'. The advt also lists 32 titles in the Tales for the Nursery series (here called 'Nursery Tales'), 33 items, but the advt says 'thirty-two Sorts'. (See fig. 13)
[Bod., bound with others; Ball; S 27.7.84/859 (defective) and 18.6.87/415; private coll.

This title was entered by Tabart and Co. at Stationers' Hall on 29.3.06, shown as 'whole', i.e. entirely owned by Tabart.

Since no other titles by the same author are listed on the title-page, Dorothy Kilner's authorship may be doubted, bearing in mind Phillips's use of 'M. Pelham' on some of his books; but a copy sold at Sotheby's in 1987 had belonged to descendants of the Kilner family, which would seem to support the attribution.

The pricing of the book is rather uncertain as the cost of the version with plain plates is shown as one shilling on the title-page and ninepence on the cover; by 1808 it had risen to one shilling and sixpence.

The author's Advertisement on p.[iii], dated Jan. 1806, disclaims any poetical beauty, but says that the book is free of any evil tendency; and she hopes that children will enjoy committing the poems to memory. The author is all too humble: this is a delightful collection of simple, childish poems (the easiest are placed at the beginning of the book) and the plates are also good.

Review: This title is included in a list, approved by *The juvenile review*, 1817, of books which 'contain little pieces of childish poetry, some of which are very pretty.'

(2) Title as (1) to ... Library, New Bond-street; and to be had of all booksellers. By W. Marchant, 3, Greville-street, Holborn. 1808. [Price ninepence without prints, one shilling and sixpence with prints, or half-a-crown with the prints coloured.]

12.4×10.4 cm. Pp.60+4pp. Tabart's bklist. The illusd version has 12 pls dated Augt 1806. Yellow pr stiff-paper wrps with list of 4 titles on front 'recently published by Tabart and Co.' On lower v. a list of Nursery Tales, 34 bks inc. several parts. [Bod., no pls; BL, no pls; PLM, illusd

This title was listed in the *English catalogue of books*. 1808.

(3) Title as (1) to ... printed for Richard Phillips, 7, Bridge-street, Blackfriars; and to be had of all booksellers. 1811. [Price 6d. without plates, 1s.6d. with plain plates, and 2s.6d. with coloured plates.]

12.5×9.8 cm. Pr by J. Adlard, 23, Bartholomew Close. Pp.64 inc. 4pp. advts. [BL, no pls, rebound

89 (1) [KILNER, Dorothy] New dialogues for the amusement of good children. By M. Pelham, author of The Village School, Perambulation of a Mouse, First Principles of Religion, Miscellaneous Thoughts, &c. London: printed for Tabart and Co. at the Juvenile and School Library, 157, New Bond Street. By Barnard and Sultzer, Water Lane, Fleet Street, 1804. Price one shilling plain, or eighteen pence coloured.

14×8.3 cm. Pp.69+3pp. Tabart's bklist starting on p.[70]. Wood-engvd headpieces to 7 dialogues (on v. of headpiece the space is left blank). Blue pr bds dated 1804. [CUL, lower cover missing

Entered at Stationers' Hall by R. Phillips on 3.8.04.

This is an attractive book with large, clear print and excellent illustrations. It was chosen by Maria Sandby for her little brother because it looked pretty when she visited Tabart's Juvenile Library (see E. Kilner's *A visit to London*, 94 below).

Review: The *Guardian of education*, vol. iv, p.412: 'M. Pelham, we are very sure, from the style of these Dialogues, is no other than the *original M.P.* In saying which we shall recommend it sufficiently, for who does not know and approve of M. P.'s books? And

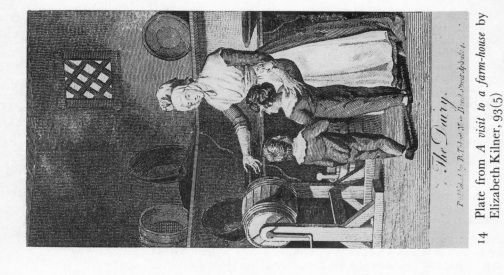

Page 43

The Toad.

Pub.ᵈ Aug.ˢᵗ 1803 by Tabart & C.ᵒ New Bond Street.

13 Plate from *Jingles*, ascribed to Dorothy Kilner, 88(1).
Sotheby's

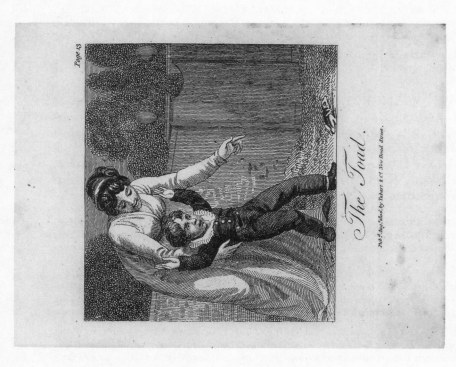

The Dairy.

Published by B. Tabart Nᵉʷ Bond Street Apᵈ 1804.

14 Plate from *A visit to a farm-house* by
Elizabeth Kilner, 93(5)

here let us give our readers a caution – Beware of impostors! for M. P.'s signature is put to some books which this respectable author would never own we are certain.'

(2) Title as (1) to ... By W. Heney, No.76 Fleet-street. 1806. Price one shilling plain, or eighteen pence coloured.

13.9×8 cm. Pp.69+1p. bklist. 7 wood-engvd headpieces to 7 dialogues. Stiff yellow pr wrps dated 1805, with advts.
[PML; S 16.3.70/218

90 (1) [KILNER, Dorothy] New Royal primer; or Reading made easy, by M. Pelham, author of The Doll's Spelling Book, Village School, New Dialogues, &c. &c. This title was advertised in 1804, with many cuts, price 1s., but it has not been traced.

91 (1) [KILNER, Elizabeth] A puzzle for a curious girl. [3 lines Shakspeare.] London: printed for B. Tabart, Juvenile Library, New Bond-street; and J. Harris, Corner of St. Paul's Church-yard: by T. Davison, White-Friars.

•13.9×8.4 cm. Pp.128. No FP but 12 engvd chapter-headings. Marbled bds, red roan sp g.
[V & A

The illustrations were engraved from designs by Dayes. The FP first appeared in 1803 (but dated 1804), making 13 engravings.

Tabart published the first three editions of this successful story-book in 1801–2, 1803 and 1806, but calling the last 'a new edition'. Phillips published the 'third' edition in 1810; and then, in 1814, B. and R. Crosby published the fourth: in 1818 Baldwin, Cradock and Joy, the 5th: and by 1819 the much-travelled book was in the hands of John Souter.
  The author's pseudonymous initials, 'S.W.', are shown in her other books. Her identity was not generally known until, in June 1988, a group of books was sold by Messrs. Sotheby (2.6.88/228) which had belonged to descendants of the Kilner family, including a number by 'S.W.' A copy of A visit to a farm-house was attributed on the title-page to Elizabeth Kilner and the advertisements in First going to school by Dorothy Kilner had been amended by a member of her family so that two of 'S.W.'s books were ascribed to 'E.K.' A puzzle for a curious girl is the first title known to be by Elizabeth Kilner and it shows that she had inherited the story-telling skills of the earlier generation of her family.
  This well-told story tells how a prying girl picked up some scraps of information, embroidered them, and spread abroad a mischievous fabrication which caused great trouble to her parents. Mrs. Field, in The child and his book, includes this tale among those 'in which a writer of real talent has clothed the dry bones of morality with living flesh and blood'. The production also is attractive, with well-planned pages and effective illustrations as chapter-headings. It was among the books bought by the young people in E. Fenwick's Visits to the Juvenile Library – 'one of the best books that was ever written for children', said Mrs. Fenwick generously.

Reviews: The Guardian of education, vol. ii, p.112: 'This is a very entertaining little book. ... The story is told in a manner which we think cannot fail of making a lasting

"Not to keep you in suspense, my only motive for going to Mrs. Hilcox's was to purchase a pound of wax."

Laura. "A pound of wax! Dear mamma, is it possible? Then why did you make such a mystery of it?"

Mrs. Belfast. "I had promised to buy it for the lame Miss Herbert, who wished to make some wax ornaments for her chimney-piece; but as she had been several times laughed at for not succeeding in her experiments, she particularly begged me not to mention it to any one till the work was completed; and that being now the case, there is no longer any occasion for secrecy."

Laura. "And why were you gone such

CHAP. XII.

THE MYSTERY DISCLOSED.

MRS. Belfast, on her daughter's entrance, laid aside her writing, and seating herself by her, thus began: "Not

15 Double-page spread from *A puzzle for a curious girl* by Elizabeth Kilner, 91(2), showing the well-laid-out pages

impression upon the mind of every child that reads it; and the publisher has given the work the advantage of good paper and type, and many engraved copper-plates'.

The juvenile review's opinion was equally favourable: 'Curiosity is natural to children and when confined to proper objects is laudable, but when exercised in endeavouring to discover what any person wishes to conceal it is highly culpable, as it leads frequently to artifice, slander, and that species of falsehood which is denominated invention. These and other results of improper curiosity are illustrated in a lively and pleasing manner in this little work, which we strongly recommend to the notice of our readers.'

(2) Title as (1) to ... Shakspeare. Second edition. London: printed for B. Tabart, Juvenile Library, New-Bond-Street; and J. Harris, Corner of St. Paul's Church-yard. 1803.

13.3×8.4 cm. Pr by T. Davison, White-friars. ½-title. Pp.130 (p.[131] = printer's impt)+3pp. (in copies without FP), 5pp. or 8pp. advts. Engvd FP dated Oct. 9 1804 in some copies+12 engvd headpieces to chapters. Marbled bds, red roan sp g. (See fig. 15)
[BL; Opie: V & A; Baldwin; CUL; UCLA, imp.; Gum. 4660; PML; Miami; S 27.2.67/83, with FP, and 2.6.88/232 without; private coll.

Advertisements in Tabart's booklists dated 1804 call for 12 engravings and those of 1805 for 13. As the title-page is dated 1803 and the FP 1804, it is likely that the 13th illustration was added to later copies, so those without it are not necessarily defective but may be the earlier issue of that edition.

(3) Title as (1) to ... Shakspeare. A new edition. London: printed by C. Squire, Furnival's-Inn-court, for Tabart and Co. at the Juvenile and School Library, No.157, New Bond-street, and to be had of all booksellers. 1806.

13.4×8.4 cm. Pp.119+5pp. bklist beginning on v. of p.119. Plates as in (2) with FP. Marbled bds, red roan sp g.
[Opie; Osborne; Wayne; S 13.10.77/2636 and 10.10.79/195; Baldwin; CBY 528; Melb.; private coll.; Som.

(4) Title as (1) to ... Shakespeare. The third edition. London: printed by W. McDowall, Pemberton Row, for Richard Phillips, Bridge Street, and to be had of all booksellers. 1810.

13×7.8 cm. Pp.124. Plates as in (3). Marbled bds, red or green roan sp g.
[V & A; S 2.6.75/165 and 12.10.81/133; private coll.; Som.

(5) A fourth edition published by B. and R. Crosby, dated 1814. Engvd FP+12 illusns. Roan-backed bds.
[S 20.7.82/64

(6) Title as (4) to ... Shakespeare. The fifth edition. London: printed for Baldwin, Cradock, and Joy, 47, Paternoster-row. 1818.

14×8.4 cm. Pr by C. Baldwin, New Bridge Street. Pp.126+18pp. bklist. Illusns as in (3). Marbled bds, green roan sp g.
[Opie; V & A; S 13.10.77/2637, 12.10.81/21 and /104; Baldwin

(7) Title as (6) to ...Shakespeare. A new edition, revised and improved. Entered at Stationers' Hall. London: printed for John Souter, at the Juvenile and School Library, 73, St. Paul's Church-yard, by Jas. W. and Chas. Adlard, 23, Bartholomew-close. 1819.

13.7×8.6 cm. Pp.117 (p.[118] = advts). 6 h/c pls pubd by J. Souter, April 20, 1818. Marbled bds, green roan sp g.
[V & A, 2 copies, one as above, another in brown-paper-covered bds, red roan sp g.

92 (1) [KILNER, Elizabeth. Pseudonym 'S.W.'] Scenes at home, or A sketch of a plain family. By S.W. author of A Puzzle for a Curious Girl, A Visit to a Farm House, &c. London: printed for B. Tabart and Co. at their Juvenile and School Library, New Bond Street. 1810.

13.4×8.4 cm. Pr by E. Hemsted, New Street, Fetter-lane (on v. of TP; but by E. Hemsted, Great New-street, Gough-square, at foot of p.144). Pp.144. Engvd FP+one other pl., both 'Pub. Feb. 1811 by F. Tabart & Co. Clifford Street, Bond Street'. Marbled bds, red roan sp g. Osborne has another copy with black roan sp g. [Osborne; Gum. 5123

There is a misprint in pagination – 141 appears as 14 . The book was reprinted in America by David Hogan, Philadelphia, in 1812. Welch 1392. 'F. Tabart' was Francis, Benjamin's son.

This is an uneventful, pleasantly-told story of a penurious but respectable family, their difficulties and how they solved them. The book contains plenty of common-sense as well as moral advice and is also very readable – like all this author's stories.

(2) THE WARREN FAMILY, OR SCENES AT HOME. By S.W. author of A Puzzle for a Curious Girl, A Visit to a Farm House, etc. Embellished with 4 engravings. London: published by James and Bain, at their Juvenile and School Library, Little Brook-street, New Bond-street. 1813.

12.7×8.1 cm. Text pr by E. Hemsted, Great New-street, Gough-square; but TP pr by J. Catnach, 153, Swallow-street. Pp.144. H/c FP engvd by C. Knight after H. Corbould+3 h/c pls (two have impts shaved off), one sgd as FP. The two sgd pls do not appear in Tabart's 1810 edn. Marbled bds, ¾ red roan, sp g. [Osborne

The shaving of the plates was evidently meant to remove Tabart's imprint. This edition is made up of a new title-page and the sheets of Tabart's 1810 edition.

(3) Title as (2) to ... Embellished with four engravings. Second edition. London: published by James and Bain, at their Juvenile and School Library, Little Brook Street, New Bond Street. 1814.

13.9×8.5 cm. Pr by Schulze and Dean, 13 Poland-street, Oxford-street. Pp.142+2pp. advts. FP and one other pl engvd by C. Knight after H. Corbould+2 other pls. Plain brown-paper-covered bds, red roan sp g. [V & A; Osborne

93 (1) [KILNER, Elizabeth. Pseudonym 'S.W.'] A visit to a farm-house, or An introduction to various subjects connected with rural economy. Embellished with plates. By S.W. author of A Puzzle for a Curious Girl. London: printed by R. Taylor, Black-Horse-court; for Tabart and Co. at the Juvenile and School Library, No.157, New Bond-street; and to be had of all booksellers. 1804. [Entered at Stationer's Hall.]

13.8×8.5 cm. Pp.iv+168+8pp. bklist. Engvd FP dated Apr 1 1804+7 pls same date. Marbled bds, red or green roan sp g. [BL; Osborne; Opie; UBC; Birm.; private colls, one in tree calf

The plates were drawn by Dayes. This title was entered at Stationers' Hall by

R. Phillips on 14.5.04. It was reprinted in America in 1817 by Benjamin Warner, No.147, Market-st., Philadelphia. Welch 1393.

This delightful book sets out to investigate 'the simple arts by which the nourishment of man is produced' and other 'wonders of creation'. The story – mostly in the form of conversations – conveys instruction pleasantly and interestingly and the plates are excellent. There are only 8 in the 1804 and in some 1805 editions, not 10, as Osborne suggests (p.816); 2 more were added in 1807.

In E. Fenwick's *Visits to the Juvenile Library* this was one of the books selected by some of the 'blooming boys and girls'.

Reviews: The *Guardian of education*, vol. iii, p.376: 'This is another production from the same pen which furnished the very pleasing and ingenious story, called "A Puzzle for a Curious Girl" ... the subjects to which it relates ... are such as may be placed before children again and again, without tiring or disgusting them. ... The pretty plates, with which this book is embellished, add much to its attractions.'

The juvenile review, 1817, said that 'The author of this pretty work announces in the preface that it was written with the view of exciting the attention of children, who live in the country, to the interesting objects with which they are surrounded, and of affording useful information to those who live in town. In both these points we may affirm that the writer will succeed, for we have not met with any book of the kind written in so engaging a style.'

(2) Title as (1) to ... with beautiful plates. By S. W. author of A Visit to London, and A Puzzle for a Curious Girl. Second edition. London: printed by R. Taylor and Co. Black-Horse-court. For Tabart and Co. at their Juvenile and School Library, No.157, New Bond-street; and to be had of all booksellers. 1805. [Entered at Stationers' Hall.]

13.3×8.3 cm. Pp.iv+168+8pp. bklist, 50 items+23 Nursery Tales. Engvd FP+7 other pls or FP+9 pls (see note below). Green marbled bds, black roan sp g.
[Exeter; Birm.; BL; private colls; S 5.2.68/40 has FP+9 pls and so have 25.2.76/47 and 12.10.81/133; Renier, 10 pls; Bod J

It seems probable that two of the plates were not ready for printing in the 1804 edition or even for the earlier copies dated 1805, but were inserted in a later issue that year.

(3) 3rd edition not traced.

(4) 4th edition not traced.

(5) Title as (1) to ... author of A Visit to London, and A Puzzle for a Curious Girl. Fifth edition. London: printed by J. Arliss, & Co. Gutter-lane. For B. Tabart, at the Juvenile and School Library, No.157, New Bond-street; and Richard Phillips, Bridge-street, and to be had of all booksellers. 1807. [Entered at Stationers' Hall.] Price half a crown.

13.8×8.3 cm. Pr by Arliss & Huntsman, 32, Gutter-lane, Cheapside (on p.168). Pp.iv+168+6pp. (or more?) bklist in V & A copy. Engvd FP+9 pls, some dated April 1804, others n.d. but impt may have been shaved. 2 pls are new and n.d. Marbled bds, red roan sp g. (See fig. 14)
[V & A; UCLA; private coll.; NYCL; Bod J

(6) Title as (5) to ... London and A Puzzle for a Curious Girl. Fifth edition. London: printed for Richard Phillips, Bridge-street, and to be had of all booksellers. 1811. (Entered at Stationers' Hall.) [Price half-a-crown.]

13.4×7.9 cm. Pr by James Gillet, Charles-street, Hatton Garden. Pp.iv+176 (inc. 8pp. bklist). Engvd FP dated Apl 1804+9 pls all pubd by B. Tabart, the two extra being The Pleasant Ride and The Bees.

[BL, rebound; Osborne; Baldwin; V & A, bound in green pr pictorial bds, on front, at top, '. . .? Library, Bartholomew Close'. On lower v. 'Juvenile books, published by Knivett, Arliss, and Baker. Juvenile Library, Bartholomew Close'; S 5.2.68/40; private coll., wmk 1808; Renier

(7) Title as (6) to . . . "A Visit to London." Sixth edition. London: printed by and for W. Darton, Jun. 58, Holborn-hill, and to be had of all booksellers. 1815. (Entered at Stationers' Hall.) [Price half-a-crown.]

13.5×8.2 cm. Pp.iv+168+8pp. Darton's bklist containing a number of Tabart's titles. No FP present in copy seen, other pls as in 1811 but slightly more worn, with impt of W. Darton, Junr. Oct., Oct. 1st, or Oct 5th 1815. Marbled bds, red roan sp g. [BL; S 27.2.67/290 and 13.10.77/2638

94 (1) [KILNER, Elizabeth. Pseudonym 'S. W.'] A visit to London, containing a description of the principal curiosities in the British Metropolis. By S. W. author of The Visit to a Farm-House, and The Puzzle for a Curious Girl. With six copper plates. London: printed by J. Adlard, Duke-street, Smithfield, for Tabart and Co. at the Juvenile and School Library, No.157, New Bond-street; and to be had of all booksellers. 1805. [Entered at Stationer's Hall.]

13.6×8 cm. Pp.ii+191 [192]+16pp. bklist in some copies. Engvd FP, n.d., +5 other pls, some dated Jan. 1805. Marbled bds, red roan sp g. (See frontispiece) [UCLA; Wayne; Baldwin; Gum. 3862; Miami

P.[192] contains a list of contents. One plate depicts the interior of Tabart's shop. This title was entered at Stationers' Hall on 9.1.05. It was reprinted in America in 1817 by Benjamin Warner, Philadelphia. Welch 1393. In E. Fenwick's *Visits to the Juvenile Library* it was one of the books bought from Mr. Tabart.

This is a lively and interesting story about the Sandby family's experiences in London in 1805. One day Maria and her mother are taken by friends to visit Tabart's bookshop and Maria, served by Mr. Tabart himself, is allowed to choose a number of books.

Reviews: The author of *The juvenile review*, having written a very favourable notice of *A visit to a farm-house*, says that this book 'is equally attractive, though from the quantity of objects it embraces, not quite so easy for young children.'
   The *Guardian of education*, vol. iv, p.173: 'The attention of the young reader is agreeably kept up from the beginning to the end of the book; a constant regard is paid to moral instruction, wherever it can be introduced with propriety.'

(2) Title as (1), except date: 1808.

13.6×8.1 cm. Pp.[iv]+188. FP+5 undated pls. Marbled bds, red or green roan sp g. [Osborne; Gum. 3863; BL; UCLA; private coll.; Renier

The list of contents is on p.[iv], not at the end of the book as in 1st edition.

(3) Title as (1) to . . . Printed for Tabart & Co. at the Juvenile and School Library, No.157, New Bond-street; and to be had of all booksellers; by B. McMillan, Bow Street, Covent Garden. 1810. [Entered at Stationers' Hall.]

13.9×8 cm. Pp.[iv]+196. Engvd FP (n.d.)+5 pls (2 dated Dec. 11 1804, pubd by R. Phillips) inc. one folding dated 1st Jan. 1807 by R. Phillips, New Bridge Street, Blackfriars. Marbled bds.
[Birm., imp., rebound; UCLA; Bath; Bod J; S 20.4.71/371 and 27.7.83/250

(4) Title as (1) to ... plates. A new edition, with additions and improvements. London: printed by and for W. Darton, Jun. 58, Holborn-hill; and to be had of all booksellers. Price half-a-crown. 1813. [Entered at Stationers' Hall.]

13.5×7.8 cm. Pp.[iv]+217. Engvd FP+5 pls (or 7 in some copies) inc. one folding, dated Octr 9th, 1813. The date of the single pls is almost illegible but probably 1813. Mottled green paper bds, red roan sp g.
[BL, imp.; Baldwin; S 24.2.69/32 and 23.5.83/70; CUL and private coll. with 7 pls, inc. one folding

William Darton published another edition in *c*.1820 with additions and improvements by T.H. In later editions the text was considerably rewritten and some subjects were removed (including the visit to the Juvenile Library) and new ones introduced. All the plates were dated as the folding plate in (4).

95 (1) LENOIR, Monsieur. The logographic-emblematical French spelling-book; or, French pronunciation made easy.

Tabart's edition has not been traced but the *Critical review*, vol. xv, p.447, reviewed the 3rd edition, corrected and considerably improved, published by Tabart, Old Bond-street, 1808, as follows:

> Monsieur Lenoir is truly a Frenchman! We do not condemn his method, though we cannot altogether commend the idea of teaching a child to speak without understanding what it says. But that we may not be too hasty we will subjoin one or more of the many of Monsieur Lenoir's *certificates*, attesting the efficacy of this method. [Here follow some certificates.]
>
> M. Lenoir ... enabled my sister ... to read French fluently and at first sight, and communicated to her the most exact and accurate pronunciation, in the course of six-and-thirty lessons ...

Another certificate declares that M. Lenoir taught a girl of seven in 48 lessons to read fluently and without hesitation and with most accurate pronunciation, *even without understanding a syllable of what she was reading*.

In fact, 'Monsieur Lenoir's certificates ... [are] not only vastly entertaining but really edifying.'

96 (1) [LE PRINCE DE BEAUMONT, Jeanne Marie] The history of Prince Fatal and Prince Fortune. And the story of the three wishes. With three copperplates. A new edition. London: printed for Tabart and Co. at the Juvenile and School Library. No.157, New Bond-street; and to be had of all dealers in books. Price sixpence. 1804.

12×7 cm. Pr by R. Taylor & Co. Black-Horse-court. Pp.27 [32] inc. 5pp. bklist. H/c engvd FP (date illegible in copy seen)+2 other pls dated Sep. 1804. Pr yellow stiff-paper wrps, advt on lower v. and advt also on v. of TP.
[UCLA, bound with others; PML, wmk 1804

A new edition was entered at Stationers' Hall by R. Phillips on 12.10.04. The plates are engraved after W. M. Craig. Both these stories are included in Mme de Beaumont's *Magasin des enfans*, first published in London in 1756.

No objection was made by the liquorish cat,
Who began without speaking to eat up the rat,
Who as briskly began the rope for to gnaw.

Which began round the Butcher, its noose to draw,
Who kicking began the Bull for to slaughter,
Who in haste began to swallow the Water.

16   Panorama from *A true history of a little old woman* ... by M. G. Lewis,
96A(2), showing four incidents in the story. *Brian Alderson*

96A   (1) [LEWIS, Matthew Gregory] A true history of a little old
woman, who found a silver penny. [3 lines verse. Thomson's *Winter*.]
London: printed for Tabart and Co. at the Juvenile and School
Library, 157, New Bond-street; and to be had of all booksellers.
C. Squire, printer, Furnival's-Inn-court, Holborn. 1806.

13.3×10.5 cm. Pp.20+4pp. or 14pp. advts in some copies. 12 h/c pls pr on both sides
of 6 leaves, dated May 27, 1806, +h/c 4-fold panorama dated May 1806 showing
illusns to last 4 episodes. In some copies these 4 scenes are cut and bound as 4 single
pls, making 16 in all. Yellow pr stiff-paper covers, advt on front of *The London primer*
and Dr. Mavor's *English spelling book*; and bklist on lower v.
[Opie, 2 copies, slight differences in quality of plates; Hockliffe, imp.; Spencer; Bod J;
V & A, imp.; Osborne; UCLA, with undated panorama; PML; CBY 286; S 13.10.77/
2558

See Appendix D for a discussion of the engraving of the illustrations.

The authorship of this spirited versification of the cumulative tale about the old woman
and her pig is revealed in M. Baron-Wilson's *Life and correspondence of M. G. [Monk]
Lewis*, 1839, pp.202–15. (For this information I am indebted to Mrs Iona Opie.)

The poem ends with a cynical moral:

> No finger stirs, in vain you kneel and sue,
> The work brings benefit to none but you:
> Must, to exert themselves, your friends be won?
> Make it their *interest*, and the work is done!

The comic drawings reflect the funny story and the free colouring of the panorama is

Which began to extinguish the flame as quick.
Which began that moment to burn the stick.
Which began in a hurry the Dog to lick.

Who began post haste the Pig to bite.
Who began to jump over the stile in a fright.
And so the old woman got home that night.

particularly attractive. The book was still in print *c.*1855, when it was published by William Darton.

(2) Title as (1) to ... Library, New Bond-street; ... booksellers. W. Marchant, Printer, 3, Greville-street, Holborn. 1808.

13×10.6 cm. Pp.20+12pp. bklist in some copies. 12 h/c pls+one folding panorama (or, the panorama cut into 4 sections and bound as 4 leaves). Pls dated May 27, 1806. Yellow stiff-paper pr wrps, advts on front and back. (See fig. 16)
[PML, wmk 1808; Lilly; Opie; Miami; McKell; S 13.10.77/2559; private coll.

(3) Title as (1) to ... London: printed for Richard Phillips, 7, Bridge-street, Blackfriars; and to be had of all booksellers. J. Adlard, Printer, 23, Bartholomew Close. 1812.

12.6×10.2 cm. Pp.20. 12 h/c pls pubd by Tabart & Co. dated as (1)+folding panorama as (1). Pr stiff-paper wrps, undated, showing 'Price one shilling and sixpence, coloured. London; printed for the booksellers'. On lower v. list of 9 Darton titles, 'Lately published'.
[Private coll. with covers as above; BL, imp.; bound with others; Phila., rebound; S 27.2.67/291 and 10.12.80/63

97 (1) THE LIONESS'S BALL; being a companion to The Lion's Masquerade. London: printed for C. Chapple, Pall Mall; B. Tabart, New Bond-street; J. Harris, St. Paul's Church-yard; Darton and Harvey, Gracechurch-street; and all other booksellers. [H. Reynell, Printer, 21, Piccadilly.] [N.d. but *c.*1808.]

12×10 cm. Pp.16. H/c engvd FP+5 h/c pls attributed to W. Mulready. Pr pink wrps.
[BL, imp.; Gum. 3799, imp.; McKell; Osborne; UCLA

This title was advertised in Mrs. Cockle's *The fishes grand gala*, Part II, 1808, as 'At Easter will be published ...' The Dedication makes it clear that the author was not Mrs. Dorset.

98 (1) THE LIONESS'S ROUT; being a sequel to The Butterfly's Ball, The Grasshopper's Feast, and The Peacock "At Home." By a lady. London: printed for B. Tabart, at the Juvenile Library, No.157, New Bond Street.

12.8×9.9 cm. Pr by E. Hemsted, Great New-street, Fetter-lane. Pp.32. H/c or plain FP dated March 1808+2 other h/c or plain pls, one dated as FP. Pr orange wrps, cover-text reads: 'The Lioness's Rout; being a sequel to The Butterfly's Ball, and The Peacock "At Home." Adorned with plates. By a lady. London: published by Tabart and Co. Juvenile Library, New Bond-street; and J. Harris, Corner of St. Paul's Church-yard. 1808.'
[McKell; BL; Osborne, plain; UCLA; Melb.

Has been attributed to Mrs. Dorset, but not confirmed. The coloured plates are bright and gay, especially the splendid frontispiece showing a huge cake surrounded by animals – camel, giraffe, monkey, horse, tiger, and so on. On p.4 there is a misprint in the 4th line: 'Insests' for 'insects'.

99 (1) [LYNCH, Mr. Possibly W. R. Lynch, q.v.] The nursery concert; or Musical exercises of duty and affection, for children, including My Father, Mother, Brother, Sister. Set to music by S. Bennet, Organist. London: printed for Tabart and Co. at the Juvenile and School Library, New Bond Street, and to be had of all booksellers. Price eighteen-pence. 1808.

14.5×11.4 cm. Pr by Diggens, St. Ann's-lane. Pp.iv+12. FP engvd by Tomlinson, Jany 1st 1809. Advertisement dated Nov. 1, 1808. Each poem is accompanied by 2pp. music. Yellow stiff-paper pr covers, on lower v. Tabart's bklist.
[Opie; Baldwin; CBY 239; S 14.10.77/2863 and 27.7.84/859

The poems in this book are not those written by Mary (Belson) Elliott or Ann Taylor. They are also found in the 1821 edition of Blair's *The first, or Mother's catechism* and are there ascribed to 'Mr. Lynch'. Hence the attribution to this author, who may be the W. R. Lynch who alternates with W. R. Johnson, q.v., 77–80 above. The first verses of the four poems are set out in 12 (6) above.

100 (1) LYNCH, W. R. The world described, in easy verse. Illustrative of the situation, manners, and produce, of all nations. For the use of young persons. With coloured engravings and a map. By W. R. Lynch, Esq. author of the Poetical Histories of England, Greece, and Rome. A new edition, illustrated by notes. London: printed by

W. Lewis, Finch-lane; for Sir Richard Phillips and Co. Bride-court, Bridge-street; and may be had of all booksellers. 1820. Price 5s. half-bound.

15×8.5 cm. Pp.viii+195 [196]+36pp. bklist of Sir Richard Phillips. Folding FP map dated July 1st 1820 pubd by R. Phillips+3 h/c pls×3 and 11 plain pls×2. Marbled bds, red roan sp g.
[Private coll.

This book is included here (though having no connection with Tabart) to show the confusing reference to the Poetical Histories of W. R. Johnson, 77–80 above, which were published by Tabart.

The book-list in Mavor's *The English spelling-book*, 1822, published by Longman, Hurst, Rees, Orme, and Brown advertises *The world described* . . . as by Mr. T. Lynch Johnson, which adds to the confusion.

101 (1) MANDEVILLE, Harriet. Familiar conversations, for the use of young children. Interspersed with stories, and adorned with cuts, by their very good friend, Harriet Mandeville. In two volumes. Vol. I. [Vol. II.] The third edition. London: printed by J. Vigevena, Huggin Lane, for B. Crosby & Co. Stationer's Court, and B. Tabart, 157, New Bond Street. [c.1802]

9.6×7.7 cm. Pp.85; 76; +2pp. Crosby's bklist in each vol. Wct FP+2 other wcts in each vol. Plain blue or yellow wrps, pr labels on front.
[Private coll., 2 vols; private coll. vol. II only. (See fig. 18)

See E. Somerville's *A grandmother's stories*, 155, for a similar production.

A mother and child hold instructive conversations on subjects such as reason, kindness to animals and good behaviour, interspersed with illustrative stories, the whole written in very easy language and pleasantly narrated.

102 (1) MARMONTEL, Jean-François. Belisarius, the Roman general. By Marmontel. With four coloured plates. London: printed for Tabart and Co., at the Juvenile and School Library, No. 157, New Bond-street; and to be had of all dealers in books. Price one shilling. 1805.

13.6×8.8 cm. Pr by R. Taylor and Co., 38, Shoe-lane. Pp. 70+2pp. bklist. H/c engvd FP+3 h/c pls all dated Nov. 1805. Purple (or beige?) pr wrps, bklist on lower v.
[Hockliffe, no TP; UBC

Cover-text reads: The life of Belisarius, the Roman general. Abridged from the French of Marmontel. With four coloured plates. Price one shilling. Published by Tabart & Co. at the Juvenile and School Library, No.157, New Bond-street, where have lately been published, a great variety of superior books for schools and young persons, from 5s. to 6d. each, with which families, schools, and booksellers, in town and country, may be supplied on the best terms. Price one shilling.

The plates are of fine quality and the colouring is beautiful. The story is also very enjoyable.

(2) Title as (1) to ... printed for B. Tabart, at the Juvenile and School Library, No.157, New Bond Street: and to be had of all booksellers. Price one shilling. 1807.

13.9×8.8 cm. Pr by J. Diggens, St. Ann's-lane. Pp.72. H/c engvd FP pubd Nov. 1805 by Tabart & Co. +3 h/c pls, same date. Yellow pr covers, bklist on lower v.
[Opie; Bod J

(3) Title as (1) to ... printed for R. Phillips, No.7, Great Bridge-street; and to be had of all booksellers in town and country. Price one shilling. 1811. J. Adlard, Printer, Duke-street, West Smithfield.

13.8×8.5 cm. Pp.72. H/c engvd FP headed 'Vol. IV p.131' +3 other h/c pls headed respectively 'Vol. IV, p.137' 'Vol. IV, p.143' and 'Vol. IV, p.169', all n.d. Pr yellow stiff-paper covers, advts on lower v.
[UCLA; S 2.6.75/149

103 (1) MAVOR, William Fordyce. The British Nepos; consisting of select lives of illustrious Britons, who have distinguished themselves by their virtues, talents, or remarkable advancement in life; with incidental practical reflections. Written purposely for the use of schools, and carefully adapted to the situations and capacities of youth, by William Mavor, LL.D. Vicar of Hurley, Berkshire, and chaplain to the Earl of Dumfries. Third edition, with twenty-four portraits. [5 lines Latin. Virgil.] London: printed for Richard Phillips, No.71, St. Paul's Church-yard; by T. Gillet, Salisbury-square. And sold by T. Hurst, Paternoster-row; John Harris, (successor to Mrs. Newbery) St. Paul's Church-yard; Lackington, Allen, and Co. Finsbury-square; Benj. Tabart, New Bond-street; Wilmot and Hill, in the Borough; Wilson and Spence, York; H. Mozley, Gainsborough; and all other booksellers. 1802. Price four shillings and sixpence, bound.

17.1×9.6 cm. Pp.x [xii]–[17]+18–454. Engvd FP, Thurston del., W. Taylor sculpt., +2 (should be 4) pls×6 portraits on each+wood-engvd tailpiece, all n.d. Copy seen lacked 2 pls×6. Calf, sp g.
[BL, imp.; Liv U

Richard Phillips published the first edition in 1798, 2nd edition 1800. The Dedication to Lord Loughborough is signed 'W. Mavor' and dated Oct. 10 1798 from Woodstock.

This was one of the books bought for the children when they visited Tabart's Juvenile Library in E. Kilner's *A visit to London*.

Reviews: The *Monthly review*, June 1799: 'In presenting this work to the public, Dr. Mavor has not only made a valuable and much wanted addition to the school library, but has furnished a book which is well calculated for the parlour window, and for the shelf in the room behind the shop of those tradesmen who devote to reading some of the hours which they can steal from business; justly persuaded that money, without knowledge is an acquisition of little value.'

The *Christian spectator*, No.ix: 'The actions of these great men are told in a plain and pleasing manner; and, what is no small difficulty in a work adapted for juvenile capacities, the incidental reflections suggested by particular circumstances, or traits of character, are so naturally made, that the reader cannot but feel the effect of the example with a force equal to the pleasure excited by the story.'

The *Young gentleman's and lady's magazine*, Feb. 1799: 'The selection is extremely judicious, and the execution is correspondent. The principles throughout are entitled to our unqualified praise; and we have no doubt the author wrote with a view to the inculcation of those maxims, civil, moral, and religious, which have raised Great Britain to such an exalted height among the nations of the earth ...'

Writing in 1817, the author of *The juvenile review* said that this work had 'deservedly gone through twelve editions, and if merit determines its duration, it will last as long as the language in which it is written' – extravagant praise for a book which posterity has forgotten.

(2), (3) and (4). The 4th, 5th and 6th editions have not been found, but Phillips published a 7th edition as follows:

(5) Title as (1) to ... reflections. Written purposely for the use of schools, and carefully adapted to the situations and capacities of youth. By William Mavor, LL.D. Vicar of Hurley, Berkshire; chaplain to the Earl of Moira; and author of The New Universal History, Natural History for Schools, etc. etc. etc. Seventh edition with twenty-four portraits. [5 lines Latin. Virgil.] London: printed for Richard Phillips, No.6, Bridge Street, Blackfriars, by R. Taylor and Co. 38, Shoe-lane. 1806. Price five shillings, bound.

17×9.6 cm. Pp.xi [xii]+[15] 16–462+8pp. bkslist. Engvd FP, Thurston del. W. Taylor sculp., +4 pls with 6 portraits on each dated June 1805. Red embossed cloth, g sides and sp.
[BL

R. Phillips entered the 7th edition at Stationers' Hall on 19.2.06. The 8th edition was printed for Phillips in 1807 and the copyright was acquired by Longmans, who published the 11th edition in 1816.

104 (1) MAVOR, William Fordyce, and PRATT, Samuel Jackson. Classical English poetry, for the use of schools, and of young persons in general. Selected from the works of the most favourite of our national poets, with some original pieces. Compiled and written by Dr. Mavor and Mr. Pratt. London: printed for Richard Phillips, 71, St. Paul's Church-yard. Sold by [7 London congers and] Benj. Tabart, New Bond-street; Wilson and Spence, York; E. Balfour, Edinburgh; J. Archer and H. Colbert, Dublin; E. and J. Larkin, Boston, New England; and by all other booksellers. Price 4s.6d. in boards, or 5s. bound. 1801. T. Gillet, Printer, Salisbury-square.

17.5×10 cm. Pp.xxiv+432 (inc. 3pp. Phillip's bklist). FP dated March 28th 1801 engvd by Dadley after Burney. Calf, rebacked, sp g.
[BL; S 5.2.68/25

This is the first edition.

Review: The *Critical review*, vol. xxxiii, 1801, p.104, gave this anthology a long and scornful notice, condemning both the arrogance of the editors in including some of their own poems in a *classical* collection and their carelessness in correcting the printing.

(2) Title as (1) to ... Classical poetry, for the use of schools, and young persons in general. Selected from the works of our most favourite national poets. Compiled by Dr. Mavor and Mr. Pratt. London: printed for Richard Phillips, No.6, Bridge Street, 1807. Price 5s.6d. bound. T. Gillet, Printer, Wild-court.

17.3×9.5 cm. Pp.xxiv+456 inc. 8pp. Richard Phillips's bklist.
[BL, rebound]

In 1813 Longmans published the 8th edition of this book.

105 (1) MAVOR, William Fordyce. The elements of natural history, for the use of schools, and young persons, founded on the Linnaean arrangement, with popular descriptions in the manner of Goldsmith and Buffon. Illustrated with a frontispiece and fifty copper plates, representing one hundred and eighty of the most curious objects. By William Mavor, LL.D. Vicar of Hurley, Berkshire, chaplain to the Earl of Dumfries, author of the Universal History, of the British Nepos, the Abridgment of Plutarch's Lives, the Universal Short Hand, &c. [Quotes from Edgeworth's Practical Education and Miss More's Strictures on Female Education.] A new edition, revised. London: printed for Richard Phillips, No.71, St. Paul's Church-yard, by T. Gillet, Salisbury-square. Sold by T. Hurst, Paternoster-row; Benj. Tabart, No.157, New Bond-street; Wilson and Spence, York; H. Mozley, Gainsbro'; E. Balfour, Edinburgh; and by all other booksellers, with the usual allowance to schools. 1802. (Price 4s.6d. in boards or 5s. bound.)

17×10 cm. Pp.xi [xii]+343+4pp. Phillips's bklist, starting on p.[344], +1p. direction to binder (copy seen possibly incomplete). FP engvd by Dadley after Burney, dated May 6 1802+44 pls out of 50 listed. Calf, sp g.
[BL

The plates are printed on both sides of 22 [25?] leaves. The book was first published in 1799.

(2) Title as (1) to ... Phillips, No.6, New Bridge Street. By T. Gillet, Salisbury Square. Sold by Tabart & Co. No.157, New Bond-street; Wilson and Spence, York; H. Mozley, Gainsbro'; and by all other booksellers, with the usual allowance to schools. 1805. Price 4s.6d. in boards, or 5s. bound.) [*sic.* no opening bracket]

17.2×10 cm. Pp.xi+342–? (imp.) Col'd pls, some missing. FP as (1). Calf.
[Private coll. imp.

(3) 5th edition printed for R. Phillips, No.6, Bridge-street, Blackfriars: by T. Gillet, Salisbury-square. 1806. (Price six shillings, bound.) Pp.329. FP as (1)+50 other pls. Calf, sp g.
[UCLA

106 (1) MAVOR, William Fordyce. The English spelling book, accompanied by a progressive series of easy and familiar lessons, intended as an introduction to the first elements of the English language. By William Mavor, LL.D. Vicar of Hurley in Berkshire;

chaplain to the Earl of Dumfrie [?s] and author of The British Nepos, Universal History, Natural History for Schools, &c. &c. London: printed for Richard Phillips, No.71, St. Paul's Church-yard: sold by Thomas Hurst, Paternoster Row; Benjamin Tabart, 157, New Bond Street; Wilson and Spence, York; H. Mozley, Gainsborough; and by all booksellers and stationers; with full and liberal allowance to schools. By T. Gillet, Salisbury-square. [Price eighteen-pence bound.]

Wood-engvd FP×2 dated 1802. Wood-engvd picture alphabet (26 letters)+9 illusns; 6pp. advts at end. Sheep.
[S 21.10.76/1680 with reproduction of TP

Osborne gives 1st edition as 1801. The 182nd edition was published by Longmans 13 years later – in 1814 – and Routledge published a revised and improved edition in c.1890. In 1822 Longmans published the 273rd edition with a note that nearly 2,000,000 copies had been sold in 19 years; and in 1885 *The English spelling book*, illustrated by Kate Greenaway and engraved and printed by Edmund Evans, was published by George Routledge and Sons.

(2) Title as (1) to ... Dumfries, and author of The British Nepos, Universal History, Natural History for Schools, &c. &c. A new edition, revised and improved. London: printed for Richard Phillips, No.71, St. Paul's Church-yard; sold by Thomas Hurst, Paternoster Row; Benjamin Tabart, 157, New Bond-street; Wilmot and Hill, in the Borough; Wilson and Spence, York; H. Mozley, Gainsborough; and by all booksellers and stationers; with full and liberal allowance to schools. By T. Gillet, Salisbury-square. [Price eighteen-pence bound.] 1804.

17×9.6 cm. Pp.168 inc. 4pp. bklist. Engvd FP×2 dated July 14 1803, showing, above, a school-dame reading to a group of little girls; and, below, a schoolmaster instructing one little boy, with another seated on a stool beside him, and a class of diligent boys in the background. Between, are 5 lines of poetry (Thomson). Pp.6–8 contain a picture alphabet showing animals and birds; there are other text wcts and pictorial headpieces to fables. Calf.
[BL

This remarkably successful work attempted to present a survey of all knowledge in a small compass, its contents ranging from reading and spelling lessons to natural history, from fables, moral tales and moral observations to gymnastics, the arts and sciences, geography, poetry, prayers and the catechism.
In his Preface, dated May 1, 1803, from Woodstock, the author says that his aim has been to provide 'as great a variety of useful matter as the price will permit' for the benefit of poor children who may have no other book, unless it be a Bible. At a time when school-books could be very drear, this is probably one of the most humane lesson-books for young children. E. Kilner puffed it in *A visit to London*, 1808.

(3) Another printing, with otherwise identical specification to (2), shows the author as 'chaplain to the Earl of Moira'.
[Baldwin

(4) ... The English spelling book. Fifteenth edition. Richard Phillips. 1805. Engvd FP×2, wood-engvd picture alphabet of animals and birds, 12 illusns of animals and 6 of fables. Sheep.
[S 10.12.80/41

(5) Title as (1) to ... introduction to a correct knowledge of the English language. By William Mavor, LL.D. Vicar of Hurley in Berkshire; Chaplain to the Earl of Moira; and author of the British Nepos, Universal History, Natural History for Schools, &c.

&c. The thirty-fifth edition, revised and improved. London: printed for Richard Phillips, No.6, New Bridge Street, Blackfriars. Sold by Tabart and Co. 157, New Bond Street; Champante and Whitrow, Jewry-street; Wilson and Spence, York; H. Mozley, Gainsborough; and by all booksellers and stationers; with full and liberal allowance to schools. [Price eighteen-pence, bound.] 1806. T. Gillet, Printer Wild-court Wild-street.

17×9.9 cm. (Printer's impt on last p. adds 'Lincoln's Inn Fields'.) Pp.162+6pp. advts. Preface dated 'Woodstock, Feb. 12, 1806'. Calf, blind-stamped, no spine label present.
[Miami

(6) An edition dated 1811 printed for Richard Phillips has been reported but not traced.

107 (1) MAVOR, William Fordyce. Select lives of Plutarch, containing the most illustrious characters of antiquity; abridged from the original for the use of schools. By William Mavor, LL.D. Rector of Stonefield, Vicar of Hurley, Berkshire, Chaplain to the Earl of Moira, &c. &c. A new edition. London: printed for Richard Phillips, No.6, New Bridge Street, Blackfriars; sold by Lackington, Allen and Co. Finsbury Square, Champante and Whitrow, Old Jewry; Tabart and Co. Juvenile Library, Bond Street; and by all other booksellers. [Price 5s. bound, with full allowance to schools.] 1806.

17.3×10.5 cm. Pr by C. Stower, Paternoster-row, Cheapside. Pp.[viii]+466+6pp. bklist pr by Lewis, Paternoster-row. Calf, black label, g, on sp.
[BL

An earlier undated edition in BL and S 12.11.73/95, printed by T. Davidson [sic], Lombard-street, White-Friars (FP dated 1800), did not carry Tabart's name. In the edition of 1806 the life of Solon has been added.

Review: The *Anti-Jacobin review*, vol. 7, p.421: 'A book well suited to the indolent spirit of the age, in which *Newspapers*, *Dictionaries*, and *Beauties*, are the chief objects of study, with the generality of readers. The first for learning the science of politics, and the two last for the acquisition of general knowledge.'

108 (1) MEMOIRS OF DICK, THE LITTLE PONEY; supposed to be written by himself; and published for the instruction and amusement of pretty masters and misses. A new edition. London: printed for J. Harris, corner of St. Paul's; and Tabart and Co. at the Juvenile and School Library, 157, New Bond Street; by Slatter and Munday, Oxford. 1804. Price two shillings.

13.2×8.2 cm. Pp.xii+164+4pp. Tabart's advts. ½-title. FP engvd by J. Scott after Howitt+TP vignette. Yellow, or marbled bds, green roan sp g.
[BL; Melb.; ? S 2.6.75/48

The Dedication is dated 14 Dec. 1799 and the Editor's Advertisement, 5 April 1804. This story was first published as a separate book by J. Walker and sold by E. Newbery in 1800 (Roscoe J241) but it had previously appeared in the *Young gentleman's and lady's magazine*, 1799 (Roscoe J393). It was reprinted in America in 1802 by Benjamin Johnson and Jacob Johnson, Philadelphia. Welch 832.1.

The Dedication is to 'The hopeful sons of the most noble the Marquis of B...'. The Advertisement says that 'Dick is still alive and well; and on lately hearing how many blooming Boys and lovely Girls interested themselves in his welfare, expressed his wish, that he could have an opportunity of obliging them, occasionally, by taking a ride on his back round the beautiful paddock in Berkshire, where it is probable he will close his days ...'

The story tells how Dick ran free with his dam on Hounslow Heath until he was stolen by gypsies, who cropped his tail and ears – an event giving rise to a lecture on the cruelty of mutilating defenceless animals. He was sold at a fair and in a variety of homes he was sometimes well, and sometimes unkindly, treated; and he carefully explains the details so that children may learn how to behave towards their ponies. He ends up in a good home and now has time to dictate his memoirs. This book is, in fact, a precursor of *Black Beauty*.

Mrs. Fenwick puffed the story in her *Visits to the Juvenile Library*.

(2) An identical edition was also printed in 1804 but with the price of half-a-crown. [Miami

Most of Tabart's advertisements show the price as 2s. but the booklist in Aikin's *Poetry for Children*, 1805, quotes 2s.6d. Some other advertisements in 1805 give 2s. as the price.

(3) Title as (1) to ... amusement of little masters and misses. A new edition. London: printed by C. Squire, Furnival's-Inn-court, for Tabart and Co. at the Juvenile and School Library, No.157, New Bond Street; and to be had of all booksellers. [Price two shillings.] 1806.

13.5×8.5 cm. Pp.xii (should be x but misprinted) + 165 + 5pp. bklist beginning on v. of p.165. FP as in (1). TP wct vignette. Marbled bds, black roan sp g. [Osborne

Later editions were published by Whittingham and Arliss [1816] with the Dedication dated 1799 but Editor's Advertisement dated September 1816 [Osborne]; and by Arnold *c*.1823 with 18 woodcuts [Gum. 4016].

109 (1) MEMOIRS OF THE LITTLE MAN AND THE LITTLE MAID: with some interesting particulars of their lives. Never before published. London: published by B. Tabart, at the Juvenile and School Library, No.157, New Bond-street. 1807.

13.2×11.1 cm. Pr by C. Squire, Furnival's-Inn-court, Holborn. Pp.12+2pp. bklist. XII h/c pls dated May 1807. Pr yellow wrps with picture of Tabart's shop on lower v. Cover-text reads: 'Authentic memoirs of the little man and the little maid ... lives. Illustrated with beautiful engravings. London ... 1807.' (See fig. 17)
[Osborne; Hockliffe; Bod.; PML; CBY 335; S 21.10.76/1692

On p.1 'wooed' is misprinted as 'woed'. Plate VI is misnumbered IV and this is not corrected in later printings. There is a notice on the verso of the title-page that the ballad would be 'speedily' set to music; advertisements show that the composer of the music was Dr. Calcott and that the price of the book was 1s.6d. or 2s.6d. with music. See Appendix D for a full discussion of the book's printing history.

Horace Walpole attributed an earlier and shorter version of this rhyme to Sir Charles

IX.

London.Published March 1,1807.by.B.Tabart,157,New Bond S.!

Plate IX, version dated March 1, 1807

IX

London.Published May.1,1807.by. B.Tabart.157.New Bond Street.

Plate IX, redrawn version dated May, 1807

17   *Memoirs of the little man and the little maid*, 109

Sedley. The ODNR gives an extended note on its sources and reprints and quotes 6 stanzas. Reprinted in America in 1811 by Wm Charles, Philadelphia. Welch 838. 1 and 3–4; by Henry Whipple, Salem, Mass., in 1814 and 1818. Welch 838. 2 and 5.

(2) As (1) but with the plates interleaved with Dr. Calcott's musical setting. [Private colls; S 20.2.73/541

(3) Title as (1) to ... published by B. Tabart & Co. at their Juvenile and School Library, New Bond-street. 1808.

13.2×11 cm. Pr by C. Squire, Furnival's-Inn-court. Pp.12+(in some copies) 2pp. advts. This 'new edition' appears to have been issued in two printings, themselves subject to variations: (a) continues the use of the May 1807 plates; (b) introduces an alternative and different cutting of the original illustrations on plates dated March 1807. The only copy seen thus has the music gathered at the start and has the plates interleaved with the text pages. Yellow, or brown, stiff-paper covers, picture of Tabart's shop on lower v. Cover-text includes 'A new edition ... 1808' and omits 'beautiful' before 'engravings'.
[UCLA, (a) imp., no music; Lilly; FCB (a) pp.183–196; S 21.10.76/1693 with music; private coll. (a); private coll. (b).

(4) Another edition published by Tabart and Co. with plates dated 1816. Marbled papers wrps.
[S 2.6.82/129 with title only+12 h/c pls, no text; Ball, untraced

(5) Title as (1) to ... lives. Illustrated with engravings. London: published by Tabart & Co. at their Juvenile and School Library, No.39, New Bond Street. Printed by G. Sidney, Northumberland Street, Strand. 1818.

13.1×10.9 cm. Pp.12. No FP, XII h/c pls dated May 1816 by B. Tabart, 85 Piccadilly. Pl VI still misnumbered IV. Yellow stiff-paper pr covers, text includes 'A new edition ... 1818'.
[Opie, no music; Gum. 4017; S 28.2.84/11

Sotheby (25.2.76/34) sold a copy of Souter's edition, dating it c.1808, which is unlikely, since it has a presentation inscription dated 6 October 1829 and is watermarked 1827. It has the May 1807 plates, but now given J. Souter's imprint, and the text pages have been given a double-rule frame. This copy contains no music but copies with music were advertised.
[Private coll.

110 (1) MINCE PIES FOR CHRISTMAS: consisting of riddles, charades, rebuses, transpositions and queries; intended to gratify the mental taste, and to exercise the ingenuity of sensible masters and misses. By an old friend. London: printed for Tabart and Co. at the Juvenile and School Library, No.157, New Bond-street. 1805. By T. Gillet, Salisbury Square.

13.3×8.2 cm. Pp.vi+189+3pp. bklist. H/c or plain FP dated Dec. 25 1804. Marbled bds, red or black roan sp g.

[V & A; Osborne, only 172pp.; Renier; CUL; UCLA; Phila.; Bath; S 24.2.69/303

A pencil note in V & A's copy says that the frontispiece is by Blake, but this is not confirmed. On p.119 'Charades' is mis-spelt 'Crarades'.

Dedicated 'to Miss Eliza Phillips, a young lady of seven, with wit and beauty sufficient for seventeen, the Editor inscribes this little volume, as a token of his affectionate regard; and sincerely wishes her, many happy returns of this season. Dec. 22, 1804.'

Review: In the *Guardian of education*, vol. iv, p.97, Mrs. Trimmer quotes the Preface and launches out into a commentary on the editors of children's books, amongst whom 'so much *cookery* is going on, ... that the shops with which they abound greatly resemble those of the *pastry-cook*, from the circumstance of their furnishing some things that are good and wholesome; and others which are fit only to corrupt the taste of the plain eater, or to gratify the vitiated appetite of those who, by luxurious indulgence, have lost all relish for that which is simple and nutritious. ... For our own parts, we cannot adopt the *nonchalance* of the Editor; who, if children reject what he has provided, tells them "he has no objection to their going and *cramming* themselves with what they like better, providing HE has neither the cook or the apothecary to pay"'.

To cut short Mrs. Trimmer's diatribe, she recommends that the hurtful ingredients should be picked out, leaving 'nothing but what is wholesome behind ... with the aid of ... a pair of scissors, leaving behind a considerable quantity of *innocent amusement*; for, with the mixture of some *highly exceptionable things*, this book contains a variety of good *Riddles, Charades*, &c.'

Mrs. Trimmer takes exception to riddles or charades which mention the Bible, or any character therein (including a rather funny one whose solution is 'Balaam's ass'), or plays less than respectfully with royalty – 'What is majesty deprived of its externals?' Answer: 'A jest'.

(2) MINCE PIES FOR CHRISTMAS, and for all merry seasons: consisting ... as (1) to ... ingenuity of all sensible masters and misses. By an old friend. A new edition. London: printed for Tabart and Co. at the Juvenile & School Library, 157, New Bond Street. 1807. [Price half a crown.]

13.4×8.4 cm. Pr by Squire, Furnival's-Inn-court, Holborn. Pp.vi+186+6pp. bklist, 46 titles. FP as in (1). Marbled bds, green roan sp g.
[V & A; Baldwin; Osborne; Gum. 4045; Phila.; Melb.; private coll.; NLS; Bod J

Dedicated 'To Miss Eliza Phillips, a young lady who, on this day, completes her 7th year ... Dec. 25, 1804.'

(3) Title as (2) to ... Library, Clifford-street, Bond-street – 1812, – [Price half-a-crown.]

13.7×8.5 cm. Pr by Galabin and Marchant, Ingram Court, Fenchurch Street. FP as (1). Pp.vi+192 (inc. 6pp. advts). Marbled bds, roan sp.
[Opie; UCLA; de Grummond

Dedication as in (2).

111 (1) MODERN LONDON: Being the history and present state of the British metropolis. Illustrated with numerous copper-plates. London: printed for Richard Phillips, No.71, St. Paul's Church-yard, by C. Mercer and Co. Northumberland-court, Strand. 1804.

26.1×19.3 cm. Many handsome engravings of views and scenes in London. After p.501 follows a section with fine hand-coloured engraved pictures of 'The Itinerant Traders of London in their ordinary costume; with notices of the remarkable places given in the background.' Among these is a plate entitled 'Band Boxes' (published April 25, 1804, by Richard Phillips, 72, St. Paul's Church Yard), drawn by Craig, showing a man with a variety of boxes of all shapes and colours fastened to a pole over

MOTHER GOOSE.

The rich old squire, & the poor youth,
Who open first our play;
Are placed before a Dame, whose truth
Does the old Beau dismay,

57

had brought out all their play-things; besides which, Mrs. Bond had provided a great many new ones, and gave them leave to run about in a large field, that was full of flowers; and there was a pretty summer-house at one corner of the field, where they were not yet allowed to enter; but Harriet whispered to her companions, that the summer-house was full of cakes and sweetmeats; and that when the cows were milked, they

VOL. II, D

vol. 2. p. 63.

18 Double-page spread from *Familiar conversations* by Harriet Mandeville, 101 (1)

19 Scene from the Harlequinade, *Mother Goose*, 112. A horizontal slit across the picture allows upper and lower flaps to be lifted, revealing more scenes below. *Sotheby's.*

his shoulder, and in the background, a view of Tabart's Juvenile Library. On the facing page is a note: 'The Bibliothèque d'Education, or Tabart's Juvenile Library, seen to the left of the Plate, is in New Bond-street, at the corner of Grafton-street. It is a very admirable and unique Institution, where all elementary books of science and education are to be found, in addition to every moral and amusing publication that can "teach the young idea how to shoot, Or pour the fresh instruction o'er the mind."'
[BL

Although this is not one of Tabart's publications, it is included because it shows the close connection between himself and Richard Phillips.

111A (1) THE MONTHLY PRECEPTOR: not traced, but see the *School magazine, or the Monthly preceptor,* 150 below.

112 (1) [Cover-title] MOTHER GOOSE [Harlequinade]. Sold by B. Tabart & Co. [Imprint on 2nd leaf] Published by B. Tabart & Co. July 1st 1809.

18.6 cm high; 38.5×30.5 cm when all flaps are turned up. Engvd and h/c throughout. Orange and black marbled wrps with buff pictorial onlays. Front onlay shows large wood-eng. of Mother Goose; rear onlay has large wood-eng. of a negro clashing cymbals. (See fig. 19)
[Private coll. ex S 1.6.89/389

113 (1) NATURAL HISTORY OF THE ROBIN-RED-BREAST. To which is added a selection of complimentary verses, addressed to His Serene Littleness. Adorned with a striking likeness. By an old friend. London: printed for B. Tabart, at the Juvenile and School Library, 157, New Bond-street, and to be had of all booksellers. Price one shilling. 1808.

13×8.7 cm. Pr by J. Diggens, St. Ann's Lane. Pp.[iv]–[5] 6–54. H/c FP. Pr yellow wrps, bklist on lower v. of Tabart's publications.
[S 10.12.80/44, 10.12.85/474 and 1.12.88/81

114 (1) NOURJAHAD, of The folly of unreasonable wishes, an Eastern tale, with three coloured engravings. London: printed for Tabart and Co. at the Juvenile and School Library, No.157, New Bond-street; and to be had of all booksellers. Price sixpence. 1805.

12.1×7 cm. Pr by V. Griffiths, Bell-Savage Yard. Pp.36. H/c FP dated Augst 12 1805+2 undated h/c pls. Pr yellow wrps.
[UCLA, bound with others; S 14.3.72/457 and 9.6.75/772; PML

Entered at Stationers' Hall by R. Phillips on 9.9.05. Reprinted in America *c.*1817 or later by W. Jackson, 71 Maiden-lane, New-York (American imprint on cover only; TP shows N. Hailes, London Museum, Piccadilly, 1817; Welch 953 with reference to Tabart's edition of 1805.)

(2) An edition of 1808, no details known except engvd h/c FP+2 pls, wrps. [S 9.6.75/77]

(3) An edition published by N. Hailes, London Museum, Piccadilly, 1817, presumed from TP of American edition described in Welch 953.

115 (1) A NUMERATION, ADDITION AND MULTIPLICATION TABLE was entered by Tabart and Co. on 9.12.08 at Stationers' Hall but it has not been traced.

116 (1) THE PAGAN MYTHOLOGY OF ANCIENT GREECE AND ROME, VERSIFIED. Accompanied with philosophical elucidations of the probable latent meaning of some of the fables of the ancients, on a theory entirely new. Illustrated with impressions from engravings on wood by J. Berryman. Dedicated to Her Royal Highness the Princess Charlotte of Wales. [1 line Virgil. 4 lines Pope.] London: printed for the author: and sold by J. M. Richardson, 23, Cornhill, opposite the Royal Exchange; J. Wallis, Jun. Universal Juvenile Library, 188, Strand; and B. Tabart, 165, New Bond Street. 1809.

16.9×10.1 cm. Pr by Mercier and Co. King's Head Court, St. Paul's Church Yard. Pp.vii [viii blank], [i]–vi, [7]–148. Wood-engvd FP+21 wood-engs, each tipped in and blank on other side, by J. Berryman.
[UCLA, rebound

117 (1) PARNELL'S HERMIT [Harlequinade]. Published by Tabart & Co. Jany 31st 1810.

A folded sheet, 19.3×30.7 cm, with flaps, each with a h/c picture and engvd verse; 19.3×7.8 cm when folded. The flaps meet in the middle horizontally and, when lifted, reveal more scenes and descriptive verses underneath. Text and h/c pictures engvd throughout. Enclosed loosely in pink pictorial paper covers measuring 22.3×8.5 cm and lettered on front 'Parnells Hermit. Sold by Tabart & Co.' Three well-executed engs on both front and back.
[Hockliffe; private coll.

All the engravings are well drawn and executed and the colouring is careful and bright.

Dr. Thomas Parnell, Archdeacon of Clogher, 1679–1718, was the author of *The Hermit*, a popular and admired poem first published in 1722. It tells how an angel, disguised as a human being, commits apparently wicked deeds, such as returning evil for good, or even murder; it then goes on to explain how each of these actions has prevented greater harm from occurring (a distorted moral which must have bewildered young readers). This fable in its oldest literary form is in the Koran, and a different version is in the Talmud. [See W. E. A. Axon: *Literary history of Parnell's 'Hermit'*, 1895? Also *The pretty pilgrim*, 136 below.]

Welch 973 mentions American editions of the poem published by Samuel Wood, at the Juvenile Book-Store, No.357, Pearl-street, New-York. So it was evidently considered fit for juvenile consumption in America.

118 (1) PEACOCK, Lucy. Ambrose and Eleanor; or, The adventures of two children deserted on an uninhabited island. Translated from the French, with alterations, adapting it to the perusal of youth. By Lucy Peacock, author of The Visit for a Week, &c. The third edition. London: printed for J. Johnson and J. Harris, in St. Paul's Church-yard; R. and L. Peacock, at the Juvenile Library, No.259, Oxford Street; C. Law, Avemaria Lane; and B. Tabart, New Bond Street. 1807.

17.3×10.2 cm. Pr by E. Hemsted, Great New Street, Fetter Lane. Pp.iv+292. No illusns. Tree calf, black or red label on sp, g.
[BL; Gum. 4394; Reading U; UCLA; Ball; Baldwin; private coll.

First published in Paris in 1788 under the title of *Lolotte et Fanfan*, by François Guillaume Ducray-Dumenil, and this abridged translation was first published in 1796. It is an interesting and romantic Robinsonade about a shipwrecked traveller (a colonel) who is cast up on an almost-deserted shore where he finds two seven-year-old English children who have been there, alone, for four years. They were marooned there with a good sailor, who died, and they learned to fend for themselves. The years go by, the party is joined by another shipwrecked Englishman, the colonel educates and civilises the children, and then he and the other man mysteriously disappear (having been captured and taken away by visiting Spaniards). The boy and girl leave their island in a little boat which they have all helped to make and, after many adventures and remarkable coincidences, are reunited with their two friends. Eventually, the colonel finds his own family and, what is more, discovers that Ambrose and Eleanor are his grandchildren. They all go to France and see the sights of Paris but some months later the main characters in the story return to the island, where a colony is founded.

119 (1) PEACOCK, Lucy. A chronological abridgment of universal history: to which is added, an abridged chronology of the most remarkable discoveries and inventions relative to the arts and sciences. Translated from the seventh edition of the French [of Mathurin Veyssière de la Croze]. By Lucy Peacock. Printed for J. Johnson and J. Harris, St. Paul's Church-yard; R. and L. Peacock, 259, Oxford Street; C. Law, Ave Maria lane; J. Mawman, in the Poultry; and B. Tabart, New Bond Street. 1807.

16.5×9.5 cm. Pr by Law and Gilbert, St. John's Square, Clerkenwell. Pp.xi+257 [pp.260 inc. 3pp. advts]. No illusns.
[BL, rebound; Briggs

The whole of the history is presented in questions and answers in a manner unlikely to arouse any interest in the subject. Nevertheless, this book was reprinted in America, printed in Boston by David Carlisle for Caleb Bingham, 1802, with the title *A historical grammar; or A chronological abridgment* ... (Copy in BL).

120 (1) PEACOCK, Lucy. The Knight of the Rose: an allegorical tale, designed for the amusement and moral instruction of youth. By Lucy Peacock. The second edition, improved and enlarged. London:

printed for J. Johnson, and J. Harris, in St. Paul's Churchyard; R. and L. Peacock, 259, Oxford Street; C. Law, in Ave Maria Lane; and B. Tabart, New Bond Street. 1807.

17.5×9.8 cm. Pr by B. McMillan, Bow Street, Covent Garden. Pp.[iv]+240. No illusns. Marbled bds, red roan sp g; or blue paper covers; or sheep.
[BL, rebound; UCLA; Osborne, with 12pp. Crosby's advts dated 1813; Miami; PML, with cat. of Baldwin, Cradock and Joy, wmk 1819

First published in 1793 by Hookham and Carpenter, J. Marshall, S. Hazard of Bath, and the author. The leaf following TP carries Advertisement on recto and list of Lucy Peacock's books and recommendations on verso.

In her Advertisement the author admits to having borrowed the idea of this story from the second book of Spenser's *Faerie Queene*. She also admits that 'allegory is an unfavourable vehicle to convey instruction' to children, but she has designed this book 'for the perusal of youth'.

120A (1) PERONELLA. A tale for the nursery. Advertised in 1805 but not found as a separate work. It is included in *Tabart's collection of popular stories*, part I.

121 (1) [PERRAULT, Charles] La barbe bleue. Tabart's French version of Blue Beard was often advertised but has not been found. In 1804 it was 'just published' and 'with the same embellishments' – probably meaning the same engravings as the English version.

122 (1) PERRAULT, Charles. Blue Beard; or, Female curiosity: and Little Red Riding-Hood: tales for the nursery. From the French of C. Perrault. With copperplates. Fifth edition. London: printed for Tabart and Co. at the Juvenile and School Library, No.157, New Bond-street; and to be had of all booksellers. Price sixpence. 1804.

13.2×7.5 cm. Pr by R. Taylor, Black Horse Court, Fleet Street. Pp.36. 3 h/c pls engvd after Craig. Yellow stiff-paper pr wrps, advt on lower v.; advt also on v. of TP.
[PML

Welch 986.1 does not mention this separate production of the story but only its inclusion in *Tabart's collection of popular stories*.

(2) 6th edition not traced.

(3) Title as (1) except Seventh edition.

12.1×7.1 cm. Pr by Taylor, Black Horse Court. Pp.36. H/c FP+2 h/c pls, all dated Sep. 18 1804, engvd after Craig. Advt on v. of TP.
[UCLA, bound with others

(4), (5) 8th and 9th editions not traced.

(6) Title as (1) except Tenth edition.

12.6×7.7 cm. Pr by Taylor, Black Horse Court. Pp.36. 3 h/c pls dated Sep. 18 1804. Buff-orange paper wrps, cover-title: Tabart's improved edition of Blue Beard ... [Private coll., wmk 1801

(7) Title as (1) except Tenth edition [*sic*] and date ... 1806.

12×7.9 cm. Pr by W. Heney, 76, Fleet-street. Pp.34+1p. bklist, 34 titles, pasted to r. of lower cover. H/c FP dated Nov. 1804+2 other h/c pls dated Sep. 18 1804, the third representing Little Red Riding-Hood and the wolf. Pr yellow stiff-paper covers, text reads: 'The renowned History of Blue Beard; with plates, taken from the splendid pageant represented at the Theatre-Royal Drury Lane. London: published by Tabart and Co. ... and sold by all booksellers and toy-shops throughout the Empire. 1809. Marchant, Printer, 3, Greville-street.' [Private coll., S 2.7.74/256; PML

123 (1) PERRAULT, Charles. [Bluebeard] The renowned history of Bluebeard; with plates, taken from the splendid pageant represented at the Theatre-Royal, Drury Lane. Tabart. 1809. [CBY 398a

This must have been a longer version of the story as it was advertised in 1809 price 1s. plain, 1s.6d. coloured. Not traced.

124 (1) PERRAULT, Charles. Cendrillon. Tabart's French version of Cinderella was advertised from 1804 – 'Just published' – to 1809, 'new and beautiful edition', price 6d. with plates drawn by Craig. Not traced.

125 (1) PERRAULT, Charles. Cinderella; or The little glass slipper: a tale for the nursery. From the French of C. Perrault. With three copperplates. Sixth edition. London: printed for Tabart and Co. at the Juvenile and School Library, No.157, New Bond-street; and to be had of all booksellers. Price sixpence. 1804.

12.1×7 cm. Pr by Taylor, Black Horse Court. Pp.36. 3 undated pls. Marbled bds, ½ mottled calf. [Lilly

Advertised in 1804 'with representations of three of the principal scenes in the performance at Drury Lane Theatre'. The plates are engraved after Corbould or Craig. The numbering of the above and subsequent editions appears to be haphazard. Welch 987.1 quotes 16th edition 1804, q.v.

Review: The *London Magazine*, No.11, Nov. 1820, vol. ii, in an article headed 'The Literature of the Nursery', recalled the joys of fairy tales and remembered that 'We used to gaze on Cinderella's face, where she sat among the cinders, as if it were a lily in a wilderness of foul weeds. ...' (This did not specifically refer to Tabart's edition.)

(2) Title as (1) except 'Fourteenth edition'.

12.3×7.7 cm. Pr by R. Taylor, Black Horse Court, Fleet Street. Pp.36. H/c FP+one other h/c pl, both dated Aug. 7 1804.
[Renier, imp., no covers

(3) Title as (1) to ... copperplates. Sixteenth edition. London: printed for Tabart and Co. at the Juvenile and School Library, No.157, New Bond-street; and to be had of all booksellers. Price sixpence. 1804.

12.7×7.8 cm. Pr by Taylor, Black Horse Court. Pp.36. H/c FP dated Aug. 7 1804+2 other pls, same date. Blue pr stiff-paper covers, advt of Tabart's Library on lower v. (Osborne), or gold-coloured stiff-paper wrps (PML). Advt on v. of TP.
[Osborne; PML, wmk 1801; UCLA

(4) Title as (3) to ... three copper-plates. Eleventh edition. London: printed for Tabart and Co. at the Juvenile and School Library, No.157, New Bond Street; and to be had of all booksellers. Price sixpence. 1806.

12.3×7.8 cm. Pr by Squire, Furnival's-Inn-court. Pp.35, p.[36] = bklist. Pls as in (3) but one n.d. Yellow pr stiff-paper covers, advt on lower v.
[CUL; UCLA, bound with others

Advt on v. of TP.

(5) Title as (4) to ... slipper: ... three copper-plates. Twelfth edition ... New Bond-street, and to be had of all booksellers. Price sixpence. 1807.

11.9×8.2 cm. Pr by J. Diggens, St. Ann's Lane. Pp.35, p.[36] = list of 4 titles. H/c FP+2 (?) pls. Yellow stiff-paper pr covers, Tabart's advt on lower v.
[CUL, 2 pls; Hirsch, 2 pls.

[The 2 copies recorded had only 2 plates each.]

126 (1) [PERRAULT, Charles] Hop o' my Thumb: a tale for the nursery. With three copperplates. A new edition. London: printed for Tabart and Co. at the Juvenile and School Library, No.157, New Bond-street: and to be had of all dealers in books. Price sixpence. 1804.

12×7 cm. Pr by R. Taylor & Co., Black-Horse-court. Pp.32. H/c FP (date illegible)+2 other h/c pls dated July 1804. Pr green wrps, advt on lower v. Advt also on v. of TP.
[UCLA, bound with others; PML

The plates are engraved after designs by Craig. This title was entered at Stationers' Hall by R. Phillips on 8.8.04. It is an English version of Perrault's story, 'Le Petit Poucet'.

In Mrs. Fenwick's *Visits to the Juvenile Library* the children who are taken to Mr. Tabart's shop are allowed to choose several fairy-tales, including this one.

(2) Title as (1) to ... three copper-plates. A new edition. London: printed for B. Tabart, at the Juvenile and School Library, No.157, New Bond Street; and to be had of all booksellers. Price sixpence. 1808.

11.4×7.8 cm. Pr by J. Diggens, St. Ann's Lane. Pp.35 (last leaf a paste-down). H/c FP (paste-down)+2 other h/c pls dated July 1804. Plain yellow stiff-paper covers.
[Renier

Advertisement on v. of TP.

127 (1) [PERRAULT, Charles] Hop o' my Thumb [Harlequinade]. Published by Tabart & Co. Jany 1st 1810.

2 sheets, unfolded and uncut, both made up of 4 panels, each panel having a h/c illustration and verses, ready to be made into a turn-up or harlequinade. Size of printed portion of sheets, without margins, 29.5×17.0 cm.
[UCLA; D. C. Muir's Memorial Catalogue dedicated to Percy H. Muir, with illusn.

128 (1) [PERRAULT, Charles] *Little Red Riding Hood.* The history of Little Red Riding-Hood, in verse. Illustrated by engravings. London: published at the Juvenile Libraries of B. Tabart, New Bond-street, and J. Harris, St. Paul's Church-yard. Printed by E. Hemsted, Great New Street, Fetter-lane. 1807.

12.3×9.9 cm. Pp.11 p.[12] = Moral. H/c or plain stipple-engvd FP+11 other h/c or plain pls; the FP, virtually a second TP, is dated Jany 1 1808, by B. Tabart and Jno. Harris. Greyish pr paper covers. Text of lower v. includes 'Illustrated with her portrait, and the most remarkable events of her life ...'
[Renier; S 3.3.77/268; private coll.; Baldwin, h/c

The story is told in unusually simple, direct poetry and the illustrations are very graphic and prettily coloured. An elegant booklet.

Review (but not specifically referring to this edition): The *London Magazine*, No.11, Nov. 1820, vol. ii, in an article headed 'The Literature of the Nursery', recalling the joys of fairy tales, said 'Then how sweet it was to accompany poor little Red-riding-hood, on her walk by village lanes, girded with hedges – not without taking a wistful peep at the "cheese-cakes" and the "little pot of butter", in the basket which she bore on her left arm! Those niceties were for her old grandmother; but her grandmother never enriched her toast out of the pot which little Red-riding-hood carried! The deceitful monster's fatal reply to the innocent ejaculation – "Grandmama what great teeth you have got!" – continued to startle us at every reading, with undiminished effect, as if we had heard the gnash of the ravenous seizure, and the crackling of the unfortunate child's bones!'

(2) Title as (1) except ... 1808.

13.2×11 cm. Pp.11, p.[12] = Moral. H/c engvd FP as in (1)+11 h/c engs.
[BL, rebound, with pls IX, X and XI out of order; Ball

(3) Title as (1) to ... Second edition. London: published at the Juvenile Libraries of B. Tabart and Co. New Bond-street, and J. Harris, St. Paul's Church-yard. Printed by E. Hemsted, Great New-street, Fetter-lane. 1808.

14×10.7 cm. Pp.11 (+[2] in some copies). FP+11 pls dated July 1816 by Tabart & Co. 85, Piccadilly. Pr orange or yellow stiff-paper covers with title: 'The Renowned History of ...' and some copies have cover-impt: 'London: printed for John Souter, at the School Library, 73, North Side of St. Paul's Church-yard. 1s. plain, 1s.6d. coloured. 1819.'
[V & A, with date on cover crossed out and '1808' written in ink. On lower v. bklist of John Souter, 9 titles; PML, pls wmk 1814; S 16.10.75/1236; private coll. with Souter's covers, 1819

(4) There was also a Souter edition of 1819, his address shown as 'at the School Library, 73, North Side of St. Paul's Church-yard.'

129 (1) PERRAULT, Charles. Puss in Boots, and Diamonds and toads: tales for the nursery. From the French of C. Perrault. With three copperplates. London: printed for Tabart and Co. at the Juvenile and School Library, No.157, New Bond-street; and to be had of all booksellers. Price sixpence. 1804.

12×7 cm. Pr by Taylor, Black Horse Court. Pp.35 [36]. H/c FP+2 other h/c pls, n.d. [UCLA, leaves trimmed, bound with others

Entered at Stationers' Hall by R. Phillips on 9.7.04. Advertisement on v. of TP reading 'Published by Tabart and Co. ... where is constantly kept on sale the largest collection of books of amusement and instruction in the world, from one penny to five guineas in price.'

These two tales are English versions of Perrault's stories, 'Le Chat Botté' and 'Les Fées'. The frontispiece is an amusing picture of Puss, heavily booted, lying in wait for rabbits. The plates are engraved after Craig.

This title was one of the fairy tales bought by the lucky children who visited Tabart's bookshop in Mrs. Fenwick's *Visits to the Juvenile Library*, 43 above.

Review but not specifically of Tabart's edition. The *London magazine*, No.11, Nov. 1820, vol. ii, in an article headed 'The Literature of the Nursery', recalled the pleasure of reading about Puss in Boots, declaring 'We may, we believe, boast of having seen the most favoured specimens of the present generation of cats; but we candidly confess we have never had the good fortune to meet with one individual whose talents and carriage were at all comparable to his of the "*Boots*". There is nothing we think, in Dante or Cobbett, more tremendous than his threat uttered to the trembling reapers: "Good people! if you do not tell the king, who will shortly pass this way, that the meadow you are reaping belongs to my master, the marquis of Carabas, *you shall be chopped as small as mince-meat!*" – And yet how insinuatingly respectful was the same blusterer to the unsuspicious Ogre, who treated him "as civilly as an ogre could do," – and of whom puss in return made a meal! The consummation of this interesting history is worthy of its noble course: the master of the cat married a princess, and 'the cat became a great lord, – nor ever after pursued rats and mice *but for his amusement!*'

(2) Title as (1) except ... copperplates. Sixth [*sic*] edition...

12.9×7.5 cm. Pr by R. Taylor, Black Horse Court, Fleet Street. Pp.35 [36]. Pls as in (1). Stiff yellow pr wrps, advts on lower v. [PML, wmk 1804

(3) Title as (1) to ... nursery from the French of C. Perrault. With three copper-plates. Fourth [*sic*] edition. London: printed for Tabart & Co. at the Juvenile and School Library, No.157, New Bond-street, and to be had of all booksellers. Price sixpence. 1806.

11.9×7.7 cm. Pr by C. Squire, Furnival's-Inn-court. Pp.33+3pp. bklist starting on v. of p.33. H/c FP (impt illegible)+1 pl. (of 2) dated July 1804. Plain blue card covers. [Hockliffe

(4) Title as (1) to ... three copper-plates. Fourth edition [*sic*]. London: printed for Tabart and Co. at the Juvenile and School Library, 157, New Bond-street, and to be had of all booksellers. Price sixpence. 1807.

11.5×8.2 cm. Pr by J. Diggens, St. Ann's Lane. Pp.33. H/c FP (date illegible)+2 h/c pls dated July 1804 on one, the other shaved in copy seen. Plain yellow stiff-paper covers.
[UCLA

The text has been reset since 1804.

130 (1) [PERRAULT, Charles] Riquet with the Tuft: a tale for the nursery. With three copperplates. A new edition. London: printed for Tabart and Co. at the Juvenile and School Library, No.157, New Bond-street; and to be had of all dealers in books. Price sixpence. 1804.

12.2×7.6 cm. Pr by R. Taylor and Co., Black-Horse-court. Pp.34+2pp. bklist. 3 h/c pls dated July 1804. Blue or pink paper covers.
[Baldwin; PML

Entered at Stationers' Hall by R. Phillips on 3.8.04. The plates are engraved after designs by Craig.

(2) Title as (1) to ... copper-plates ... New Bond Street; and to be had of all booksellers. Price sixpence. 1806.

11.9×7.7 cm. Pr by Squire, Furnival's-Inn-court. Pp.32+4pp. bklist. H/c pls as in (1). Plain blue card covers.
[Hockliffe

(3) Gum. 4779 lists an edition of 1809 with 3pp. bklist at end in yellow wrps. Not traced.

131 (1) [PERRAULT, Charles] The sleeping beauty in the wood. With three copperplates. A new edition. London: printed for Tabart and Co. at the Juvenile and School Library, No.157, New Bond-street; and to be had of all dealers in books. Price sixpence. 1804.

11.5×7.7 cm. Pr by R. Taylor and Co. Black-Horse Court. Pp.34+2pp. bklist. 3 h/c pls dated July 1804. Green or gold stiff-paper pr wrps, advt on lower v. and on v. of TP.
[PML, wmk 1804; S 22.4.77/2340; Osborne, rebound; private coll.

Entered at Stationers' Hall by R. Phillips on 28.7.04. It was advertised in *c.*1806 as having three engravings from designs by Craig and described as 'in Lilliputian folio, a legend for the nursery, performing at this time with great applause, at the Theatre-Royal, Drury-lane'.

In [1837] T. Hughes advertised this title in *A new and original book of forfeits* as one of his series of 'Children's Threepenny Books. ... Tabart's Editions' with plain engravings.

(2) Title as (1) to ... copperplates ... New Bond Street, and to be had of all booksellers. Price sixpence. 1806.

12×7.5 cm. Pr by C. Squire, Furnival's-Inn-court. Pp.34+2pp. bklist. Pls as in (1). Plain blue card covers.
[Hockliffe

132 (1) PERRIN, Jean Baptiste. A new and easy method of learning the spelling and pronunciation of the French language. Pr for Lackington, Allen, and Co. Finsbury-square; Law and Scatcherd and Letterman, Ave Maria-lane; Crosby and Co. Stationers-court; Boosey, Broad-street; Darton and Harvey, Gracechurch-street; Dulau and Co. Soho-square; Tabart, New Bond-street; Symonds, Paternoster-row; and Harris, St. Paul's Churchyard.

Listed in MLA, Aug. 1805, but no copy traced.

133 (1) POLISH TYRANT [Harlequinade]. Tabart & Co. 1809.

H/c engvd sheet folded into four panels, each with movable flaps.
[Bookseller's cat. *c.*1970

134 (1) PORTER, Jane. The two Princes of Persia. Addressed to youth. [2 lines verse] By I. Porter. London: printed by J. Cundee, Ivy-lane, for Crosby and Letterman, Stationers'-court, Ludgate-hill; and J. [in Osborne's copy; B. in UCLA's] Tabart, New Bond-street. 1801.

17.1×9.8 cm. Pp.xxiii+117 [118]+2pp. Crosby and Letterman's bklist. ½-title. FP engvd by C. Rivers after J. Ramsay dated March 16, 1801. Wct TP vignette+wct tailpieces in text. Calf, sp g.
[Osborne; UCLA

The author's Introduction recalls her youth: 'Once, the nurse's story of the tripping fairy, the witch riding her broomstick, the turban'd giant, and the sheeted ghost, were the earliest accounts of the universe which were offered to an infant's mind. Those legendary times, with the age of chivalry, are passed away. False as were the traditions then inculcated, there are many old people who even now look back with a doting regret upon the usages of those years . . .

'I yet remember the jocund festival of Christmas. A season, which fifty years ago, was spent by the country gentleman within the walls of his own paternal mansion. The enlivening mirth in the parlour, was then answered by the honest laugh of the kitchen; where over the Yule-log, the happy servants welcomed their rustic neighbours to share their cheese and ale.

'On these nights, yet a little prattling child, I have stood between the knees of my grandfather's white-headed Robin, and listened with open mouth, and extending eyes, to the annual narrative of the airy coach-and-six, with its headless coachman; which on every St. Mark's eve was seen driving into the great gate of the deserted manor-house in the bottom, where it vanished into the ground, and was never more heard of, until that day the succeeding year, when it again began its round. How often have I ran by the side of this good old creature, and traced with him the tiny steps of the fairy race, where he told me their bright robes had trailed the green sward into a freshness more lively than the rest of the field. Here the elfin people danced, by moon-light, and hummed those sighing ditties, which I had heard in my chamber when sleeping, towards the shrubbery.

'These tales, whilst they aroused my imagination, gave me a habit of ascribing all natural appearances to fanciful causes. . . . Thus reason was permitted to sleep. . . . The path was erroneous, but gemmed with ten thousand glittering meteors: infant credulity mistook them for stars: and for a time the delusion was enchanting. But all this is done away, with many better things!'

In this book, a wise Persian teacher and philosopher instructs two princely pupils by telling them apposite stories about heroic and moral events. The exotic settings and picturesque background to his lectures put this book perfectly in tune with the contemporary enjoyment of oriental tales.

Reviews: In the *Guardian of education*, vol. i, Mrs. Trimmer was at her most patronising: '... humbler youths of British origin may be innocently amused with the story, and if they will give patient attention, they may also derive moral instruction from this Book.'

The *Critical review*, vol. xxxii, 1801, p.463, said: 'Many excellent moral lessons are here communicated in the swelling language of the East ... and the work has the advantage, that it contains nothing which may not be addressed to children. The manners of the East are well preserved; and young people will feel their curiosity excited by the language and customs which the writer has adopted for their instruction and amusement.'

The *Anti-Jacobin review*, vol. 8, p.421: 'We recommend it to those who are solicitous for their offspring to profit by the dictates of virtue.'

135 (1) PRATT, Samuel Jackson. Pity's gift: a collection of interesting tales, to excite the compassion of youth for the animal creation, (ornamented with engravings.) Selected by a lady from the writings of Mr. Pratt. The tenth edition. London: printed for Harris & Co. J. Marshall, J. Johnson, and Tabart & Co. Price two shillings.

15.4×9.4 cm. No printer shown. Pp.viii+147 [148]. 15 wcts, a few signed 'TK' and one signed 'T. Kelly', copied from Longmans' and E. Newbery's 3rd edition of 1801. Buff paper bds, red roan sp g.
[Private coll.

Thomas Kelly was a wood-engraver working in Dublin around 1800. The book is printed on laid paper, no watermark. The long ſ is used, otherwise this is almost a line-for-line reprint of the 3rd edition, 1801, which did not show Tabart's name. There is a cancel TP. There is no printer's imprint and this book is possibly an Irish (probably Dublin) piracy. Another difference from the genuine 3rd edition is that this suspect copy shows at the end of each chapter the title of the work from which the piece was selected. Until the Act of Union, 1800, Irish reprints of London editions were not piracies but now the British were able to extend the Copyright Act of 1801 to Ireland, so that open reprinting became impossible and reprints had to have a disguised imprint.

136 (1) THE PRETTY PILGRIM: or The marvellous journey of Evelina Evans. London: printed by J. Vigevena, Huggin Lane, for B. Crosby and Co. Stationer's-court, and B. Tabart, 157, New Bond-street. [? *c*.1803–04]

13.3×8.5 cm. (yellow covers) or 12.7×7.4 cm. (pink covers). Pp.84+6pp. Crosby's bklist. Long ſ. Stipple-engvd FP by P. Roberts after W. Hopwood+one wct pl. Yellow or pink paper over bds, label on front showing 'Price one shilling'.
[UCLA, 2 copies, both lacking pp.81/82, one lacking FP

This unwholesome story was clearly inspired by Parnell's poem. 'The Hermit' (see note to 117, *Parnell's Hermit*). Evelina is a disobedient daughter: one day she is kidnapped by a man who says he is on a pilgrimage to the Holy Land. They suffer hardships but, worse, he forces her to steal and commit other crimes. When she is cowed and completely subdued he returns her to her home, where he tells her relieved parents that he stole her to make her repent of her disobedience. He then explains that the apparent crimes had had good results – for instance, by stealing a little child from its over-fond father the parent had been 'brought back to a sense of his duty', and so on. An unusual and horrifying tale.

137 (1) PROVERBS; or, The manual of wisdom: being an alphabetical arrangement of the best

English,	French,
Spanish,	Italian,

and other proverbs. To which are subjoined the wise sayings, precepts, maxims, and reflections of the most illustrious ancients. [4 lines prose. Lavater's Aphorisms.] Second edition. London: printed for Tabart and Co. at the Juvenile and School Library, No.157, New Bond Street. 1804.

16×9.4 cm. Pr by Slatter and Munday, Oxford. Pp.vi+146. No illusns. Calf, g sides and sp.
[UCLA; BL

This book was advertised as 'by a celebrated Divine' (Dr. Mavor has been suggested). The price was 2s.6d. in boards. The first edition has not been located.

The alphabetical arrangement of the proverbs begins at 'A good word is as soon said as a bad one' and ends with 'Young men should excel in fortitude, old men in prudence. *Bion.*'

R.R. **Note** The identity of 'R.R.' is uncertain. 'R. Ransom' has been suggested but I have not found out why. Another candidate is Richard Roe, stenographer, writer and bass singer, who died in 1853. He gave glee and ballad entertainments in London and wrote books on metre and rhythm. However, the verses in *The good boy's soliloquy*, 139 (q.v.), which inspired this suggestion obviously refer to the group of names (John Doe, Richard Roe, etc.) which are used in a law case to denote the plaintiff and defendant (see Brewer's *Dictionary of phrase and fable*) and are in the same class as 'Tom, Dick and Harry'. Even so, 'R.R.' could still be Richard Roe bluffing his readers.

138 (1) R.R. The assembled alphabet; or, Acceptance of A's invitation; concluding with a glee for three voices. Being a sequel to the 'Invited Alphabet.' By R.R. London: published by B. Tabart and Co. Juvenile and School Library, New Bond-street. 1809.

13.6×11.5 cm. Pr by E. Hemsted, New Street, Fetter Lane. Pp.36+2pp. music on 2 leaves. 26 plain or guarded h/c pls engvd by Charles Knight, 5 dated June 1 1809. Yellow pr card covers, on lower v. advt of *The invited alphabet* 'Just published', and

'Speedily will be published by the same author, Infantile Erudition, concluding with a glee for three voices: to which are added The Figure Dancers ...' (See fig. 20)
[Opie, plain; Osborne, no music; Hockliffe, imp.; Lilly; PML; 2 private colls; Nottm U

Some copies have watermark 1808. The three voices of the glee are those of 'Child, or pupil', 'Mother, or mistress' and 'Father, or master'.

The full-page illustrations are elegant and very prettily coloured. Each one, in an octagonal frame, represents a young boy in a landscape clasping a large letter of the alphabet, almost as big as himself. The first plate has at foot 'The whole Designed by R:R: and Engraved by Charles Knight ...'

(2) S 21.4.77/2134 lists an edition published by William Darton, Jun. in 1813; CBY 9.

139 (1) [R.R.] The good boy's soliloquy; containing his parents' instructions, relative to his disposition and manners. London: printed by and for W. Darton, Jun. 58, Holborn Hill. 1811.

11.7×8.7 cm. Pp.16. Copperplate FP dated April 15th 1811 pubd by W. Darton, Junr. +15 copperplates. Blue paper covers with text and copper engs on upper and lower sides.
[PML; S 21.4.77/2133

This book is included here, though never published by Tabart, because it not only completes the quartet of children's picture-and-rhyme books by 'R.R.' but may contain a clue to the author's name. The tongue-in-cheek verses describe exactly the naughty deeds that a good boy should NOT do. The pictures subversively depict *how* he does them. The poem concludes with the lines:

> I must, in short, from morn till night,
> Endeavour to do what is right;
> And must as much, the whole day long,
> Endeavour to avoid what's wrong;
> For what is right or wrong I know,)
> What is becoming or not so;)
> And hence I should the better grow,)
> As long as I am RICHARD ROE.

The note addressed 'To the Reader' says that he must consider the soliloquy as spoken by himself 'and the name at the conclusion as representing your own name; and consequently, that you may change Richard Roe into John Doe, John O Noakes, Peter Stile, or any other.' It is a delicious book, asking to be included, on the slightest pretext, in any work dealing with early children's literature, as a counterblast to excessive morality.

140 (1) R.R. Infantile erudition: concluding with a glee for three voices. To which are added The Figure Dancers. The whole intended as a supplement to the Invited and Assembled Alphabets. By R.R. London: published by Tabart and Co. at their Juvenile and School Library, New Bond Street. 1810.

13.6×11.8 cm. Pr by E. Hemsted, 19, Great New-street, Fetter Lane. Pp.40. Engvd FP dated January 1810, signed 'R.R. delt.' 'C. Knight sculpt.' +2pp. music+5 fp pls+2

illusd diagrams – Game of Addition and Game of Multiplication. Yellow pr stiff-paper covers dated 1810, text as TP with addition of printer's name and address. On lower v. advt of *The invited alphabet* and *The assembled* alphabet.
[CBY 106; Lilly; 2 private colls; PML and S 21.4.77/2132 with covers bearing Darton's impt

For suggested authorship see note to *The assembled alphabet*, 138, and *The good boy's soliloquy*, 139.

(2) A Darton edition of *c.*1812 was advertised in 1812 in Mary Elliott's *The orphan boy*.

141 (1) R. R. The invited alphabet; or, Address of A to B; containing his friendly proposal for the amusement and instruction of good children. Virginibus puerisque canto. Hor. *I sing for girls and boys.* By R. R. London. Published by B. Tabart and Co. Juvenile and School Library, New Bond-street. 1809.

13.6×11.5 cm. Pr by W. Marchant, 3, Greville-street, Holborn. Pp.11 [12]. 25 engvd, h/c or plain, pls with text above+one engvd pl showing the letters, each in a square frame, scattered about higgledy-piggledy, with text above. Yellow stiff-paper pr covers dated 1809, text incs 'Illustrated with twenty-five engravings.' On lower v.: 'Speedily will be published, by the same author, The Assembled Alphabet ... also, Infantine Erudition ...' At foot of 1st pl: 'The whole designed by R. R. and engraved by Charles Knight.'
[Opie, as above and also below; Osborne, plain; Gum. 150, plain; Hockliffe, plain; Bod, h/c; Birm., plain; UCLA: 2 private colls; Nottm U

For suggested authorship see note to *The assembled alphabet*, 138, and *The good boy's soliloquy*, 139.

The Opie Collection has another copy, same TP, uncol'd, in marbled bds, ¾ red roan, sp g. And a 3rd copy on thinner paper, uncol'd, with cover as the first.

The elegant and picturesque plates show children demonstrating the deaf-and-dumb language letter by letter, surrounded by labels containing the letters, great and small, in Roman, Italic, Old English, German writing styles. The author's note says that his design is to lure children 'to the vestibule of learning'.

CBY 8 lists a copy published by Darton *c.*1808. This date is improbable since Darton's imprint betwen 1807 and 1809 was 'W. and T. Darton'; moreover, Mr Lawrence Darton actually visited the National Book League exhibition in 1946 and noted the title-page of the book – the imprint was 'W. Darton, Jun.' This collection (later acquired by Mr Oppenheimer) was sold at Sotheby's and no copy of this book '*c.*1808' was included; but there *was* a Darton edition with watermark 1818 in that sale (21.4.77/2136), imprint W. Darton, Jun., and I suggest that '1808' may have been a misprint for '1818'.

(2) Title as (1) to ... London: published by W. Darton. Jun. Juvenile and School Library, 58, Holborn Hill. [Price eighteen pence.]

13.3×12.1 cm. Pr by W. Darton, Holborn-hill. Pp.11 [12]. 25 plain pls+engvd page as in 1809. Red pr covers, bklist on lower v.
[V & A; Bod., with price erased; S 21.4.77/2135

GOOD NATURED FREDERICK

Oh, give him my Hat & my Stocking's Mama.
Page. 3.

Chigh Sculp

Lon Pub. Janr.1.1807. by B. Tabart & Cᵒ New Bond Stᵗ

21 Plate from *Simple stories, in verse,* 153(1). *Sotheby's*

U *or* you

London: Pubᵈ June 1.1809 by Tabart & Cᵒ New Bond Street

20 The letter U from *The assembled alphabet by R. R.,*
138(1)

142 (1) THE RENOWNED HISTORY OF VALENTINE AND ORSON. Embellished with engravings. London: printed for Tabart and Co. at the Juvenile and School-Library, No.157, New Bond-street. By Lewis & Roden, Paternoster-row. 1804.

14×8.6 cm. Pp.119+3pp. bklist starting on v. of p.119. H/c engvd FP dated April 2 1804+4 h/c pls. Purple pr bds, same text back and front in decorative border. [Hockliffe; CBY 385

This is a longer version of the story than the sixpenny edition. Either this book or *The adventures of...*, 3, q.v., was one of the tales bought for the children at Tabart's shop in Mrs. Fenwick's *Visits to the Juvenile Library*. Curiously enough, the booklist is headed 'The only Bookseller's Shop devoted solely to Books of Education'. It is for his non-educative and delightfully illustrated books that Tabart is now remembered.

An advertisement in Perrault's *Riquet with the Tuft* says that this book is 'the famous Romance, which is now performing at the Theatre Royal Covent Garden, with coloured engravings, intended to represent the principal scenes'. The plates are, indeed, beautifully drawn and coloured.

(2) Title as (1) to ... Orson. A new edition. Embellished with engravings. London: printed by Lewis and Roden, Paternoster Row, for Tabart and Co. at the Juvenile and School Library, New Bond-street; and to be had of all booksellers. Price 2s.6d. bound. 1813.

13.7×8.2 cm. Pp.120 inc. 1p. advts on p.120, 8 items. H/c FP (no date visible)+one other h/c pl dated April 2 1804. Wct tailpiece. Brown paper-covered bds, brown leather sp, g bands. [Osborne

The only copy seen was probably imperfect.

143 (1) RICHARD COEUR DE LION, an historical tale. With three copper-plates. London: printed for Tabart and Co. at the Juvenile and School Library, No.157, New Bond Street. And to be had of all dealers in books. [Price sixpence.] 1805.

12.4×7.7 cm. Pr by Barnard and Sultzer, Water Lane, Fleet Street. Pp.[3] 4–32+4pp. bklist, 26 numb'd items. H/c FP+2 other pls dated 4 June 1805. Buff or blue pr wrps. Advt on v. of TP. [UCLA, bound with others; Ball; PML, wmk 1801; private coll.

Entered at Stationers' Hall by R. Phillips on 9.9.05. This was one of the books bought from Mr. Tabart in Mrs. Fenwick's *Visits to the Juvenile Library*.

(2) As (1) to ... copper-plates. A new edition. London: ... B. Tabart, 1808.

Pp.36. 3 h/c copperplates dated as in (1), first and third pasted inside covers. Plain yellow paper wrps. [Hobbyhorse cat. 13/166; Renier

144 (1) ROBIN HOOD [Harlequinade]. Cover-text: Sold by B. Tabart & Co. 1st flap: Published by Tabart & Co. June 1 1809.

A sheet 18.5×30 cm. folded into 4 panels with 8 flaps (4 above, 4 below) superimposed. H/c engvd illustrations and engvd text. When lifted, flaps reveal more scenes underneath. Russet-col'd card covers, title on front and wct of Harlequin. On lower v. wct of peasant woman with barrel; or, alternatively, of a jester on front and a pedlar on lower v.
[BL; UCLA, private coll.

145 (1) [ROWSE, Elizabeth] [Game] A grammatical game in rhyme. By a lady. [At foot of game:] Price 10s.6d. with requisites for playing the game. London. Published for the author by Saml. Conder, Cheapside. Jany. 22^d 1802.

An engvd sheet in 9 sections, 41.5×33.7 cm, mounted on linen, in a slip-case. The rules are engvd on the sheet, which consists of a small-shell design of 88 circles, with 12 h/c pictures, played with a teetotum. The book of instructions, 17.8×10.6 cm, 27 [28] pp., describes the nine parts of speech. TP shows: 'Printed for the author, and published by Darton and Harvey, sold also by Tabart, Bond-street; Conder, Cheapside; Gurney, Holborn; Willmott and Hill, Borough; Smith, Bath; and Flower, Cambridge.' Marbled wrps. The slip-case has an oval letter-press label showing 'Published for the author, by S. Conder, Cheapside, London. 1802.'
[Whitehouse, p.34; Gum. 3275; S 19.3.81/105 and 26.7.84/628

The author's name is found on the title-page of *Outlines of English history, in verse*, by Elizabeth Rowse, 1808, published by J. Burditt et al: 'By the same author, A Grammatical Game in Rhyme, – price 10s.6d. And Mythological Amusement, – price 7s.6d.'

The title was entered at Stationers' Hall by E. Rowse on 3.3.02 with the word 'Whole', showing that the rights in the work belonged solely to her.

Review: The *Anti-Jacobin review*, vol. 11, p.400: 'The design is ingenious, and the Map, and book of definitions are very neatly executed. These definitions are written in verse, which, though not highly polished, is correct, clear, and perfectly level to infantine capacities ... and we heartily wish, "the Author may win the Game!"'

146 (1) [ROWSE, Elizabeth] [Game] Mythological amusement. London. Published by Conder and Jones, Cheapside, June 1st, 1804.

H/c engvd sheet 14¾×19", mounted in nine sections on linen, contained in a slip-case with a label on the front. Price 7s.6d.

The design consists of 51 diamond-shaped panels carrying pictures of the gods and goddesses of mythology. Book of Rules: Mythological Amusements. By the author of A Grammatical Game, in Rhyme. London: published by Conder and Jones, Cheapside; sold also by J. Harris, St. Paul's Church-yard; Darton and Harvey, Gracechurch-street; B. Tabart, Bond-street; and by the Author. Darton and Harvey, Printers, Gracechurch-street. 1804.
[Whitehouse; extra details from Mr Lawrence Darton

For author's name, see note to *A grammatical game*, 145 above.

Review: The *Critical review*, July 1804, p.344, said that 'This is a pretty little contrivance to entrap the attention of children. Instruction is exhibited by way of a game in which a tee-totum is spun and the child has to repeat the name and particulars of the heathen deity whose station happens to be at the number turned up. The fair author complains that we neglected her Grammatical Game; we do not recall having received it or we certainly should have made it an object of notice.'

147 (1) [SALIGNAC DE LA MOTHE FENELON, François de]. The adventures of Telemachus, son of Ulysses. With four coloured plates. London: printed for Tabart and Co. at the Juvenile and School Library, No.157, New Bond-street: and to be had of all dealers in books. Price one shilling. 1805.

13.3×8.2 cm. Printed by R. Taylor and Co., 38, Shoe Lane. Pp.66+6pp. advts. H/c FP+3 h/c pls dated Dec. 1805. Pr yellow stiff-paper covers, bklist on lower v. Cover-text reads: 'The History of Telemachus, the son of Ulysses. Abridged from the French of Fénélon . . .'
[UCLA; Osborne; Gum. 3598; S 8.7.76/201, 27.7.84/859

A pencil note in the BL copy, 1807, attributes the beautifully drawn and coloured engravings to Blake.

(2) Title as (1) to . . . Printed for B. Tabart, at the Juvenile and School Library, No.157, New Bond Street: and to be had of all booksellers. Price one shilling. 1807.

14×8.5 cm. Pr by J. Diggens, St. Ann's-lane. Pp.69+3pp. bklist starting on v. of p.69. H/c FP+3 other h/c as in (1). Pr yellow or pinkish stiff-paper covers, bklist on lower v.
[BL; Gum. 3599; UCLA; Opie

148 (1) SANDHAM, Elizabeth. The perambulations of a bee and a butterfly, in which are delineated those smaller traits of character which escape the observation of larger spectators. By Miss Sandham, author of The Twin Sisters, &c. [2 lines verse – Gay] London: printed by W. Lewis, Paternoster-row; for B. Tabart and Co. Clifford-street, New Bond-street; and may be had of all booksellers. 1812.

13.6×8.1 cm. ½-title. Pp.xii+132. Engvd FP+2 pls. Blue paper-covered bds, red roan sp g.
[V & A, in brown-paper-covered bds, red roan sp with gilt bee; Gum. 5104; private coll., BL; Baldwin; UCLA

Miss Sandham's sternly moral preface expresses the hope that young people 'may receive [from this book] even from the limited remarks of a Bee and a Butterfly a gentle hint or two of what they may expect to meet with in their future walks through life.'

The long ſ is used in sigs A and B of the story, but not in the prelims.

Review: *The juvenile review* stated somewhat sententiously that 'The observations of these diminutive travellers, and their strictures on human manners, are expressed in lively terms, and with great propriety; young readers will derive considerable amusement from this little work, and they may also find improvement by attending to the slight sketches of the human character, with its various absurdities, as remarked by the Bee and the Butterfly.'

(2) Title as (1) to . . . London: published by Tabart and Co. No.85, Piccadilly, opposite the Green Park; and may be had of all booksellers. 1816.

As (1) but pr by G. Sidney, Northumberland Street, Strand. No long f. Engvd FP dated May 1816+2 pls as in (1). Brown-paper-coverd bds, green roan sp g.
[Morgan; S 22.4.77/2270 and 3.6.75/490; Baldwin; UCLA; BL; private coll.

(3) 3rd edition not located.

(4) Title as (1) to ... butterfly; ... the Twin Sisters, the School-fellows, &c. [2 lines verse. Gay.] Fourth edition. London: printed for Tabart and Co. at the Juvenile Library, 39, New Bond Street; and John Souter, at the School Library, 73, St. Paul's Church Yard; and may be had of all booksellers. Jas. Adlard and Sons, Printers, 23, Bartholomew Close. 1819. (Price 2s.6d. half-bound.)

13.9×8.2 cm. Pp.xii+132. On p.132 printer's impt = G. Sidney, Northumberland Street, Strand. FP pubd by John Souter, March, 1819+one other pl, same impt. Brown-paper-covered bds, black roan sp g.
[CUL; Baldwin

(5) The bee and butterfly; or, Industry and idleness: in which are delineated those smaller traits of character that usually escape observation. [2 lines verse. Gay.] By Miss Sandham, author of the School-fellows, the Boy's School, &c. New edition. London: printed for John Souter, at the School Library, 73, St. Paul's Church Yard; 1824. [Price 2s., or 3s. coloured.]

14×8.6 cm. Pr by Jenkinson, 19, Old Boswell Court. Pp.139+4pp. Souter's bklist. FP as in (4)+2 other pls, same date.
[Osborne, rebound

149 (1) THE SCHOOL ATLAS, or Key to the Geographical Copy-Books, containing the same fifteen maps, finished and neatly coloured, as examples to be copied by those who fill in the Geographical Copy-Books.

This title was advertised in 1808 as 'published by Tabart and Co.', price 5s. in boards. Not traced, but probably sold by B. Tabart like the Copy-Book itself. The author may have been the Rev. J. Goldsmith. See 50, *The geographical copy-book*.

150 (1) THE SCHOOL MAGAZINE, or The monthly preceptor in every branch of knowledge. ... Price one shilling and sixpence each ... Conducted by a Society of Clergymen and men of letters ... Printed for Tabart and Co. at the Juvenile and School Library, No.157, New Bond-street: sold by Craddock and Joy, Ave Maria-lane, near St. Paul's; by Martin Keene, Dublin; by Walter Berry, Edinburgh; and by all other booksellers and stationers.

In 1809 vol. iv of *Tabart's collection of popular stories* carried an advertisement for this title, describing it as 'the *Monthly preceptor* revived, with Twelve Guineas worth of Prizes per Month'. A note was added: 'As this will be one of the very best books that can be read in Schools by the senior Scholars, Schoolmasters or Governesses who take upwards of twenty-five copies, will be entitled to a copy gratis, and also an allowance of twenty per cent.'

The *Monthly preceptor* has not been traced but the advertisement says that 'it was a few years since in course of publication ... its temporary discontinuance ... the subject of regret'. Nor has the 1809 issue of the *School magazine* been found but in that year Tabart published the *Juvenile miscellany*, 84, which was also discontinued for lack of support.

(2) THE SCHOOL MAGAZINE, or Journal of education (also: TABART'S SCHOOL MAGAZINE, or Journal of education).

No TP: the above are page headings on pp.[1] and [73] respectively. 21×12 cm. Pp.200. Lacking all before p.[1] except h/c pl showing 'Shepherds of the Landes' – peasants walking on stilts. At foot of p.[1] is printed: No. 1. – March, 1817; and on p.[73]: No. II.–April, 1817. P.[137] has text-title as on p.[73] with, at its foot: No. III.–May, 1817. Five further h/c or plain fp pls, some with two subjects, +two folding pls. Marbled bds, green roan sp g, title: School Magazine.
[BL

The contents include various school subjects and material which was also printed separately or elsewhere, e.g. Richard Phillips' *Walk to Kew*. The plates are well executed with good colouring. The inscription on front free endpaper is dated 1820.

SCOLFIELD, William: see [GODWIN, William]

SCRIPTURE HISTORIES: a title sometimes used in advertisements for William Godwin's BIBLE STORIES, 49, q.v.

151 (1) [SEMPLE, Elizabeth] The magic lantern; or, Amusing and instructive exhibitions for young people. With eleven coloured engravings. By the authoress of Short Stories, Summer Rambles, The Red and Black Book, &c. &c. London: printed for Tabart and Co., 157, New Bond-street; and to be had of W. Gibbons, Bath; M. Keene, Dublin; and of all other booksellers. Price 6s. half-bound. [Printed by J. Adlard, Duke-street.] [*c.*1806]

16.8×9.4 cm. Pp.200+2pp. Tabart's bklist. H/c FP dated Mar 4 1806+10 h/c pls. Marbled bds, ¾ red roan, corners and sp g.
[BL; V & A; UCLA; CBY 527, 752; Phila.; Miami; S 22.4.77/2250, pr on good paper, wmk 1806; and /2251, on inferior paper, no wmk, and pls have been reworked; Osborne; 2 private colls

A handsome book with unusual illustrations, showing coloured subjects against a flat white background. A father entertains his children on ten evenings with magic-lantern slides and tells the stories which they illustrate.

Reprinted in America by Benjamin Johnson, Philadelphia, in 1807, Welch 1153 (mistakenly attributing authorship to E. Sandham).

Elizabeth Semple's many books for children were published over a period of at least 40 years by E. Lloyd, John Harris, Longmans, Darton, Harvey and Darton and B. Tabart – and, later on, by Grant and Griffith. Until quite recently her identity was unknown and her titles could only be ascribed to 'E.S.', the initials with which she signed her dedication to 'Helen' in *The godmother's tales*, J. Harris, 1808. However, the Darton and Harvey records at Reading University have revealed a receipt dated October 17th 1814 signed 'Eliz[th] Semple' for ten pounds 'for a Manuscript entitled "The Oracle"'. This book's author can be shown, through cross-references, to be that same 'E.S.' (see Osborne, p.930). There is also a note from Longmans in their archive at Reading, dated 30 Sep. 1814, to the Exeter bookseller, E. Upham, concerning a transaction relating to 'Copyright of Oracle' involving ten pounds on account of Mr. Semple paid to Upham's account. It will be remembered that in those days a wife's or daughter's earnings belonged to her husband or father. An earlier account with Longmans, in 1808, showed E. Upham acting as agent, or bulk bookseller, for this lady's *Juvenile dramas* – but in this case the author's name was not mentioned.

Review: The *Anti-Jacobin review*, vol. 11, p.400, noticed two of E. Semple's earliest books, *Summer rambles* and *Short Stories* (both published in 1801) and some of the remarks in the review are equally applicable to *The magic lantern*: 'These elegant little volumes are written by a lady, whose merits are not yet sufficiently known to be duly appreciated . . .'.

152 (1) [SHARPE, Richard Scrafton] The conjuror, or The turkey and the ring. A comic tale. London printed for R. Dutton, Gracechurch Street and sold by Mr. Harris, Mr. Hughes & Mr. Tabert [*sic*].

12.5×9.3 cm. Pp.16. Engvd FP, engvd TP+6 pls. Blue stiff-paper pr covers, text includes 'By the author of Old Friends in a New Dress. Printed and sold by R. Dutton, Gracechurch Street. 1808. Price 1s. plain or 1s.6d. coloured.' On lower v. advt of Dutton's titles: The Master Cat . . ., The Fairy . . ., Little Thumb and the Ogre . . . and Aunty Ann's Drawing Book. (See fig. 22)
[BL; UCLA; V & A; CUL; Opie; Lilly; PML, wmk 1807; S 22.4.77/2306 and 1.12.88/188; private coll.

The story is told in verse of Robin Rostrum who, tiring of his sparse fare, decides to better himself by setting up as a magician. Disguised in a tall hat, false beard and whiskers, he is first commissioned to find a lost diamond ring. Having, by lucky chance, given the thieves the impression that he has discovered them, he obtains the ring and to demonstrate his magic powers, he secretly forces a turkey to swallow it. Then the bird is slain publicly and the ring is revealed. But the Knight, his client, demands another magical feat before paying him. He claps his hat on a robin which has flown into the room, calls in Robin Rostrum and asks him what is under the hat. In dismay the conjuror exclaims, 'Poor Robin! are thou caught at last?' at which 'the Knight amaz'd, his hat withdrew, And pleas'd away the Robin flew.'

153 (1) SIMPLE STORIES; IN VERSE. Being a collection of original poems; designed for the use of children. [2 lines verse] London: printed by R. Juigné, 17, Margaret-street, Cavendish-square, for B. Tabart and Co. at the Juvenile and School Library, New Bond-street. 1809.

15.1×9.3 cm. ½-title. Pp.x+43. FP+12 other pls engvd by Charles Knight dated Jany 1809. Marbled bds, red roan sp g. (See fig. 21)
[Baldwin; UCLA; CBY 340, col'd; Phila.; Renier, imp.; S 25.2.76/44 and 22.4.77/2307, latter h/c in sheep; and 23.11.78/92, 27.7.84/930 and 18.6.87/420; private coll.

The charming illustrations and well-printed pages add considerably to the appeal of this little book, whose artless verses are intended, says the author's Preface, 'to convey Instruction under the fascinating garb of Amusement'. She feels no '*dread* of the censure of the Guardian of Education, should that most useful Work be still

22 Plate from *The conjuror* by R. S. Sharpe, 152(1). *Sotheby's*

FRONTISPIECE. *Page 199.*

Pra:Chesham del. et sculp.

23 Frontispiece of *Leading strings to knowledge* by Elizabeth Somerville, 156(1)

continued, as it is not the *want of talents* which that most excellent Critic considers, but the moral tendency of the Work; in which the Author feels satisfied of her *intentions* ...' She is, perhaps, too modest about her simple poems.

(2) A COLLECTION OF SIMPLE STORIES. London: F. G. Tabart & Co., 12, Clifford Street, New Bond Street.
[OFCB pp.129–34

Andrew W. Tuer included some abridged poems and line-drawing copies of engraved plates from this book in *Stories from old-fashioned children's books*, 1899–1900, with the above title. This edition has not been traced, but it would probably have been published *c.*1812. F. G. Tabart was Benjamin's son, Francis Gerard (see Introduction).

154 (1) SIX STORIES, IN ENGLISH AND FRENCH; to which is added, The Jubilee; or, Twenty-fifth of October, 1809. By a mother, for the use of her own children. London: printed for Tabart and Co. Juvenile-Library, New Bond-street; and sold by Meyler, How, and Binns, Bath. 1810.

13.4×8 cm. Pr by Galabin and Marchant, Ingram-court. Pp.vi+[3] 4–137. FP engvd by Knight after Corbould, dated Jany 1810. Marbled bds, red or green roan sp g.
[UCLA; private coll.; Bod J

There is a mistake in the numbering of the preliminary pages: p.iv is numbered vi and v is vii, but vi is correctly printed. The stories are printed in English and French on opposite pages and in the English version the syllables are divided.

Review: The juvenile review said 'These stories are extremely easy and pretty; they are written by a mother for the use of her own children, and we have no doubt that they will be approved by *all* mothers as well as by their little ones.'

(2) Title as (1) to ... FRENCH. By the authoress of Stories by a Mother, for the use of her own children. London: printed for Darton, Harvey, and Darton, Gracechurch-street. 1812.

13.7×8.1 cm. Pr by Darton, Harvey, and Co. Gracechurch Street. Pp.[iii]+4–195. Engvd FP+5 pls. Plain brown-paper-covered bds, green roan sp g.
[BL; S 23.11.77/40

In 1824 M. J. Godwin & Co. republished this book, titled *Six stories for the Nursery in words of one and two syllables. Intended as a sequel to the 'Mouse-Trap.'* See A. W. Tuer, *Forgotten children's books*, pp.429–38.

155 (1) [SOMERVILLE, Elizabeth] A grandmother's stories. Vol. I. – comprising The old Harper. The Misfortunes of Ingratitude. Benevolence its own Reward. Story of the little Girl at the Gate-house. The good Father; or, Punishment frequently necessary. Honesty rewarded. London: printed by J. Vigevena, Huggin Lane, for B. Crosby & Co. Stationer's Court, and B. Tabart, 157, New Bond-street. [*c.*1801]

9.9×8.2 cm. Pp.77+(in UCLA's copy) 1p. Crosby's advts pasted inside lower cover. Wct FP+2 other wcts. Pale green stiff-paper covers, label on front.
[UCLA; Hockliffe, 2 vols bound together in marbled bds, red roan sp g.

The last two titles are transposed in the text. The story, The good Father, cannot have pleased any child-reader as it only describes the father's methods of disciplining a naughty boy.

Vol. II. – Comprising The History of an Old Rat. Frances and Laura. Ingratitude Punished. [Imprint as vol. I]

Pp.85, pp.[86–87] = Crosby's advts. Wct FP+2 wcts. Covers as vol. I.
[UCLA; Hockliffe, bound with vol. I, no FP but 3 wcts.

The book is well produced with excellent illustrations. The author's name is disclosed in B. Crosby's booklist in Harriet Mandeville's *Familiar conversations*, 101, q.v. and on the title-page of *The new children in the wood* ... by Elizabeth Somerville, 1802. For a similar production see *Familiar conversations*, 101 above.

This title was advertised by Jacob D. Dietrick in the Hagerstown *Maryland Herald*, May 31, 1805. Vol. II (and perhaps vol. I, but not recorded) was published in America by I. Cooke & Co., New Haven, printed by Sidney's Press in 1813, Welch 466.

156 (1) SOMERVILLE, Elizabeth. Leading strings to knowledge: or, Dame Wise and her pupils. In progressive lessons of one, two, three, four, &c. syllables. By Elizabeth Somerville, author of James Manners; Flora, or The Deserted Child; Village Maid, &c. &c. [4 lines verse] Brentford: printed by and for P. Norbury; and sold by T. Ostell, Ave-Maria Lane, London: also by Longman, Hurst, Rees, and Orme, Paternoster-row; Champante and Whitrow, Jewry-street, Aldgate; Earle, Albemarle-street; Tabart, Bond Street; Peacock, Oxford Street; and Didier and Tebbet, St. James's-street. 1806.

13.4×8.1 cm. ½-title. Pp.viii+208. FP 'Fras. Chesham del. et sculp.' Marbled bds, leather sp g. (See fig. 23)
[Private coll.

This is a cautionary tale about the results of wrong-doing, with stress laid on the near-sadistic punishments dealt out by Dame Wise to her bad pupils. Nevertheless, there is plenty of interest and variety in the story and by the end of it the naughty children were reformed by her plan of tuition, 'which per-haps the ad-mir-ers of the new sys-tem of mo-dern phi-lo-so-phi-cal con-fu-sion, may re-pro-bate and hold in con-tempt; un-til dear bought ex-pe-ri-ence shall con-vince them of their er-ror, and teach them that hu-man wis-dom is un-stable, fail-a-ble, and er-ro-ne-ous, when not un-der the gui-dance of re-li-gi-on'.

Review in the *Guardian of education*, vol. v, p.297: 'The design of this little volume is, to entice children to learn to read with pleasure, by engaging their attention to an interesting narrative; and the work seems well calculated to the purpose, for it abounds with moral instruction suited to young children, communicated in a way that is likely to make useful and lasting impressions upon their minds.'

157 (1) SOMERVILLE, Elizabeth. Lessons for children of three years old. By Elizabeth Somerville. London: printed by J. Vigevena, Huggin Lane, for B. Crosby & Co. Stationer's Court, and B. Tabart, 157, New Bond-street.

9.4×8.3 cm. Pp.93+1p. Crosby's bklist, all pr on rectos only. No illusns. Bound with *Lessons; or, Short stories . . .*, q.v., in brown-paper-covered bds, pr label on front showing title of this part only.
[Osborne

Published in 1800 by Sampson and Low. This edition was probably published *c.*1802. It is a very early reader, in words of one syllable.

158 (1) SOMERVILLE, Elizabeth. Lessons; or, Short stories, in two and three syllables. Containing The Little Beggar. A New Doll. The Rose Bush. The Good Child's Fairing. Old Robin and his Dog. The Brother's Return from School. The Flower Garden. Little Bell and James. The Birth Day. By Elizabeth Somerville. London: printed by J. Vigevena, Huggin Lane, for B. Crosby & Co. Stationer's Court, and B. Tabart, 157, New Bond-street.

9.4×8.5 cm. Pp.[5] 6–115+2pp. Crosby's bklist. No illusns. Bound with *Lessons for children of three years old*, 157, q.v.
[Osborne

This forms the second part of Mrs. Somerville's reading lessons. The text is printed on both sides of the leaves. The two parts, with their small format, large, clear print and interesting contents, make a charming little book for children who are beginning to read.

159 (1) SONGS FOR THE NURSERY, collected from the works of the most renowned poets, and adapted to favourite national melodies. London: printed for Tabart and Co. at the Juvenile and School Library, No.157, New Bond-street, and to be had of all booksellers. Price sixpence. 1805.

12.8×10.2 cm. Pr by R. Taylor & Co. Black-Horse-court. Pp.75+5pp. bklist beginning on v. of p.75. No illusns.
[Bod., bound with others

V. of TP carries Tabart's advertisement of the Juvenile and School Library. This book appears to have had no illustrations until the edition of 1808, although the date 1806 on the plates indicates an earlier edition. It was entered at Stationers' Hall by R. Phillips on 9.1.05 and was reprinted in America in 1812 by Archibald Loudon, Carlisle. Welch 1238. It is quoted widely by Iona and Peter Opie in ODNR.

In Mrs. Fenwick's *Visits to the Juvenile Library* it was given as compensation to a child who had received *The French and English primmer*; and E. Kilner puffed it in *A visit to London*.

Review: 'A very foolish book, intitled "Songs for the Nursery", has, we lament to say, obtained a place in the infant library, and thus the very means by which benevolent principles might have been implanted, have been perverted to the worst of purposes, that of filling the infant mind with false ideas. What, for instance, can be more ridiculous than the idea of "a dish running after a spoon," or the moon being *in a fit*? But we will quit this unpleasant subject . . .'. *The juvenile review*, 1817.

(2) Title as (1) to . . . Library, New Bond-street: and to be had of all booksellers. [Price sixpence without prints, one shilling and sixpence with prints, or half-a-crown with the prints coloured.] 1808.

[Unillustrated version] 13.1×10 cm. Pr by Marchant, 3, Greville-street, Holborn. Pp.59+5pp. or 3pp. bklist. On v. of TP Tabart's advt of his stock. Yellow pr stiff-paper covers, on lower v. advt of Nursery Tales.
[Opie

[Illustrated version] As (2) but 24 h/c or plain pls dated 1806 or May 15 1806 or May 1806. Yellow pr stiff-paper covers, advts on front and lower v.
[Private coll., h/c; Spencer; Lilly; S 22.4.77/2354, h/c

One extra shilling, or two shillings coloured, seem modest prices to pay for the addition of so many delightful illustrations.

(3) Title as (2) to . . . London: printed for Richard Phillips, No.7, Bridge-street, Blackfriars, and to be had of all booksellers. [Price . . . as (2)]. 1812.

12.3×10 cm. Pr by J. Adlard, 23, Bartholomew Close. Pp.59+5pp. bklist. Engvd FP pubd by Tabart & Co. dated May 1806+20 pls, some with verse beneath and some dated as FP. Buff (or once yellow?) pr stiff-paper covers, advts on lower v.
[BL, plain, text of covers almost illegible

An edition of 1818 was printed by W. Darton, Jun., with plates dated June 15, 1818, by Wm Darton, followed by many more Darton editions.

160 (1) STONE, Anne. Features of the youthful mind; or, Tales for juvenile readers. By Anne Stone. [4 lines verse. Bloomfield] Margate: printed by J. Warren, on the Marine Parade, for J. Harris, Corner of St. Paul's Church-yard; W. J. and J. Richardson, Royal Exchange; Darton and Harvey, Gracechurch Street; B. Tabart, 157, New Bond Street; and R. and L. Peacock, Juvenile Library, 259, Oxford Street. 1802.

16.9×9.5 cm. Pp.xii+129 (p.[130] = errata). No illusns.
[BL, rebound

The printer's address on p.129 is given as Thanet-Press, Margate. Pp.[vii]–xii = list of subscribers. The dedication to Lady Charlotte Clinton, Nov. 1st 1802, shows that Lady Charlotte was Anne Stone's pupil. The list of subscribers contains 156 names but, even so, the author apologises 'for the omission of the names of several subscribers' which, to put it shortly, she had lost.

The book contains very moral tales, two being concerned with race relations between a white girl and East Indian negroes and with the slave trade. The author explains that it was written some years earlier 'when so many works of a similar nature had not appeared', but publication was delayed until she visited Ramsgate 'for the benefit of sea-bathing' for her health. There, many ladies of fashion encouraged her to print it.

But, unfortunately, 'in consequence of pecuniary considerations, she was forced to employ her time in private tuition, and had not sufficient leisure to attend the press regularly; typographical errors have therefore occurred ...'.

161 (1) THE STORY OF GRISELDA. With three copperplates. London; printed for Tabart and Co. at the Juvenile and School Library, No.157, New Bond-street; and to be had of all dealers in books. Price sixpence. 1804.

12.5×8 cm. Pr by R. Taylor and Co., Black-Horse-court. Pp.36. H/c FP dated July 1804+2 other h/c pls, same date. Pink pr stiff-paper covers, title on front: 'Tabart's improved edition of Griselda: with coloured plates. Price sixpence.'
[UCLA; S 14.3.72/457; PML

The plates are engraved after designs by Craig. A new edition was entered at Stationers' Hall by R. Phillips on 25.7.04. T. Hughes advertised this book in his list of 'Tabart's Editions', with plain engravings, 3d., in *A new and original book of forfeits* [1837].

This story has long been regarded as representing the epitome of suffering and endurance. Griselda, a poor country girl chosen to be the bride of a cruelly self-centred marquis, is made to undergo the torment of having her two little children taken from her and (so she thinks) killed, in order to test her absolute obedience to her husband's wishes. She bears sorrows and humiliations without complaint until, after some years, the marquis, satisfied of her complaisance, restores the children to her with declarations of his lasting love.

(2) THE STORY OF GRISELDA. A tale for the nursery. With three copper-plates. A new edition. London; printed for B. Tabart, at the Juvenile and School Library, 157, New Bond-street, and to be had of all booksellers. Price sixpence. 1809.

11.3×7.5 cm. Pr by J. Diggens, St. Ann's Lane. Pp.35 (last leaf pasted to lower cover). H/c FP dated July 1804+2 other h/c pls, same date. Plain yellow wrps.
[UCLA; Melb.; S 22.4.77/2382; Renier

In this edition the FP is the 2nd plate in (1). The colouring of the plates is richer and more skilfully applied than in (1). The text has been reset since 1804.

162 (1A) [SWIFT, Jonathan] Gulliver's travels. Part I. The voyage to Lilliput. With three coloured engravings. London: printed for Tabart and Co. at the Juvenile and School Library, No.157, New Bond-street; and to be had of all booksellers. Price sixpence. 1805.

12×7.7 cm. Pr by V. Griffiths, Bell-Savage-yard. Pp.36. H/c engvd FP+2 h/c pls, one dated Oct. 1 1805. Pink pr paper wrps, on front 'Tabart's Improved Edition of the Voyages & Travels of Capt. L. Gulliver ...', on lower v. advt of Tabart's Juvenile and School Library. All 4 parts could also be had in publisher's binding of marbled bds, green or red roan sp g. (See fig. 24)
[Private coll.; 4 parts in one bound vol.: Osborne, Lilly, 3 private colls

(1B) Title as (1A) but ... Part II. The voyage to Brobdingnag ...

12.3×8 cm. Pr by V. Griffiths, No.1, Paternoster-row. Pp.36. H/c engvd FP n.d., +2

Part I 'The voyage to Lilliput', 162(1A)

Part IV 'A voyage to the country of the Houyhmns' [*sic*], 162(2D)

24   Frontispieces from *Gulliver's travels* by Jonathan Swift

h/c pls dated Sepr 1805. Orange-yellow pr paper wrps, on front 'Tabart's Improved Edition ...' as (1A), advt as (1A) on lower v.
[S 27.7.84/859; other locations as (1A)

(1C) Title as (1A) but ... Part III. The voyage to Laputa ...

12×7.8 cm. Pr by W. Heney, 76, Fleet-street. Pp.36. H/c engvd FP+2 pls dated Dec. 1 1805.
[Locations as in (1A)

(1D) Title as (1A) but ... Part IV. A voyage to the country of the Houyhnms ...

12×7.4 cm. Pr by W. Heney, 76, Fleet-street. Pp.33+3 pp. bklist starting on v. of p.33. H/c engvd FP+2 h/c pls, 2 dated Dec. 1805.
[Locations as in (1A)

(2) Parts I, II and III have not been located of the edition of 1809 and they may not have been printed.

(2D) GULLIVER'S TRAVELS. Part IV. A voyage to the country of the Houyhmns [*sic*]. With three coloured engravings. London: printed for B. Tabart, at the Juvenile and School Library, No.157, New Bond Street; and to be had of all booksellers. Price sixpence. 1809.

11.6×7.6 cm. Pr by J. Diggens, St. Ann's Lane. Pp.33+2pp. bklist starting on v. of p.33, last leaf a paste-down. H/c FP+2 h/c pls dated Dec. 1805. Yellow pr paper wrps, front titled 'Tabart's Improved Edition' as (1A), advt of Tabart's Juvenile and School Library on lower v. (See fig. 24)
[Private coll.

163 (1) TABART, Benjamin. A catalogue of books, for the amusement and instruction of youth, and for the use of schools, systematically arranged by B. Tabart, at the Juvenile & School Library, No.157, New Bond-street, corner of Grafton-street. London printed by Exton, 87, Great Portland-street, for B. Tabart; price one shilling, to be returned to the purchasers of the value of five shillings. [1801]

16.5×10 cm. No pagination, signed A⁴, B–G⁶ = pp.80. (No sig. on E). Yellow/buff paper covers, sewn. Cover-text: 'A Catalogue of Books, sold at the Juvenile Library, 157, New Bond-street. 1801.
[Bod.

The Prefatory Advertisement on pp.[v]–[viii] explains that 'The following Catalogue exhibits a List of the best Books which are now in use, in this country, for the instruction of Youth, from the age of *Two* Years to that of *One and Twenty*.'

The books are classed in ages: two years, four years, eight years, 15 years, 21 years (for 'persons, who at a mature age, may be desirous to correct for themselves the disadvantages of an imperfect early education') and 'A class of the books for the direction of Parents and Teachers, in the education of Youth, is added. Many of these are excellent. – But, it is in writing down to the exact level of the capacity of young people, that the Authors of Books of Education have been the least successful.'

This most unusual catalogue is not, of course, limited to books published by Tabart (who only appeared as a publisher in the year of its publication) or even by Phillips, but provides a survey of all the books that Mr. Tabart felt he could recommend. He stresses that 'Particular and anxious care has been taken to introduce every Book and convenience of Education that might be truly useful and acceptable to LADIES.'

Extracts from Benjamin Tabart's notes on the contents of his catalogue will be found in Appendix C.

164 (1) TABART, Benjamin (editor). Fairy tales, or The Liliputian [*sic*] library, containing twenty-six choice pieces of fancy and fiction, by those renowned personages, King Oberon, Queen Mab, Mother Goose, Mother Bunch, Master Puck, and other distinguished personages at the Court of the Fairies. Now first collected by Benjamin Tabart. Adorned with coloured engravings. London: printed by G. Sidney, Northumberland Street; published by Tabart and Co. at their Juvenile and School-Library, 165, New Bond Street. 1817.

17.1×10 cm. Pp.vi+353+1p. bklist, 12 items. Wct FP×2+5 engvd pls, one subject each. Calf, g., red leather label on sp.
[UCLA

The frontispiece (headed 'Frontispiece' in black letter) represents two scenes from 'Cinderella' as in *Popular fairy tales*. The other five plates are quite different from those in *Popular fairy tales*; they measure c.8.3×5.3–5.9 cm and might be of continental origin. The stereotyped text is as in *Popular fairy tales*.
Review: The *Quarterly review* (xxi, Jan. 1819, pp.91 et seq.) printed a long article on fairy tales inspired by Benjamin Tabart's volume, but making little reference to it after the opening sentences:

> Since our boyish days the literature of the nursery has sustained a mighty alteration: the tone of the reading public has infected the taste of the *spelling* public. Mr. Benjamin Tabart's collection is, as we understand, considered an acceptable present to the rising generation; yet, though it is by no means devoid of merit, it recalls but faintly the pleasant homeliness of the narrations which used to delight us in those happy times when we were still pinned to our nurse's apron-strings, and which are now thought too childish to deserve a place even in the tiny library of the baby ... Scarcely any of the chapbooks which were formerly sold to the country people at fairs and markets have been able to maintain their ancient popularity.... The old broadside-ballads have given way to the red stamp of the newspapers; and pedlars burn their ungodly story-books like sorcerers of old, and fill their baskets with the productions sanctified by the Imprimatur of the Tabernacle. As for the much lamented Mr. Marshall, now no longer of Aldermary Church-yard, whose cheap and splendid publications at once excited and rewarded our youthful industry, he hath been compelled to shut up his shop long ago. Not a soul in the trade would bid for the copy-right and back stock of Tommy Two Shoes. His penny books are out of print, one and all, and therefore, if things continue to go on as they have done of late years, there is really no telling what sums of money a good copy of the genuine edition of the Life and Death of Cock Robin may not soon fetch under the hammer of Mr. Evans, especially if it should chance to be a 'tall copy', with 'uncut margins', graced with 'clear impressions' of the 'numerous wood cuts,' and retaining its 'original gilt paper binding'. ... The most important addition to nursery literature has been effected in Germany, by the diligence of John and William Grimm ...

For later editions see TABART, B. *Popular fairy tales*, 166 below.

165 (1) TABART, Benjamin. The national spelling-book or A sure guide to English spelling ... the whole compiled from the dictionaries of Walker, Sheridan and Jones ... By B. Tabart.

Entered at Stationers' Hall by Mr. Tabart himself on 23.5.18, stating that it was his own property. Tabart's publication has not been traced.

(2) TABART, Benjamin. The national spelling-book, or, A sure guide to English spelling and pronunciation; arranged on such a plan as cannot fail to remove the difficulties and facilitate general improvement in the English language. By Benjamin Tabart. New edition, revised and corrected, by the Rev. T. Clark, author of The National Reader, (illustrated by 100 engravings;) and of the English Primer, or Child's First Book, (with 200 engravings.) London: printed for John Souter, at the School Library, 72, St. Paul's Church Yard. Price one shilling and sixpence.

17.3×10.1 cm. (No printer shown). Pp.viii+[9] 10–168. Engvd FP×2 with verses between pictures; wct TP vignette, no other illusns. Calf.
[BL; Columbia U

Listed in the *English catalogue of books* as 'Tabart's Spelling Book ...', May 1819. Souter. The Preface is signed 'B. Tabart'. Listed also in MLA, May 10 1819, printed for J. Souter, price 1s.

(3) Title as (2) to ... pronunciation, ... London: Souter and Law, School Library, 131, Fleet Street. Price one shilling and sixpence.

17.8×10.4 cm. Pr by C. and J. Adlard, Bartholomew Close. Pp.viii+9–168+12pp. bklist of Sherwood, Gilbert, and Piper. Wood-engvd FP×2 with verses between pictures+TP vignette showing a Druid teaching two children. Calf.
[Private coll.

The printers' imprint would date this edition 1845 or later. An entry in the booklist mentions London University College.

TABART, Benjamin [editor], Popular fairy tales. **Note** This often-reprinted book is difficult to categorise as all the following copies are undated. The item listed in its alphabetical position as 164 TABART, Benjamin ... Fairy tales ... 1817, should be regarded as part of the canon, but five of its plates are different from those in all the other issues.

There are many variants. The first point of difference is the inclusion or omission of the publisher's address in the title. It seems possible that, taking printers' addresses into consideration, the variants *with* Phillips's address are the earliest of these issues.

The second point is the occasional omission of the printer's name in the text. The third point is the number of plates. The total number present varies and yet the books do not always seem to be defective; and some copies do not have the plain wood-engraving on p.353. There are also considerable differences in bindings.

For these reasons it has not been possible to place Sotheby's catalogue entries but they are as follows: 9.6.75/809, 26 plates and tailpiece; 6.6.80/356, 24 plates; 27.7.83/250, 24 plates.

166 (1) TABART, Benjamin (editor). Popular fairy tales; or, A Liliputian [*sic*] library; containing twenty-six choice pieces of fancy and fiction, by those renowned personages King Oberon, Queen Mab, Mother Goose, Mother Bunch, Master Puck, and other distinguished personages at the Court of the Fairies. Now first collected and revised by Benjamin Tabart. With twenty-six coloured engravings. London; published by Sir Richard Phillips and Co., Bride Court, Bridge Street. Price six shillings bound.

17.5×10 cm. No printer shown. Pp.vi+353. H/c FP×2+1 h/c pls+2. Dark green leather, FAIRY TALES in g. on sp. and front, '1818' at foot of sp.
[Bod.

The texts of these stories are not always identical with those in *Tabart's collection of popular stories*, 167. Some have been edited, particularly in the opening paragraphs; some have been extended.

This title was listed in ECB 1818, the date on Bodley's cover, so the above entry is shown as the 1st edition; but Phillips was at Bride Court from 1820.

The Preface reads:
    'No method has ever been contrived for stimulating the curiosity of youth, equal to the stories founded on the Rosicrucian system, or what usage may denominate the mythology of modern poetry.
    'Many collections of such stories have within the last century appeared in the English language; but many of them are so obsolete in their style, so gross in their morals, and so vulgar in their details, as to be altogether unfit for the purpose to which they seem to have been adapted. Of this fact, every tender mother, and every intelligent tutor, must be so sensible, that they will hail with satisfaction the appearance of a selection of the most interesting of these stories, in which an attempt is made to elevate the language and sentiments to a level with the refined manners of the present age.
    'The titles of the several stories will bespeak the great interest of the work, and its paramount claim to a place in every family where there are children and young persons.
    'It has been the object of the Editor, besides that of collecting the best of these stories, to print the volume of such a size and price as should render it attainable to the class of readers for which it is intended. He dismisses the undertaking with the persuasion that it will be found to be one of the most entertaining volumes in any language. B. TABART.'

    (2) As (1) but h/c FP×2+12 h/c pls×2+wood-engvd illusn on p.353.
[BL, rebound

    (3) Title as (1). Printer shown as J. McGowan, Great Windmill Street. Other details as (1) except marbled bds, red roan sp g.
[V&A inscr. '1827' and only 12 pls×2; De Grummond, imp.; Private coll. in green leather, 12 pls×2.

McGowan was at Great Windmill Street from 1819 to 1827.

    (4) In 1822 Longmans advertised 'Tabart's complete collection of FAIRY TALES, with 26 engravings. 6s.'

    (5) Title as (1) but omitting publisher's address.

17.8×10.7 cm. Pr by D. Sidney, Northumberland Street, Strand. Pp.vi+353. H/c FP×2, no heading, +11 h/c pls×2, no illusn on p.353. Maroon cloth, sp g.
[Opie

D. Sidney was at the given address 1824–9.

    (6) Title as (5).

17.3×9.9 cm. Pr by D. Sidney, Northumberland Street, Strand. Pp.vi+353. H/c

FP×2 headed FRONTISPIECE+11 h/c pls×2. Green morocco, sp g. bands and FAIRY TALES on front.
[UCLA; Gum. 2465?

In UCLA's copy, between pp.68 and 76, the stories of Fortunatus, Peronella and Andolocia are mixed up through incorrect printing.

(7) Title as (5).

16.9×9.6 cm. Pr by William Clowes, Stamford Street. Pp.vi+353. H/c FP×2 headed FRONTISPIECE+11 h/c pls×2. Marbled bds, ¾ black leather, sp g. titled FAIRY TALES.
[Renier

Todd gives William Clowes as being at Stamford Street from 1826.

(8) Title as (5).

17.2×9.7 cm. Pr by William Clowes, Stamford Street. Pp.vi+353. H/c FP×2, no heading, +9 other h/c pls×2. Purple stippled cloth, sp g. titled FAIRY TALES.
[Renier, probably imp.

This entry differs from (7) in not having a heading to the FP.

(9) The Renier Collection (V & A) also has a very imperfect copy with a booklist printed by W. Lewis, 21, Finch-lane, Cornhill. Lewis was at this address from 1819–36.

Munro and Francis, Boston, USA, published an edition in 1827 with 285 pp.

167 (1) TABART'S COLLECTION OF POPULAR STORIES FOR THE NURSERY: from the French, Italian, and old English writers, newly translated and revised. [Adorned with numerous plates.] Part I. London: printed for Tabart & Co, at the Juvenile and School Library, No.157, New Bond-street; and to be had of all dealers in books. 1804. [Price half-a-crown for each part; and either of the three parts may be had separately.]

13.9×8.7 cm. Pr by R. Taylor & Co. Black-Horse-court. Pp.[ii] or [iv]+187 (p.[188] = advts). H/c or plain FP dated Sept 1804+5 h/c or plain pls dated as FP or July 6 or Aug 7 1804, or Sept 18 in some copies. Plain yellow or marbled bds, red roan sp g.
[Baldwin; UCLA; Opie; Birm.; McKell; CBY 430; Miami; NLS; S 5.2.68/40, 23.5.83/46, 4 vols. 1804–09, and 1.12.88/196

The plates chosen for the frontispiece vary in different copies. That in UCLA is signed 'Dayes del.' and another plate is signed 'Craig del.' R. Phillips entered Part I at Stationers' Hall on Sept. 14 1804.

Part I contains Whittington and his cat; The children in the wood; Peronella; Fortunatus; Griselda; The white cat; Robin Hood.

Mrs Mary Jane Godwin edited and translated these tales for Tabart – see 48, GODWIN, MARY JANE: *Dramas for children*, for a discussion of this attribution. The stories are told in admirably clear and simple language and the illustrations are well drawn and carefully executed. The text of some of the stories is not exactly the same as in the Tales for the Nursery series.

[Part II] Title as Part I to ... NURSERY: newly translated and reviewed from the French, Italian, and old English writers. [Adorned with numerous plates.] Part II. London: printed ... as Part I.

Blue Beard.

Published by Tabart & C? July 6 1804.

Jack the Giant killer.

London, Publish'd by Tabart & C? Sep. 1804.

From Part II. *Sotheby's*   From Part III

25   Plates from *Tabart's collection of popular stories*, 167(1)

THE FISH turned FISHER.

26   Plate from
*Signor Topsy-
Turvy's
wonderful magic
lantern* by Ann
and Jane
Taylor, 171(1)

13.6×8 cm. Pr by R. Taylor & Co. Black-Horse-court. Pp.[iv]+181+3pp. advts beginning on v. of p.181. FP+5 pls dated July 6 or August 11, 1804, 2 drawn by Dayes and 2 by Craig. In some copies the unsigned plates are dated Sept 18 1804, in others, Aug. 11 1804. Marbled bds, red roan sp g. (See fig. 25)
[Opie, in plain yellow bds, red roan sp g.; Birm.; UCLA; Froebel; McKell; private coll.; S 3.3.77/145 and 1.12.88/196; NLS

Part II was entered by R. Phillips at Stationers' Hall on Sept. 14 1804. The book contains Little Red Riding Hood; Toads and diamonds; Blue Beard; Puss in Boots; The sleeping beauty in the wood; Cinderella; Riquet with the Tuft; Hop o' my Thumb; Beauty and the beast; Fortunio.

[Part III] Title as Part II except ... Adorned with numerous plates. Part III ... Bond-street; and to be had ...

13.4×8.5 cm. Pr by R. Taylor & Co. Black-Horse-court. Pp.[iv]+188 [192] inc. 4pp. bklist. H/c or plain FP dated Sep. 1804+5 or 6 pls same date or Aug. 7 1804 or Apr 2 1804. Plain yellow or marbled bds, red or green roan sp g. (See fig. 25)
[Opie, Baldwin; UCLA; McKell; Froebel; private coll.; NLS; S 1.12.88/196

R. Phillips entered this title at Stationers' Hall on 12.11.04. Some copies have only 6 plates in all but do not seem to be defective. The dates of plates vary in different copies.

Part III contains Jack the Giant-killer. Tom Thumb. Goody Two-Shoes. Tommy Two-Shoes. The seven champions of Christendom. Valentine and Orson.

   (2) [Vol. I] Title as (1) to ... NURSERY: newly translated and revised, from the French, Italian, and old English writers. Adorned with numerous plates. Vol. I. London: As (1) to ... books. 1809. [Price half-a-crown for each volume; and either of the four volumes may be had separately.]

13.5×8.5 cm. Pr by B. McMillan, Bow Street, Covent Garden. Pp.[iv]+187 [188]+5pp. bklist starting on p.[188] listing both Crosby's and Tabart's bks in some copies. 6 plain pls engvd after W. M. Craig or Richard Corbould, 2 dated Sep. 18, 1804, and 4, Aug. 7 1804. Boards, red roan sp.
[V & A; Osborne; UCLA

Contents as in (1), Part I.

[Vol. II] Title as Vol. I to ... plates. Vol. II ...

13.4×8.1 cm. Pr by B. McMillan, Bow Street, Covent Garden. Pp.[iv]+181+3pp. bklist. FP (impt cropped)+5 pls dated July 8 1804. Brown-paper covered bds, red roan sp g.
[V & A; UCLA; Reading U; private coll.

Contents as in (1), Part II.

[Vol. III] Title as Vol. I to ... plates. Vol. III ...

13.9×8.3 cm. Pr by B. McMillan, Bow Street, Covent Garden. Pp.[iv]+188+2pp. bklist. FP dated Sep. 1804+5 or 6 pls. Marbled bds, green or red roan sp g.
[Opie; Reading U; V & A; UCLA; S 2.7.74/484; private coll.

Contents as in (1), Part III, plus Prince Fatal and Prince Fortune and The Three Wishes.

[Vol. IV] Title as Vol. I to ... plates. Vol. IV ...
13.5×8.6 cm. Pr by B. McMillan, Bow Street, Covent Garden. Pp.[iv]+129 sic (i.e. 219); (p.[220] = advt of the School Magazine, or The Monthly Preceptor). FP, n.d., +2 other pls dated Feby 1809. Marbled bds, black roan sp g.
[BL; Baldwin; UCLA; private coll.; TCCU

Contents: Aladdin; or The wonderful lamp. Nourjahad; an Eastern tale. Ali Baba; or The forty thieves. The history of Jack and the bean-stalk. The voyages of Sindbad the sailor.

(3) Title as Vol. IV to ... numerous coloured plates. In four volumes. Vol. I. London: printed by R. Taylor and Co. Shoe-lane, for Tabart and Co. at the Juvenile and School Library, 157, New Bond-street; and to be had of all dealers in books. 1812. [Price sixteen shillings half-bound.]

13.5×8.4 cm. Pr (on text pp.) by B. M°Millan, Bow Street, Covent Garden. Pp.[iv]+187 [188]. H/c FP dated Sep 18 1804+5 h/c pls dated as FP or Aug 7 1804. Marbled bds, green roan sp g.
[Hockliffe

Contents as in (1), Part I.

Vols. II, III and IV have not been traced and were perhaps never printed.

168 (1) TABART'S MORAL TALES, in prose and verse. Selected and revised from the best authors. In four volumes. Vol. I [II, III, IV]. London: printed for Tabart and Co. at their original Juvenile Library, New Bond-street; and to be had of all booksellers. Price 10s.6d. half-bound. J. Adlard, Printer, Duke-street, Smithfield. [1809]

13.7×8.4 cm. Grey-green, brown or marbled bds, red or green spp. g.

Vol. I: Pp.[iv]+180. 5 (or 4 in one copy) unsigned pls.
Vol. II Pp.[iii]+180. 5 pls, 4 engvd by Tomlinson.
Vol. III: Pp.[iii]+220. 5 unsigned pls.
Vol. IV: Pp.[iii]+191+5pp. R. Phillips's bklist, beginning on v. of p.191. FP+4 unsigned pls, but 'Directions to binder' call for placing of FP only.
[UCLA; Osborne, with FP only in vol. IV; S 22.10.76/1746; private colls

The four volumes include a great variety of stories and poems, 'moral' covering exotic tales, stories about animals, adventures on sea and land, Jauffret's *The little hermitage*, Marmontel's *Belisarius* and Saint-Pierre's *The Indian cottage*: amongst the poetry are Cowper's *John Gilpin* and that least moral of poems, Parnell's *The hermit* (see PARNELL'S HERMIT, 117).

In his Advertisement to vol. I, dated July, 1809, from Bond-street, the publisher says 'His [the publisher's] collection of Fairy Tales and Romances ... in four similar volumes, united to the present work, cannot fail to form an interesting feature in every juvenile library. THE BIBLE, or SCRIPTURE STORIES [by William Godwin, 49, q.v.], in two volumes, ... afford, together, all the aid which can be necessary to get afloat and direct the genius and imagination of young persons.'

TABART'S SCHOOL MAGAZINE: see THE SCHOOL MAGAZINE, 150 above.

169 No entry.

170 (1) TALES FOR THE NURSERY. The title was not specifically used by Benjamin Tabart to designate his sixpenny series of fairy and popular stories, but most of the books did include 'A tale' (or 'Tales') 'for the nursery' in their titles. The numbers refer to those in the bibliography:

The adventures of Andolocia, 1
The adventures of Valentine and Orson, 3
Aladdin, 5
Ali Baba, 7
Beauty and the beast, 9
The children in the wood, 18
[d'Aulnoy, M. C.]
    The history of Fortunio, 26
    The history of the White Cat, 27
The history of Fortunatus, 61
The history of Goody Two-Shoes, 62
The history of Jack and the bean-stalk, 63
The history of Jack the Giant Killer, 64
The history of Robin Hood, 65
The history of Tom Thumb, 66
The history of Whittington and his cat, 67
[Johnson, Richard] The seven champions
    of Christendom, 76
[Le Prince de Beaumont, M. J.] The
    history of Prince Fatal and Prince Fortune,
    96

Nourjahad, 114
Peronella, 120A
Perrault, C.
    La barbe bleue, 121
    Blue Beard and Little Red Riding Hood,
    122
    Cendrillon, 124
    Cinderella, 125
    Hop o' my Thumb, 126
    Puss in Boots, and Diamonds and toads,
    129
    Riquet with the Tuft, 130
    The sleeping beauty, 131
Richard Coeur de Lion, 143
The story of Griselda, 161
[Swift, J.] Gulliver's travels, 4 parts, 162
The voyages of Sinbad the sailor, 2 parts,
    183

171 (1) [TAYLOR, Ann and Jane] Signor Topsy-Turvy's wonderful magic lantern; or, The world turned upside down. By the author of 'My Mother,' and other poems. Illustrated with twenty-four engravings. London: printed for Tabart & Co. at the Juvenile and School Library, No.157, New Bond-street; and to be had of all booksellers: by B. McMillan, Bow Street, Covent Garden. 1810. [Price 3s.6d. bound.]

13×10 cm. Pp.[iv]+5–71; p.[72] = Phillips's bklist. Engvd FP+23 other pls. Red, green or blue roan-backed plain or marbled bds, sp g. (See fig. 26)
[Gum. 5517; Hockliffe; Opie; Baldwin; BL; UCLA; FCB pp.217–221; CBY 460; Lilly; PML; Melb.; Miami; McKell; private colls; S 13.10.77/2450, 12.10.81/123 and 23.5.83/66

The book was partially reprinted in America by William Charles, Philadelphia, in 1811. Welch 449.1.

This is an excellent production. The verses are neat, pointed and (as may be expected, considering the authors) easily to be understood by children. The Introduction, in verse, is signed 'A' and so are 9 of the poems, 11 are signed 'J', 2 'T', and 2 are unsigned. The plates (by Isaac Taylor, jun.?) are among the more proficient illustrations in children's books of the period and amusingly depict 'The horse turned driver' (showing a horse sitting in a chaise, driving the groom), 'The ass turned miller' (a donkey, whip in hand, urging on a laden miller), etc.

Nevertheless, there is a crudity – even cruelty – about some others of the themes which would not commend them to readers today: for instance, a cook being roasted by a hare or a butcher being carved up by an ox or fricassée-ed by hogs, inversions of the natural order of things which were used to express dissatisfaction with the general state of society.

The Advertisement recalls 'nursery learning of fifty years ago' and 'a little volume entitled, "The World turned upside down" ... which [the present authors] had been recommended to revise for the amusement of modern nurseries'. This could refer to Riley's publication in the second half of the 18th century, eleven of whose tales in verse obviously inspired the Taylors' work.

172 (1) TAYLOR, Joseph. Ornithologia curioso: or, The wonders of the feathered creation. Being a collection of anecdotes, illustrative of the surprising instinct, sagacity, &c. of birds. Selected by Joseph Taylor. London: printed for Lackington, Allen & Co. Temple of the Muses, Finsbury Square. Sold, also, by Tabart & Co. New Bond Street, and Harris, St. Paul's Church Yard, London: and F. Houlston and Son, Wellington, Salop. 1807.

14.4×8.6 cm. Pr by Houlston's, Wellington. Pp.216. FP engvd by Charles Knight after Corbould Junr, dated August 27th 1807. Marbled bds, red roan sp g, or blue bds, white paper sp (perhaps with label).
[Osborne; UCLA; Renier; BL; Baldwin; Bod.

A collection of entertaining anecdotes about birds, not a serious ornithological study.

173 (1) THORNTON, Robert John. School Virgil: whereby boys will acquire ideas as well as words; masters be saved the necessity of any explanation; and the Latin language obtained in the shortest time: by Robert John Thornton, M.D. Member of the University of Cambridge, and of the Royal London College of Physicians, &c. &c. &c. [One line Latin. Hor.] London: stereotyped and printed by David Cock and Co. Stereotype-Office, 75, Dean-street, Soho. Published at the Linnaean Gallery, Hinde-street, Manchester-square; – [21] congers inc.] Tabart, Conduit-street ... and may be had of all booksellers in town and country. Price of this volume, bound, with only a few cuts, eight shillings – with numerous wood-cuts, (most of the ideas of Virgil being pictured) twelve shillings. 1812.

17.3×10 cm. Pp.xxiv+623. Stipple-engvd FP dated Novr 1, 1812, J. Jenkins delt et sculpt+one other pl engvd by Burke, pubd Novr 1, 1811. Calf.
[Exeter

Variant copy
Specification as above except size, 16.8×10 cm., but with FP engvd by D. Graham+2 othe pls, one engvd by Burke (as above), the other by D. Graham. This copy is bound in marbled bds, leather sp with label 'School Virgil'.
[Private coll.

'Newberry, St. Paul's Church-yard' is among the congers, but this edition is not recorded in Roscoe; J 352, *Illustrations of the School Virgil*, 1814, has 2 leaves of letterpress and 62 leaves comprising 150 wcts. Tabart's name is not included in the imprints of the 1814 edition.

174 (1) A TOUR THROUGH ENGLAND, described in a series of letters, from a young gentleman to his sister. With copper plates. London: printed for Tabart and Co. at their Juvenile and School Library, No.157, New Bond-street. 1804. (Price three shillings and sixpence.) W. Flint, Printer, Old Bailey.

13.7×7.6 cm. Pp.x+232+8pp. advts. ½-title. Folding map dated June 25th 1804 pubd by Richd Phillips, engvd by J. A. Neele, +4 pls (Oxford, Birmingham, York and Cambridge).
[Birm., rebound

The supposed writer of these letters uses effusive and flowery language – unnatural for a young man – but this does not disguise the interest of his tour. Knowing Tabart's fondness for introducing advertisement into his books, it was to be expected that the letter-writer would visit Tabart's Juvenile Library, where he bought 'some of his delightful books'. This book was puffed in E. Kilner's *A visit to London* and E. Fenwick's *Visits to the Juvenile Library*.

(2) Title as (1) to ... plates. Second edition, revised ... Bond-street. 1806. (Price half-a-crown.) T. Curson Hansard, Printer, Peterborough-court, Fleet-street.

13.3×8.1 cm. Pp.vi+200+8pp. advts. FP+folding map by Russell Jun. sculp. 30 Noble Street, Cheapside, +5 pls (2 dated Aug. 11 1804). Marbled bds, red roan sp g.
[Renier; Osborne, rebound; Baldwin; CBY 177; S 6.4.79/486

(2A) Titles as (2) except ... (Price three shillings and sixpence.) Contents as (2) but map of Hindostan, n.d. and unsigned.
[Nottm U

(3) Title as (1) to ... plates. Third edition, revised. London: printed for Richard Phillips, Bridge-street. And to be had of all booksellers. 1811. (Price three shillings.)

13.3×8.6 cm. Pr by James Gillet, Charles-street, Hatton Garden. Pp.vi+209 [212]. Folding map FP dated March 7th 1814 'by Willm Darton Junr Holborn Hill' +6 other pls similarly dated. Plain brown paper over bds, red roans sp g.
[BL; Baldwin; private coll.; S 27.2.67/289

(4) 4th edition published by William Darton. Wandsworth's copy has a map and six plates dated March 7, 1814; Renier has a copy with a FP dated 1821, map dated July 1820 and 4 plates dated 1821.
[Renier; Wandsworth

175 (1) TRIMMER, Sarah (Kirby). Fabulous histories. Designed for the instruction of children, respecting their treatment of animals. By Mrs. Trimmer. Seventh edition. London: printed for J. Johnson, and F. and C. Rivington, in St. Paul's Church-yard; G. and J. Robinson, and Longman and Rees, in Paternoster-row; J. Hatchard, in Piccadilly; and B. Tabart, in Bond-street. 1802. Price two shillings and sixpence.

17.1×10 cm. Pr by T. Bensley, Bolt Court, Fleet Street. Pp.viii+9–172. No illusns. Calf, g bands on sp. Long f.
[UCLA; Baldwin; private coll. in tree calf with red label

Review: *The juvenile review*, 1817: 'This delightful work was written ... for the instruction of children respecting their treatment of animals; it contains the history of a young brood of robins, with anecdotes of some children who protect and feed them. We remember the extreme satisfaction this work afforded us in childhood ...'.

(2) Title as (1) to ... Trimmer. Eighth edition. London: printed for J. Johnson, and F. C. and J. Rivington, St. Paul's Church-yard; Longman, Hurst, Rees, and Orme, Paternoster-row; J. Hatchard, Piccadilly; and B. Tabart, Bond-street. 1808. Price two shillings and sixpence. [1 vol. as above]

16.2×9.1 cm. Pr by T. Bensley, Bolt Court, Fleet Street. Pp.viii+9–172. No illusns. [Baldwin, rebound

(3) Title as (1) to ... Trimmer. Vol. I [II]. Eighth edition. London: printed for J. Johnson, F. C. and J. Rivington, St. Paul's Church-yard; Longman, Hurst, Rees, and Orme, Paternoster-row; J. Harris, corner of St. Paul's Church-yard; J. Hatchard, Piccadilly; and B. Tabart, New Bond Street. 1807. [2 vols.]

16×9.1 cm. Pr by T. Bensley, Bolt Court, Fleet Street. Pp.xii+144; 164. Wood-engvd TP vignettes+wood-engvd headpieces to chapters. Marbled bds, ¾ black roan g, or ¾ green morocco g.
[BL; Miami

In *Memoirs of the little man* ... 109, 1807, Tabart advertised Fabulous Histories, by Mrs. Trimmer, 2s.6d., followed by 'A new and beautiful edition of the above, with cuts, in 2 volumes, 6s.od.' This edition was listed in MLA, February 1807, with woodcuts designed by Thornton, engraved by Nesbit and others.

176 (1) TRIMMER, Sarah (Kirby). A new series of prints, accompanied by easy lessons: being an improved edition of the first set of Scripture prints, from the Old Testament. By Mrs. Trimmer. London: printed for J. Harris, successor to E. Newbery, corner of St. Paul's Church Yard; J. Hatchard, Piccadilly; and B. Tabart, New Bond Street. 1803. [2 vols.]

11.3×9 cm. Pr by Brettell, Great Windmill-street, Haymarket. Lessons: Pp.vi+107; Prints: 24 pls, some dated June 1st 1803. Calf or marbled bds, green roan sp g.
[Exeter; ULC; Renier; UCLA; Hockliffe; Osborne, lessons only

(2) Title as (1) to ... Bond Street. 1808.

11.5×8.7 cm. Pr by E. Hemsted, Great New-street, Fetter Lane. Pp.vi+[7] 8–107; pp.[iv]+24 pls, three dated June 1st 1803. Two parts bound together, or separately, in leather, or marbled paper covers with white paper label.
[Renier; UCLA; Leics U; Cheltm; Hockliffe; Baldwin

177 (1) TRIMMER, Sarah (Kirby). A new series of prints, accompanied by easy lessons: containing, a general outline of antient history. By Mrs. Trimmer. London: printed for J. Harris, successor to E. Newbery, corner of St. Paul's Church Yard; J. Hatchard, Piccadilly; and J. Tabart, New Bond Street. 1803. [2 vols]

11.5×9 cm. Pr by J. Brettell, Great Windmill Street, Haymarket. Lessons: Pp.vi+[7] 8–176, Prints: same title but third publisher's name shown as 'B. Tabart'. Part I. Pp.[vi]+xxiv pls; Part II, pp.[ii], xvi pls, some pls in each part 'Pubd Decr 24 1802 by I. Harris St. Paul's Church yard, London, and the other Proprietors of the work.' Calf, sp g.
[BL; Renier; Exeter; Som.; Wandsworth; UCLA; Baldwin; private coll.

The initial 'J' before 'Tabart' in the volume of lessons was changed to 'B' in the set of prints. Tabart was not concerned with subsequent editions.

178 (1) TRIMMER, Sarah (Kirby). A new series of prints, accompanied by easy lessons: containing a general outline of Roman history. By Mrs. Trimmer. London: printed for J. Harris, successor to E. Newbery, corner of St. Paul's Church Yard; J. Hatchard, Piccadilly; and B. Tabart, New Bond Street. 1803. [2 vols]

11.9×9 cm. Pr by J. Brettell, Great Windmill Street, Haymarket. Lessons: pp.xiii+[14] 15–210. Prints: TP, dated 1804, does not carry Tabart's name. Pp.vi+40 engs, some 'Publish'd Decr 1, 1803, by J. Harris, St. Paul's Church Yard, London, and the other Proprietors of the Work.' Calf, sp g, or marbled paper wrps, paper label.
[BL; ULC; UCLA; V & A; Reading U; Osborne

Tabart was not concerned with subsequent editions.

179 (1) THE TRUE HISTORY OF A LITTLE BOY WHO CHEATED HIMSELF Founded on fact By a young Naval Officer London Published by Tabart & Co at the Juvenile and School Library New Bond Street 1809

11.8×11.3 cm. Pr by W. Marchant, 3, Greville-street. 14 leaves comprising TP and 12pp. text with 11 h/c engvd pls on the other side (2 leaves have text only, other sides blank)+1 more pl with blank v. Orange pr wrps dated 1809, carrying printer's impt; bklist on lower v., 8 items. (See fig. 27)
[Osborne; CBY 529; 2 private colls; S 13.10.77/2556–7; Phila.

Each plate has a single engvd word at foot, e.g. 'Request', 'Assent', etc., repeated (but not engvd) as title to accompanying verse opposite.

The publication of this book in the year after Tabart's son, Francis Gerard, became 'a young naval officer' prompts interesting speculation as to its authorship – but this must not be treated seriously. It was reprinted in America by W. Charles, Philadelphia, c.1817. Welch 1349.

The story is told in verse of a naughty boy who took a cake from a sleeping man and hid it. Later, he discovered that the cake was meant to be a birthday present for himself; he ran off to find it, but it had been eaten by a ploughboy.

Review: This title is one which *The juvenile review*, 1817, included in a list of books which 'contain little pieces of childish poetry, some of which are very pretty'.

(2) An edition of 1810 is presumed (but has not been found) on account of the cover-text of the next entry.

(3) Title as (1) to ... Published by William Darton at the Juvenile and School Library Holborn Hill 1811

12×11.3 cm. No printer shown. Pp. unnumb'd. 6 leaves with text on one side, h/c eng on other, followed by 2 leaves with text on one side only; followed by 6 leaves with text on one side, h/c eng on other. No impt on UCLA's pls but Opie's has impt on one (shaved) reading 'Jany 1811 by W. Darton Junr, Holborn Hill'. Yellowish stiff-paper pr covers, text reads 'Published by B. Tabart and Co. at the Juvenile and School Library, New Bond-street. 1810.' Lower v. of cover carries list of Tabart's bks.
[Opie; UCLA; S 19.4.71/216

(4) Title as (3) to ... London: printed by William Darton, Jun. 58, Holborn-hill. 1813. Price one shilling plain, or eighteen-pence.

11.5×9 cm. 19 leaves. Pr TP+12pp. pr text on 6 leaves+12 h/c engs on 12 leaves.
[Osborne, rebound; Gum. 5641, erroneously stating 'First edition'

Darton published further editions in 1817 and c.1850, the FP of the last being a view of Darton's shop.

180   No entry.

181   (1) VENTUM, Harriet. Surveys of Nature: a sequel to Mrs. Trimmer's Introduction; being familiar descriptions of some popular subjects in natural philosophy, adapted to the capacities of children. By Harriet Ventum, authour [*sic*] of Selina, The Amiable Tutoress, &c. London: printed for John Badcock, Paternoster-row, and B. Tabart, Bond Street; by W. Bristow, Canterbury. 1802.

15.4×9.3 cm. Pp.vi+138. No illusns, except wct tailpiece. Printer's colophon reads: 'From the Press of Wm. Bristow, Canterbury. – 1802.' Green marbled bds, brown leather sp, green pr label showing 'Price two shillings'.
[BL; Osborne; UCLA

In her Preface, dated October 1801, London, the author says that she is involved in the business of a school and constant teaching; and she has found that while Mrs. Trimmer's Introduction was a very serviceable work for the persual of her younger pupils, she found a need for something more detailed for the older ones. In this book a knowledgeable mother, armed with a pocket microscope, takes her children for walks and expounds on the birds, plants and other natural phenomena they see. Some of the natural history which she imparts is, perhaps, more colourful than scientific – for example, 'The tarantula of Italy has very fatal effects unless counteracted by the power of music upon the senses.'

Review: The *Anti-Jacobin review*, vol. 10, p.427: 'Certainly the author of this little volume is not either a profound grammarian or naturalist: to the morality of the work, however, we have not anything to object; and when its numerous typographical, grammatical, and scientific errors are corrected by a judicious parent or teacher, it may safely and advantageously be placed in the hands of children "from the age of eight to twelve years."'

FALSE PRIDE.

Engraved by Chapat.

Matilda & Sir Felix.

Page 77.

London. Publish'd May, 1807, by B. Tabart.

IDLENESS.

3

London. Published June 1.1808. by B.Tabart & C.º New Bond Street.

27   Plate from *The true history of a little boy who cheated himself*, 179(1). *Sotheby's*

28   Frontispiece of *Matilda Mortimer* by M. Woodland, 188(3)

182 (1) A VIEW OF UNIVERSAL HISTORY. Tabart & Co.

12mo. 2 folding h/c engvd maps. Roan-backed bds. [*c*.1804]
[S 2.6.75/18

No copy yet seen.

Review: The *Gentleman's magazine*, March 1805, p.251: 'This epitome will be found useful, not only to the young readers for whom it is principally intended, but to those of a maturer age who wish for much information in a little compass. ... The concluding chapter ... is not uninteresting.'

(2) A VIEW OF UNIVERSAL HISTORY, from the Creation to the year 1803. With a brief chronology. Abridged, for the use of children, from the twenty-five volumes of Dr. Mavor's Universal History. With two maps. London, printed for Tabart & Co. at the Juvenile and School Library, 157, New Bond-street, and to be had of all booksellers. [Entered at Stationers'-Hall.] Price half a crown.

13.3×8.7 cm. Pr by Heney, 76, Fleet-street. Pp.iv+171+5pp. list of Phillips's bks. Folding map FP pubd by R. Phillips, dated 1806, and another folding map by Ricd Phillips, dated March 1, 1807. Marbled bds, red roan sp g.
[Opie

The Advertisement is written, but not signed or dated, by 'Mr. Tabart' from Juvenile Library, No.157, New Bond-street. He says he 'has the satisfaction to introduce to his young Friends an Abridgment of the valuable Universal History of Dr. Mavor, which he presumes will induce them hereafter to peruse the entire work [25 volumes] with increased pleasure and diligence.'

The greater part of the book is concerned with ancient history. It is divided into 12 'periods' and only on reaching the 11th period is the reader introduced to the Crusades and events up to the discovery of America. The 12th period covers the succeeding years 'up to our own time' in 8 pages. The rest of the book, to p.171, contains a chronology beginning at 4004 BC. The concentration of facts makes dry reading and the adult style makes little, if any, concession to young minds.

(3) Title as (2) to ... London: printed ... Stationers'-Hall. [No closing bracket] Price half-a-crown.

13.5×8.2 cm. Pr by Heney, 76, Fleet-street. Pp.iv+171+5pp. Phillips's bklist. Folding map FP of the ancient world dated March 1 1807, pubd by Ricd Phillips, engvd by Neele, 272 Strand, +another folding map of 2 hemispheres dated 1809. Marbled bds, red leather sp.
[BL

(4) Title as (2) to ... 1803, with ... Price half a crown.

13.6×8.7 cm. Pr by Heney, 76, Fleet-street. Pp.iv+171+5pp. Phillips's bklist. Folding FP map pubd June 15, 1813, by C. Law, Ave Maria Lane, engvd by Neele, Strand, the edges of the globes outlined in yellow, +folding map of the ancient world framed in yellow rectangular line, same imprint, engvd by Mutlow, Russell Cot. Plain grey bds, black roan sp g.
[Private coll.; S 25.2.76/92

183 (1) THE VOYAGES OF SINBAD THE SAILOR. A tale for the nursery. With three copperplates. In two parts. Part I. [Part II.] London: printed for Tabart and Co. Juvenile and School Library, No.157, New Bond Street. And to be had of all dealers in books. Price sixpence. 1805.

11.9×7.6 cm. Pr by D. N. Shury, Berwick street, Soho. Pp.34+2pp. bklist; pp.36. Part I has h/c FP+2 h/c pls dated Feb. 14 1805. Part II has h/c FP+2 h/c pls dated March 25 1805. Plain blue card covers or stiff yellow wrps, advt on lower v.
[Hockliffe; PML, Part I; private coll. Part II, rebound; S 14.3.72/457

The bklist uses the long f. In Part II the title spells 'Sindbad'. This book was entered at Stationers' Hall by R. Phillips on 15.3.05. Mrs. Fenwick puffed it in her *Visits to the Juvenile Library*.

184 (1) [WOLLSTONECRAFT, Mary] Original stories from real life: with conversations calculated to regulate the affections, and form the mind to truth and goodness. A new edition. London: printed for J. Johnson, St. Paul's Churchyard, and B. Tabart, 157, New Bond-street, by Wood and Innes, Poppin's Court, Fleet Street. 1807.

13.1×8.5 cm. Pp.[iv]+199. No illusns. Calf, g.
[BL; Wayne

First published in 1788 by J. Johnson and re-issued in 1791 with engravings by William Blake. In 1906 Henry Frowde published an edition with an entertaining introduction by E. V. Lucas.

Mrs. Mason, the guardian of the children in this story, has always (in modern times) been ridiculed for her immense self-satisfaction and unbending rectitude. 'Providence', she says, 'has ... made me an instrument of good – I have been useful to my fellow-creatures.' She 'was never in a passion, but her quiet steady displeasure made them [the girls] feel so little in their own eyes, they wished her to smile that they might be something. ... I declare I cannot go to sleep, said Mary, I am so afraid of Mrs. Mason's eyes – would you think, Caroline, that she who looks so very good-natured sometimes, could frighten one so?'

When Caroline was stung by some wasps 'she uttered the loudest and most silly complaints' and Mrs. Mason addressed to her in lofty language a homily on fortitude of mind: 'After you have borne bodily pain, you will have firmness enough to sustain the still more excruciating agonies of the mind.'

And yet the same pen that created this monster of respectability could, in the same book, write with tenderness and deep sensibility about country scenes and the beauties of nature.

185 (1) THE WONDERS OF THE MICROSCOPE; or, An explanation of the wisdom of the Creator in objects comparatively minute, adapted to the understanding of young persons. Illustrated with five large copper-plates. London: printed for Tabart and Co. at the Juvenile and School Library, No.157, New Bond Street; and to be had of all booksellers. Price half-a-crown. Barnard & Sultzer, Printers, Water Lane, Fleet Street. [1804]

15.6×9.2 cm. Pp.viii+132+4pp. bklist. Folding engvd FP of a louse+3 other folding pls+one fp engvd pl. Marbled bds, red roan sp g.
[Opie

This title was advertised in 1804 at 2s.6d. In 1806 it was advertised at 3s.6d. By 1811 the price was 4s. These advertisements help to date the above edition as *c*.1804 and the following one as *c*.1806.

The 4 folding plates are copied from Robert Hooke's *Micrographia*, London, 1665.

This was one of the books read by the 'blooming boys and girls' who went to Tabart's shop in E. Fenwick's *Visits to the Juvenile Library* and E. Kilner's *A visit to London.*

(2) Title as (1) to ... Price three shillings and sixpence. [Barnard & Sultzer, Printers, Water Lane, Fleet Street.] [*c*.1806]

17.4×9.4 cm. Pp.xii+118 [120], p.[119] being an explanation of technical terms with advts on v. Folding FP+one fp and 3 folding pls. Leather sp.
[BL, rebound; Baldwin

Advertised in 1806 at 3s.6d.

(3) Title as (1) to ... Creator, in objects comparatively minute. Adapted to the understanding of young persons. Illustrated with five large copper-plates. London: printed for Richard Phillips, Bridge-street, and to be had of all booksellers. (Price four shillings and sixpence.) 1811.

17.3×10.4 cm. Pr by James Gillett, Charles-street, Hatton Garden. Pp.xii+118 (p.[119] = Technical Terms)+1p. advt. Folding engvd FP+one fp and 3 folding pls. Marbled bds, red roan sp g.
[Opie, lacking 5th pl.; private colls

William Darton took over this title: he advertised it from 1812 but no edition of his earlier than 1823 has been found.

186 (1) THE WONDERS OF THE TELESCOPE; or, A display of the wonders of the heavens and of the system of the universe, written in a familiar and popular manner, adapted particularly to the perusal of young persons, and especially calculated to promote and simplify the study of astronomy among persons of all ages, with twelve plates, on a plan never before attempted. London: printed for Richard Phillips, New Bridge-street, Blackfriars; and sold by Tabart and Co. at the Juvenile Library, New Bond-street, and by all other booksellers. 1805. (Price 4s.6d. half-bound.)

18.6×11.2 cm. Pr by Marchant, 3, Greville-street. Pp.iv+120. Folding engvd FP of the solar system, pubd Feb. 25 1805 by Tabart & Co. +4 fp pls and 7 folding pls dated variously Oct. 7 1806, Oct. 7 1805, Feb. 25 1805. Marbled bds, red roan sp g.
[BL; Osborne; UCLA; Melb.; Miami; Nottm U

This book was puffed in E. Fenwick's *Visits to the Juvenile Library* and E. Kilner's *A visit to London.*

Reviews: The *British critic*, vol. 26, p.334: 'We have not met with a work of the kind better calculated to amuse young persons, or so far as it goes, to instruct them, than that which is now before us.' *The juvenile review* 1817, recommended 'this pleasing volume the contents of which are calculated to strengthen and confirm the pious and grateful sentiments which naturally arise from a contemplation of the celestial orbs.'

(2) Another edition dated 1805, as (1) but some later plates:

18×11 cm. Pr by Marchant, 3 Greville-street, Holborn. Pp.iv+120. 12 pls, 7 folding, of which one is dated 1808 and others 1806. 4 fp pls. Marbled bds, red roan sp
[Opie; NLS; private coll.]

(3) ...; or, A display of the starry heavens and of the system of the universe: calculated to promote and simplify the study of astronomy. With fourteen plates. New edition. London: printed for Richard Phillips, Bridge Street. 1809. [Price 5s. boards, or 6s. bound.]

18.9×11.6 cm. Pr by B. M'Millan, Bow Street, Covent Garden. Pp.iv+128. 14 pls inc. some folding; some pubd by Tabart; impts dated 1806, 1807, 1808 and 1809. Marbled bds, red roan sp g.
[Private coll.; UCLA; NLS; Baldwin

The text has been reset since 1805. The wove paper is watermarked 1805, 1808 and 1815 [*sic*). At the end of 'Advertisement' on p.iv, 4 errata are listed.

The dates on some of the plates seem to indicate that another edition was published between 1805 and 1809, but this has not been traced.

This title was taken over by William Darton, who advertised it in 1812 (no copy found) and published an edition in 1823.

187 (1) WOODLAND, M. Bear and forbear.

This forms vol. II of *Tales for mothers and daughters*, 1807, by Miss Woodland, 191 below.

The book was reprinted in America in 1827 by W. B. Gilley, New-York. It is a novel for teenagers, telling how a sweet nature and good principles will, in the end, bring happiness out of affliction.

(2) BEAR AND FORBEAR: or, The history of Julia Marchmont: a moral tale for young ladies. By Miss M. Woodland. London: published by Tabart and Co. at the Juvenile and School Library, New Bond Street. Mercier and Co. Printers, King's Head Court, St. Paul's Church Yard. 1809.

15.4×8.5 cm. Pp.199. FP engvd by C. Knight, May 1807. Marbled bds, red roan sp g.
[BL; Osborne; Melb.

188 (1) WOODLAND, M. Matilda Mortimer.

This forms vol. III of *Tales for mothers and daughters*, 1807, by Miss Woodland, 191 below.

The book was reprinted in America in 1818 by W. B. Gilley, New-York.

Matilda was intelligent and artistic but proud and when her rich father lost his fortune, rather than live with her impoverished parents, she accepted the invitation of a wealthy friend and went to stay with her; but she found herself treated with contempt as an unpaid companion. After some unhappy experiences in the fashionable world she realised how wrong she had been and went back to her loving parents, determined to make a living by teaching art.

(2) MATILDA MORTIMER; or, False pride. A moral tale. By Miss M. Woodland. London: published by Tabart and Co. at the Juvenile and School Library, New Bond Street. Mercier and Co. Printers, King's Head Court, St. Paul's Church Yard. 1809.

14.9×9.1 cm. Pp.155. FP engvd by C. Knight, May 1807. Marbled bds, red roan sp g. [BL; Osborne

(3) Title as (2) to ... pride. For the use of young ladies. By Miss M. Woodland. London: printed for B. Tabart and Co. at the Juvenile and School Library, New Bond Street, by Ellerton and Byworth, Johnson's Court, Fleet Street. 1810.

15.1×9 cm. Pp.155. FP engvd by Charles Knight, dated May, 1807. Marbled bds, red roan sp g. (See fig. 28)
[Baldwin; private coll.

189 (1) WOODLAND, M. Rose and Agnes.

This forms vol. IV of *Tales for mothers and daughters*, 1807, by Miss Woodland, 191 below.

The book was reprinted in America in 1818 by W. B. Gilley, New York. It sets out to illustrate the evils of favouritism in a family.

(2) ROSE AND AGNES; or, The dangers of partiality. A moral tale. By Miss Woodland. London: published by B. Tabart and Co. at the Juvenile and School Library, New Bond Street. Mercier and Co. Printers, King's Head Court, St. Paul's Church Yard. 1809.

15.2×9 cm. Pp.146. FP engvd by Charles Knight dated May, 1807. Marbled bds, red roan sp g.
[Osborne; Renier

(3) An edition of 1810 was sold at Sotheby's 19.2.73/47.

190 (1) WOODLAND, M. A tale of warning.

This forms vol. I of *Tales for mothers and daughters*, 1807, by Miss Woodland, 191 below.

The book was reprinted in America in 1818 by W. B. Gilley, New-York. It is a passionate tale about an indolent mother whose child dies from her neglect. The mother dies too, from the shock.

(2) It seems likely that there was an edition of 1809 but it has not been traced.

(3) A TALE OF WARNING; or The victims of indolence. Intended for the use of young ladies. By Miss M. Woodland. London: printed for B. Tabart and Co. at the Juvenile and School Library, New Bond Street. By Ellerton and Byworth, Johnson's Court, Fleet Street. 1810.

15.1×9.4 cm. Pp.126. FP dated May 1807 pubd by B. Tabart. Marbled bds, red roan sp g.
[Private coll.

191 (1) WOODLAND, M. Tales for mothers and daughters. In four volumes. By Miss Woodland. Vol. I [II, III, IV]. London: printed for B. Tabart, at the Juvenile and School Library, 157, New Bond-street, by Mercier and Co. King's Head Court, St. Paul's Church-yard. 1807.

14.5×9.1 cm. ½-titles. Pp.viii+126; 199; 155; 146. Vols II and III have FPP dated May 1807, engvd by C. Knight; no illusns present in vols I and IV in only copy seen. Marbled bds, red roan spp g.
[BL, lacking FPP for vols I and IV

There are no individual title-pages. The ½-titles only carry words 'Tales for Mothers and Daughters' but each volume has the general title-page as in vol. I.

The titles are: Vol. I, A Tale of Warning: or, The victims of indolence. Vol. II, Bear and Forbear: or, The history of Julia Marchmont. Vol. III, Matilda Mortimer: or, False pride. Vol. IV, Rose and Agnes: or, The dangers of partiality.

M. J. Godwin published *Histories of four young ladies* ... by Miss Woodland, 2nd edition, 1814, containing the above four novels. The book was reprinted in America by W. B. Gilley, New York, 1818.

'The plan on which the following tales have been written', says the author, 'is that of taking one peculiar vice or virtue, and showing the good or evil which may possibly result.
  'In the perusal of them, it will be seen that the moral tendency of A Tale of Warning is to impress the evil consequences of indolence on the mind of the reader, and to bring to recollection the fatal error to which this vice, if indulged to excess, may lead. The intention of the tale of Bear and Forbear is to show that a mild and forbearing temper must finally make the possessor happy, however severe the temporary trials may be to which she is exposed. The authoress has endeavoured, in The Dangers of Partiality, to exemplify the fatal occurrences of exclusive preference in families, as well as to show the sacred nature of filial duty, and the reverence and love a child ought to pay a parent, however mistaken that parent may be. The object of the tale of False Pride is to inculcate that laudable activity and independence of mind which, should we be overtaken by adversity, will excite us to exert our talents for an honourable support, rather than live in splendid dependence.'

Part II

The books in this part were all advertised by Benjamin Tabart at some time but they have not been found with his imprint. Most of them were published by Richard Phillips but they are given a place here because they must have been on sale in Tabart's Juvenile Library.

192 (1) ADET, S. The first grammar; or, An easy accidence of the French language. This title was advertised in 1806 and again in 1809.

193 (1) BINGLEY, Rev. W. Animal biography; or, Authentic anecdotes of the lives, manners, and economy, of the animal creation, arranged according to the system of Linnaeus. By the Rev. W. Bingley, A.M. Fellow of the Linnean Society, and late of Peterhouse, Cambridge. In three volumes. Second edition, with considerable additions and corrections. Vol. I [II, III] Quadrupeds. London: printed for Richard Phillips, No.71, St. Paul's Church-yard; and sold by all booksellers. 1804. S. Rousseau, Printer, Wood Street, Spa Fields.

21.5×12.5 cm. Leather, sp g.

Vol. I   Quadrupeds. Pp.xxiii+504+8pp. Index. FP: 4-fold pl of lioness and cubs, engvd by Reeve.

Vol. II   Quadrupeds-Whales-Birds. Sold by T. Hurst, Paternoster-row; E. Balfour, Edinburgh; and J. Archer, Dublin. T. Gillet, Printer, Crown-court, Fleet-street. Pp.554. No illusns.

Vol. III   Amphibious animals, -Fishes, -Insects, -Worms. Impt as vol. II. C. Mercier and Co. Printers, Northumberland-court, Strand. Pp.580. No illusns.
[BL

First published in 1802. It was translated into several European languages.

'In composing these volumes, I have all the way attended to every thing that might be of use in juvenile instruction', says the author, in his Preface dated Feb. 1, 1804 and signed 'W. B.' from Christ Church, Hants (where he was the incumbent). Otherwise, these imposing, almost-unillustrated volumes would hardly be recognised as children's books, being so large and expensive (30s. in boards). But they are popularly written and most entertaining.

Reviews: The *Anti-Jacobin review*, vol. 15, p.151: 'It contains in a comparatively small compass, a compendium of natural history, prepared with taste and judgment, and arranged with regularity and perspicuity. His care and caution too, in excluding those indelicate passages, which unavoidably occur in the larger histories of this description, are highly meritorious. ... Mr. Bingley has exerted uncommon diligence and industry, in his collection of facts. The style of his narrative is easy and perspicuous; his remarks are apposite, ingenious and acute; and he suffers no opportunity to escape of conveying to his readers good religious and moral principles.'

The *Monthly review*, 1813, noticed the 4th edition and listed its publishers but these do not include Tabart or Phillips. The reviewer said: 'The labour of nearly two years, and the careful inspection of almost one thousand volumes are solid proofs of the compiler's diligence and perseverance. From the perusal of these anecdotes the young of both sexes may reap much entertainment and instruction without encountering a single passage which can alarm the modesty ...'.

(2) Title as (1) except 'Third edition' to ... Phillips, No.6, Bridge-street; and sold by all booksellers. 1805. [Price 30s. in boards.]

20.8×12.7 cm. Pr by R. Taylor and Co. No.38, Shoe-lane, Fleet-street. No binding seen.

Vol. I.   Quadrupeds. Pp.xxiii+500 [502]. No illusns.

Vol. II.   Quadrupeds, -Whales, -Birds. Pp.557. No illusns.

Vol. III.   Amphibious animals – Fishes – Insects. Pp.606. No illusns.
[BL, rebound

194 (1) BLAIR, Rev. David. An easy grammar of natural and experimental philosophy. With ten engravings.

Tabart advertised this book in 1808, bound in blue, with 10 engravings. It was entered at Stationers' Hall by R. Phillips on 21.9.07.

195 (1) BLAIR, Rev. David. An easy Latin accidence.

Advertised in 1806, price 1s. in cloth.

196 (1) BLAIR, Rev. David. A practical grammar of the English language, accompanied by numerous exercises, and adapted throughout to the use of schools. By the Rev. David Blair, author of the Class Book, First Catechism, Reading Exercises, Grammar of Philosophy, &c. &c. Fourth edition. London: printed for Richard Phillips, Bridge-street, Blackfriars. 1809. T. Gillet, Printer, Crown-court, Fleet-street. (Price half-a-crown.)

13.6×7.5 cm. Pp.ix [x]+168.
[BL, rebound

Listed in the *English catalogue of books*, 1809. Entered at Stationers' Hall by R. Phillips on 27.10.09 and again on 2.11.14. Advertised in 1808 as 'published by Tabart and Co.', the price being shown as 2s.6d. 'with an allowance of the 25th book'.

197 (1) BLAIR, Rev. David. A school dictionary; or, Entick's English dictionary, abridged and adapted to the use of schools. Containing only the roots of words, and those of importance and utility, and omitting derivative, obsolete, vulgar and unusual words. By the Rev. David Blair, author of the English Grammar, Class Book, Reading Exercises, Grammar of Philosophy, &c. &c. London: printed for Richard Phillips; and to be had of all booksellers. 1809. [Price half-a-crown.] T. Gillet, Printer, Crown-court, Fleet-street.

17×10 cm. Pp.iv+232+4pp. bklist.
[BL, rebound

A short, much-simplified, dictionary – e.g. Y has only 19 words, Z, 11. It was entered at Stationers' Hall by R. Phillips on 12.10.09.

198 (1) BOAD, Henry. The English spelling book and expositor: being a new method of teaching children and adult persons to read, write, and understand the English tongue in less time, and with much greater ease, than has hitherto been taught. Containing ... [10 lines]. By Henry Boad, Writing-master at Colchester. The twenty-third edition, revised, corrected, and enlarged, by the Rev. Thomas Smith. [6 lines verse] London: printed for R. Baldwin; W. J. and J. Richardson; Scatcherd and Letterman; T. Boosey; Longman, Hurst, Rees and Orme; G. Wilkie and J. Robinson; Lackington, Allen and Co. and R. Phillips. 1805.

18.3×10.3 cm. Pr by Rider and Weed, Little Britain, West Smithfield. Pp.xi [xii]+130+2pp. Scatcherd and Letterman's bklist. Marbled bds, ¾ black roan g (not original?).
[BL

This edition was entered at Stationers' Hall by R. Phillips and others (not including Tabart) on 8.11.05. Phillips had ⅛ share. The book was priced at 1s.4d. in 1805 and 1806 and at 1s.6d. in 1807.

199 (1) BURNEY, William. The British Neptune; or, A history of the achievements of the Royal Navy, from the earliest periods to the present time. By William Burney, A.M. Master of the Naval Academy at Gosport, &c. &c. London: printed for Richard Phillips, Bridge-street, Blackfriars; and to be had of all booksellers in the United Kingdom. 1807. (Price 7s.6d. bound and lettered; or 10s.6d. on fine paper, elegantly bound and gilt.)

18.3×10.2 cm. Pr by Squire, Furnival's-Inn-court, Holborn, Pp.vi+490. Engvd FP of the Destruction of the Spanish Armada, Sepr 1588, +6 pls+folding map of the world pubd November 1 1806 by Richard Phillips. Calf.
[BL

By no means a book for children but interestingly written and very suitable for a boy entering the Navy, with fine plates of naval triumphs and victories. It was frequently advertised by Tabart and was one of the books bought for a boy who had 'a great desire to go to sea' in E. Kilner's *A visit to London*, 1808, 94 above.

BURNEY, William The British Plutarch; consisting of the lives of our most renowned admirals and commanders ...

Advertised in 1807 at 7s.6d. bound. Probably Burney's *The naval heroes of Great Britain* below.

200 (1) BURNEY, William. The naval heroes of Great Britain; or, accounts of the lives and actions of the distinguished admirals and commanders who have contributed to confer on Great-Britain the Empire of the Ocean. By William Burney, A.M. Master of the Naval Academy at Gosport, &c. &c. London: printed for Richard Phillips, 6, Bridge-street, Blackfriars, by J. G. Barnard, 57, Snow-hill; and to be had of all booksellers at Portsmouth, Gosport, Plymouth, Chatham, Deal, Cork, Liverpool, Bristol, Hull, Greenock, Newcastle, Falmouth, Leith, and other seaports. 1806. Price seven shillings and six-pence, bound and lettered.

17×10.1 cm. Pp.vi+ii+xii (Introduction)+435+Index xvi pp. (starting on v. of p.435)+9pp. bklist starting on v. of p.xvi. Engvd FP×6 (portraits)+3 other pls×6 portraits+6 maps. Calf, g.
[BL, rebound

This title was entered at Stationers' Hall by R. Phillips on 10.11.06.

The dedication on p.[iii] is to 'The Young Gentlemen who have been educated at the Naval Academy, Gosport, Hants' and is written from Naval Academy, Cold-Harbour, Gosport, 1806. The author's chief object, set out in the Preface, 'is to present young gentlemen of the navy ... with an accurate, though concise, view of the lives and maritime exploits of our renowned naval commanders, from the time of Elizabeth to the battle of Trafalgar'. It makes solid, but interesting, reading, quite suitable for older boys, and in Elizabeth Kilner's *A visit to London*, 1808, this book was bought for one of the boys who was aspiring to go to sea; so it was undoubtedly on sale in Tabart's Juvenile Library.

201 (1) CHAMBAUD, Lewis. The treasure of the French and English languages: containing I. A vocabulary, French and English. II. Common forms of speech upon the most familiar and useful subjects. III. A collection of proverbs, common sayings, maxims, &c. Being equally necessary to the French, and other foreigners, understanding French, to learn English; and the best, if not the only help extant, for them to attain the knowledge of it. By Lewis Chambaud. The twelfth edition, corrected and improved. London: printed for R. Baldwin; W. J. and J. Richardson; W. Lowndes; Scatcherd and Letterman;

Vernor, Hood, and Sharpe; C. Law; Lackington, and Co.; T. Boosey; Darton and Harvey; Longman, Hurst, Rees, and Orme; Cadell and Davies; J. Harris; Payne and Mackinlay; and R. Phillips. 1806. G. Woodfall, Printer, No.22, Paternoster-row.

17.6×11.7 cm. Pp.vi+274. No illusns. Calf.
[Hockliffe; BL

Tabart advertised this book in 1805.

202 (1) CROXALL, Samuel. Fables of Aesop.

Tabart advertised this title in 1805 but his name does not appear among the conger of publishers in the edition of that date that has been seen.

203 (1) A DICTIONARY OF POLITE LITERATURE: or, Fabulous history of the heathen gods and illustrious heroes. Vol. I [vol. II]. Proprietors. Scatcherd and Letterman; Longman and Rees; G. and J. Robinson; Leigh and Sotheby; G. Wilkie; J. Walker; T. Hurst; H. D. Symonds; Peacock and Sons; T. Ostell; Vernor and Hood; J. Mawman; J. and A. Arch; Lackington, Allen, and Co.; Wynne and Scholey; B. Crosby and Co.; J. Harris; J. Asperne; Cuthell and Martin; W. J. and J. Richardson; Blacks and Parry; Ogilvy and Son; J. Bagster; E. Lloyd; J. Booker; R. H. Westley; Champante and Whitrow; and Wilmot and Hill. 1804. [2 vols]

13.7×8.4 cm. Pr by C. Whittingham, Dean Street. Pp. unnumbered. Pictorial TPP engvd by Woodthorpe, 29 Fetter Lane, after Burney, +7 pls dated Dec. 3 1803; vol. II, 15 pls dated Dec. 3 1803 engvd by Dadley and Angus after Burney.
[BL, rebound

Tabart advertised this title several times between 1804 and 1807, in 2 volumes with 28 copperplates engraved by Angus after Burney, price 13s. in boards. However, no edition carrying his name, or that of Phillips, has been found.

It is included here because in E. Kilner's *A visit to London* this book was bought at Tabart's Juvenile Library and given to George Sandby as a present. 'When he reads of the many great crimes that were supposed by the heathens to be committed by their divinities', said the donor, 'he will, I doubt not, find additional reason to rejoice that he has been educated in the *Christian* religion.' In Mrs. Fenwick's *Visits to the Juvenile Library*, 43, this was one of the books selected.

204 (1) DODSLEY, Robert, and other authors. Fables of Aesop.

Tabart advertised this title in 1805 and 1807, price 3s.6d.

205 (1) EDGEWORTH, Maria.

The following titles were advertised by Tabart in 1807, but this advertisement should be read with caution in view of the following notice in Bent's *Monthly literary advertiser*, Jan. 10, 1810: 'What has appeared, or may hereafter be published, bearing her name, which is not printed for her Bookseller, J. Johnson, in St. Paul's Churchyard, is spurious.' The titles Tabart advertised are *Frank; Harry and Lucy; The little dog Trusty, the orange man, and the cherry orchard; Rosamund.*

206 (1) THE ENCYCLOPAEDIA OF WIT. Advertised in 1807, price 6s. in boards, with a frontispiece representing Hogarth's Laughing Audience, but not traced. An edition of 1811 was published by B. and R. Crosby.

The *British critic*, vol, 21, p.91, said of it: 'The print is very small, and the pages very numerous ... each anecdote or jest has a title prefixed ... [which] serves to catch the eye, and the book to catch the penny.'

207 (1) EVENING AMUSEMENTS; or, A new book of games and forfeits: containing, among other games, The old soldier, – Short answers, – The trencher, Evasion, – How d'ye do? – Five vowels, Contradiction, – Key of the garden-gate, – The aviary, Buffy in the shades, – and Whittington. With full and plain directions for crying the forfeits, and numerous amusing and diverting penances, for ladies as well as gentlemen. London: printed and sold by Dean and Munday, Threadneedle-street. Price one shilling. [1826]

15.2×8.2 cm. Pp.36. H/c engvd FP dated Feb. 1 1826. Plain green covers.
[Osborne

No Tabart edition of this title has been found, but he advertised it in 1807. It is included here in case it is a reprint of Tabart's book. The list of games may be of interest.

208 (1) GOLDSMITH, Rev. J. An easy grammar of geography. Intended as a companion and introduction to the 'Geography for the Use of Schools,' by the same author. With maps. A new edition. By the Rev. J. Goldsmith. London: printed for Richard Phillips, No.71, St. Paul's Church Yard; and to be had of all booksellers, with a full allowance to schools. 1804. Printed by W. Flint, Old Bailey.

13.4×8 cm. Pp.viii+9–156 (or more). 7 folding maps, two dated 1802, both engvd by J. C. Russell (on one, 30 Noble St. Foster Lane), 5 dated 1803, of which FP engvd by Neck (?), Strand, 2 by J. C. Russell+2 unsigned. Marbled bds, red roan sp.
[Renier

This book has not been found with Tabart's imprint (however, the edition of 1803 has not been seen) but he often advertised it.

Reviews: The *Critical review*, Feb. 1804, p.237, said of Phillips's edition of 1803 that 'this little abstract contains the more strictly geographic part of [*Geography on a popular plan*] with some useful additions; particularly a vocabulary of the names of places, properly accented, and questions with their answers, as exercises ...'. *The juvenile review*, 1817, explained that 'it is in the form of a lesson-book, to be learned by heart', and asserted that the author of *The juvenile review* had always found the 'copious examination in geography in the form of questions, to be answered by the pupils from memory ... to be a source of amusement.'

As proof of the book's success, in 1811 Richard Phillips published the 31st edition, printed by W. Flint, Old Bailey; an edition of 1813 was published by Longmans.

(2) Title as (1) to ... introduction to the Geography on a Popular Plan for Schools and Young Persons, by the same author. With maps. A new edition. By the Rev. J. Goldsmith. London: printed for Richard Phillips, No.6, Bridge Street, Blackfriars; and to be had of all booksellers; with a full allowance to schools. 1805. T. Gillet, Salisbury Square. Price 2s.6d. bound.

13×8 cm. Pp.vi+144. Folding map FP+6 other folding maps dated 1802, 1803, 1805.
[BL, rebound

209 (1) GREGORY, Rev. George. The elements of a polite education; carefully selected from the letters of the late Right Honble Philip Dormer Stanhope, Earl of Chesterfield, to his son. By G. Gregory, D.D. author of Essays Historical and Moral; of The Economy of Nature, &c. &c. London: printed for R. Phillips, No.71, St. Paul's Church-yard, and sold by T. Hurst and J. Wallis, Paternoster-row; by Carpenter and Co. Old Bond Street; by Lackington, Allen, and Co. Finsbury-square; and by all other booksellers. S. Hamilton, Printer, Falcon-court, Fleet-street. (Price 4s.6d. bound.]

16.9×9.4 cm. Pp.[xii]+454 inc. 2pp. bklist. Engvd FP dated July 1st 1800.
[BL, rebound

Advertised in 1804 as Tabart's publication.

Review: The *British critic*, vol. 17, p.447: 'Dr. Gregory has condescended to extract from them [the letters] all the matter that he deemed valuable. ... His Lordship's Letters thus compressed may certainly be put into the hands of youth as models of epistolary style, and as containing much practical knowledge of mankind.'

(2) Title as (1) to ... late Earl of Chesterfield, to his son. By George Gregory, D.D. author of Essays Historical and Moral; the Economy of Nature; the New Dictionary of Arts and Sciences, &c. &c. A new edition. London: printed for Richard Phillips, No.6, Bridge Street, Blackfriars, by W. Flint, Green Arbour Court, S. Sepulchre's. [Price 5s. bound.]

17×10.2 cm. Pp.[xii]+452+4pp. bklist. FP dated Feby 10 1807. Calf.
[BL

210 (1) GREGORY, Rev. George. Letters on literature, taste, and composition, addressed to his son, by George Gregory, D.D. late Vicar of West-ham, domestic chaplain to the Bishop of Llandaff, &c. &c. In two volumes. Vol. I [II]. London: printed for Richard Phillips, Bridge-street, Blackfriars. 1808. T. Gillet, Crown-court.

16.9×8.7 cm. Pp.vii [viii]+287; iv+336 inc. 15pp. advts.
[BL, rebound

This title was advertised in 1808 as 'published by Tabart and Co.', 2 volumes, 13s. in boards or 14s. bound and lettered. It was published posthumously.

The author discusses subjects such as The Sublime, The Pathetic, The Ludicrous, Purity (not moral, but of style), Dr. Johnson, Voyages and Travels, Origin of Poetry, etc. In a letter addressed to his publisher the author said 'that this work contained the result of the observations of his whole life, on every subject of taste and literature.'

211 (1) GREGORY, Rev. George. Popular lectures on experimental philosophy, astronomy, and chemistry, intended chiefly for the use of students and young persons.

This title was advertised in 1808 as 'published by Tabart and Co.' in two volumes with 35 engravings, price 13s. in boards or 14s. bound and lettered.

212 (1) HARRY CLINTON, a tale for youth. [6 lines verse.] London: printed for J. Johnson, St. Paul's Church-yard, by T. Bensley, Bolt Court. 1804.

Pp.xii+431 [432]. No illusns.
[UCLA

This story was advertised by Tabart in 1807. It is a tale for young people, not for children.

213 (1) HAYS, Mary. Female biography; or, Memoirs of illustrious and celebrated women, of all ages and countries, alphabetically arranged. By Mary Hays. In six volumes. Volume I [–VI]. London: printed for Richard Phillips, 71, St. Paul's Church-yard. By Thomas Davison, White-Friars. 1803.

17.1×9.5 cm. Pp.xxvi+316; 404; 444; 504; 527; 476.
[BL; Bod.

Tabart advertised this title and doubtless it was on sale in his shop. He described it as 'a suitable companion at school to young ladies who are finishing their education.' However, it can hardly be described as a children's book. In her Preface the author says 'My pen has been taken up in the cause, and for the benefit, of my own sex. For their improvement, and to their entertainment, my labours have been devoted.' Mary Hays was a good friend to Mrs. Eliza Fenwick and often came to that distraught lady's rescue when she was hard up.

Review: in The *British critic*, vol. 22, p.93: 'The name of our editor must be familiar to our readers; and the whimsicality of her principles and opinions, to use no harsher term, we have before reprobated. The same unfortunate bias predominates in this work ... yet the whole, though imperfect, is an entertaining work, and shows a considerable degree of taste, good sense, and judgment ...'.

214 (1) THE HISTORY OF BRITISH BIRDS: illustrated by twelve coloured engravings of birds, their nests, & eggs. By the author of The History of Domestic Quadrupeds. London: printed for Richard Phillips, No.6, Bridge-street, Blackfriars; by C. Squire, Furnival's-Inn-court. 1807.

15.1×8.7 cm. Pp.[iv]+[5] 6–180. FP+11 h/c undated pls. Grey-green or brown bds, ¾ red leather g.
[Miami; private coll.

Tabart advertised this attractive book from 1804 to 1812 but no copy with his name on the title-page has been seen. In 1804 and 1805 it was listed at 2s.6d. with no mention of *coloured* engravings. It was occasionally advertised as *The history of seventy-four British birds*, price 5s. half-bound, the higher price doubtless applying to the coloured version. 60 above is by the same author.

'This work is dedicated to those good and humane Children, who are satisfied with the Contemplation of the Beauties of Nature, and who never disgrace themselves by robbing birds ... of their Eggs or their Young ...'. 74 different birds are described, as well as an account of eagles in general. The descriptions are written in a way to interest children, with anecdotes introduced.

215 (1) THE JUVENILE LIBRARY, including a complete course of instruction on every useful subject: particularly natural and experimental philosophy, moral philosophy, natural history, botany, ancient and modern history, biography, geography and the manners and customs of nations, ancient and modern languages, English law, penmanship, mathematics, and the belles lettres. With prize productions of young students; and a monthly distribution of prizes, value fifteen guineas, and upwards. Vol. I [to vol. VI]. London: printed by T. Gillet, Salisbury-square, Fleet-street, for R. Phillips. Sold by T. Hurst, 32, Paternoster Row, London; and by all other booksellers in Great-Britain and Ireland. [Price 6s.6d. in boards.] 1800 [to 1803].

17.9×10.2 cm. Marbled bds, ¾ brown leather, sp g.
[BL, rebound; Bod.; Miami

Vol. I: Pp.iv+428. Engvd FP×2+20 other pls, 2 folding, some×2, one leaf with a pl. on both sides.
Vol. II, 1801: Pp.410. 15 pls, of which one folding.
Vol. III, 1801: Pp.370. 17 pls, of which 6 are on 3 leaves.
Vol. IV, 1802: Pp.444. 9 pls, of which one folding and 2 on one leaf.
Vol. V, 1802: Pp.viii+432. 19 pls, 8 on 4 leaves, one folding.
Vo. VI, 1803: Pp.viii+448. 5 folding pls, 5 others, of which 2 on one leaf.

The plates are arranged differently in different sets of volumes and the numbers of plates vary. The Preface is dated July 25, 1800, from London.

This handsome production contains a variety of subject-matter, as the title shows, including Jauffret's *The little hermitage* and *Visits to the Botanic Garden at Paris*, serialized. This enterprise is very similar in design to Tabart's *Juvenile Miscellany*, 84 above.

(2) THE JUVENILE ENCYCLOPAEDIA. Title otherwise as (1) to date . . . 1802.

Vols I, II and III not traced. Vols IV–VI, pp. as (1).
[Baldwin

216 (1) MAVOR, William Fordyce. A circle of the arts and sciences, for the use of schools and young persons, containing a clear yet brief explanation of the principles and objects of the most important branches of human knowledge. Illustrated with engravings. By William Mavor, LL.D. Author of the Universal History, British Nepos, Elements of Natural History, Universal Short Hand, &c. &c. &c. London: printed for Richard Phillips, Bridge-street, Blackfriars. 1808. By T. Gillet, Crown-court, Fleet-street.

16.7×9.5 cm. Pp.480 (inc. 4pp. Phillips's bklist)+12pp. Longman's bklist. Folding engvd FP by Cooper dated Sept 9 1808+3 other pls dated various days in Sept 1808.
[BL; NLS

The Advertisement is dated May 1, 1808, from Woodstock. This is a (very dry) book of concentrated information, in question-and-answer style, on a great variety of subjects. It was advertised in 1808 as 'published by Tabart and Co., price 4s.6d. bound.'

217 MAVOR, William Fordyce. Eton Latin grammar, with notes by Dr. Mavor.

This book was first published in 1796. It was advertised by Tabart in 1804 and 1805 but not traced. Eton College Library has no edition printed before 1825. In Aikin's *Poetry for children*, 1805, it was priced at 1s.6d. with a liberal allowance to purchasers by the dozen or hundred. The 30th edition was listed in Johnson's *History of Greece in easy verse*, 1807, 79(1), but this was Phillips's advertisement.

218 (1) MAVOR, William Fordyce. A father's gift to his children; consisting of original essays, tales, fables, reflections, &c. [1 line Latin. Hor.] By William Mavor, LL.D. Vicar of Hurley, Berks. and Chaplain to the Earl of Moira. Vol. I [II]. London: printed for Richard Phillips, No.71, St. Paul's Church-yard, by Slatter and Munday, Oxford. 1805.

16.3×9.8 cm. ½-title. Pp.xii+294; xvi+301+3pp. bklist. Full calf, g.
[BL; Osborne

This title was first published by E. Newbery in 1798 as *Youth's miscellany; or, A father's gift to his children* (Roscoe J240). It was advertised in 1808 as 'published by Tabart and

Co.', two volumes, price 9s. in boards or 10s.6d. bound. Sherwood, Neely, and Jones reprinted it in 1814, and it was issued in America in 1815 by M. Carey, Philadelphia. Welch 827.

A collection of solemn pieces in prose and verse written with an earnest desire to improve young people, amusement being but little considered. The author's Advertisement to vol. I concludes: 'Few have written more than I have done, for the use of young persons; or, let me thankfully add, with more uniform encouragement; and I desire no other epitaph to mark my grave, than – Here lies "The Children's Friend."' The book is dedicated to the Countess of Moira, Nov. 30, 1804, from Woodstock. The BL copy is inscribed 'The Gift of a Father to his dutiful Son Thomas Williams – 1 June 1807'.

Reviews: The *Guardian of education*, vol. iv, p.190, said that 'Upon the whole ... we can recommend "The Father's Gift" as a proper present for any parent to bestow, who wishes to furnish his children in their youthful days with a book of pleasing instruction.' More non-committally, the *British critic*, vol. 25, p.455, wrote: 'The volumes are neatly printed, and contain a vast variety of articles.'

219 (1) MAVOR, William Fordyce. The history of England, from the earliest records, to the year 1803. By William Mavor, LL.D. Vicar of Hurley in Berkshire, author of the British Nepos, &c. &c. In two volumes. Vol. I [vol. II]. London: printed for R. Phillips, 71, St. Paul's Church-yard; and sold by all booksellers. 1804.

13.9×8.2 cm. Pr by T. Gillet, Salisbury-square. Pp.[iv]+392; [iii]+464. Folding FP map engvd by Jones and Smith, Beaufort Buildings, Strand, +16 pls dated variously Jan. 1 or Jan. 20 1804 or Feb. 2 1804, engvd by Isaac Taylor (who designed his own) or by R. Reeve after E. F. Burney, or Craig. In vol. II, 11 pls, no FP, dated as in vol. I, engvd by Isaac Taylor (who was also the artist), or by Reeve or W & I Cooke after Burney. Mottled calf, 2 black labels on each sp, g.
[UCLA

This was one of the books enjoyed by Maria Sandby in E. Kilner's *A visit to London*.

Although in 1804 this book was advertised as with 27 engravings, 2 vols., 12s., or 10s.6d. small paper, in 1805 the 2 vols were 12s. in sheep with nearly 50 copper-plates, but there was also a small edition, 2 vols, 10s. in sheep.

220 MAVOR, William Fordyce. A history of Greece, from the earliest periods, till its reduction into a Roman province.

Advertised in 1804 as 'just published', 2 vols., 10s. It was one of the books bought by the visitors to Mr. Tabart's bookshop in E. Kilner's *A visit to London*, 94; and so it qualifies for inclusion here.

221 MAVOR, William Fordyce. The history of Rome, from the foundation of the city to the termination of the Eastern Empire.

Advertised in 1804 in 3 vols., price 15s. in boards, with maps and prints. However, other advertisements in 1804 and 1805 gave the price as 13s.6d.

In E. Kilner's *A visit to London* it was one of the books chosen by a young visitor to Tabart's bookshop, which is the reason for including it here.

222 (1) MAVOR, William Fordyce. Natural history, for the use of schools, and of young persons in general; founded on the Linnaean arrangement of animals; with popular descriptions in the manner of Goldsmith and Buffon. Illustrated by forty-six copper-plates, representing one hundred and sixty-six of the most curious objects. By William Mavor, LL.D. Vicar of Hurley, Berkshire, Chaplain to the Earl of Dumfries, author of the British Nepos, Abridgment of Plutarch's Lives, the Universal Short Hand, &c. &c. &c. [2 quotes, Edgeworth and More.] Second edition, revised. London: printed for R. Phillips, No.71, St. Paul's Church-yard. By T. Gillet, Salisbury-square, Fleet-street. Sold by T. Hurst, J. Wallis, and West and Hughes, Paternoster Row; Carpenter and Co. Old Bond-street; Wilson and Spence, York; E. Balfour, Edinburgh; and by all other booksellers; with the usual allowance to schools. 1801. (Price four shillings and sixpence bound.)

17.5×9.7 cm. Pp.xi [xii]+343+4pp. advts starting on v. of p.343+1p. Directions to Binder. 44 pls (no FP seen) pr on both sides of the paper, on 22 leaves, most having 2 or more subjects. Calf, sp g.
[Private coll.; Miami

Dedicated to the author's son, William James Mavor, of the Charter-House School. In his Preface Dr. Mavor regrets that 'there is no work on this subject which is not either too jejune, or too extensive – too scientific, or too miscellaneous, for the purposes of schools'; and a footnote says that 'Buffon, with all his excellencies, is absolutely inadmissible into the library of a young lady, both on account of his immodesty and his impiety.'

This title is not one of Tabart's publications but it is mentioned in E. Kilner's *A visit to London*, 1808.

223 A NEW HISTORICAL GAME OF THE HISTORY OF ENGLAND. This was advertised in 1804, 'just published', 12s.

It may be *Historical pastime or A new game of the history of England from the Conquest to the Accession of George the Third*, first published by J. Harris and J. Wallis in 1802 (CBY 154). The next edition, published in 1803 by the same publishers, was a coloured engraved sheet, 22¼×20⅝″ with 150 numbered medallions representing events and persons in English history, mounted on linen and folded into a case.
[BL; V & A; Gum. 3276

224 OLIVER, Edward, D.D. A short practical grammar of the English language. This was advertised in 1810, price 3s.

225 PALMER, Charlotte. Grammatical harmony; or, The conjugation of verbs in rhyme. This was advertised in 1810, price 1 shilling, but has not been traced.

226 [PELHAM, Margaret]. The London primer, being a new, easy, and fascinating introduction to the English language.

This book has not been traced but it was frequently advertised by Tabart and by Phillips with, variously, 50, 60 or nearly 100 cuts, price 6d. The author may, or may not, be Dorothy Kilner. It is significant that the author of *The parent's . . . first catechism* is given as 'Margaret' Pelham, author of *The London primer*. There can be little doubt that the publisher intended to give the impression that the author was Miss Kilner because, when Richard Phillips entered the title at Stationers' Hall on 9.1.05 he showed it as by 'M. Pelham, author of *Dialogues for children*, etc.

A later edition (not specified) was entered at Stationers' Hall by Phillips on 5.9.14 and the 86th edition, with a clock face, was entered by Phillips and John Souter on 17.3.15. The title was shown as *The London primer or Mother's spelling book*.

This was one of the books bought for the children in E. Kilner's *A visit to London* when they visited Tabart's shop.

227 (1) PELHAM, Margaret. The parents' and tutors' first catechism of the dawnings of juvenile knowledge. Intended to be committed to memory, as soon as children can read, and calculated to excite their curiosity, and enlarge their minds. By M. Pelham, author of the London Primer. London: printed for Richard Phillips, and to be had of all booksellers, with the full allowance to schools. Price one shilling sewed, or 1s.1½d with a strong parchment back, and 13 to the dozen. G. Sidney, Printer, Northumberland-street, Strand. [Text of cover, no TP. N.d. but *c*.1812]

12.5×10 cm. Pp.64. Pr clock-face with movable hands; text illusns. Pr card covers.
[BL, bound with others

Entered by R. Phillips at Stationers' Hall on 4.11.12.

(2) Title as (1) to . . . minds. By Margaret Pelham, author of The London Primer. London: printed for Richard Phillips; sold by John Souter, No.1, Paternoster-row; and to be had of all booksellers. Price one shilling sewed, or 1s.1½d with a strong parchment back, and 13 to the dozen. [Text of cover, no TP. N.d. but *c*.1815]

12.3×10.3 cm. Pr by Maurice, Howford-buildings, Fenchurch-street. Pp.64. Pr clock-face with movable hands; text illusns inc. 3 fp maps with text on other side. Buff pr card covers, bklist on lower v.
[BL

228 ROBINSON, Rev. John. Ancient history for the use of schools; exhibiting a summary view of the rise, progress, revolutions, decline and fall of the various nations of antiquity.

Advertised in 1808 as 'published by Tabart and Co.', price 3s. bound.

229 (1) ROBINSON, Rev. John. A grammar of history; ancient and modern: with questions for exercise; by means of which, history may be practically taught in schools. By John Robinson, D.D. Late of Christ's College, Cambridge; Master of the Free Grammar-School at Ravenstondale; author of the Theological Dictionary, &c. Brevis esse labora. Hor. The tenth edition. London: printed for R. Phillips; sold by J. Souter, 1, Paternoster-row; and by all booksellers. 1816. Price 4 shillings bound.

14×7.9 cm. Pr by W. Molineux, 5, Bream's Buildings, Chancery Lane. Pp.vii+[8]–185 [186]+2pp. advts. One folding chart of the world and one folding map of the Roman Empire. Calf.
[UCLA

In 1808 this title was advertised as 'published by Tabart and Co.', price 3s. bound.

This book contains a succession of dry facts, broken up into numbered paragraphs devoid of any pretence at arousing the student's interest. However, Richard Phillips thought otherwise, according to an advertisement in Lynch's *World described*, 1820: 'My ingenious and learned Friend, the Rev. Dr. Robinson, of Ravenstonedale, ... has, with singular ability, succeeded in simplifying the Study of History so as to render it, for the first time, compatible with the routine of School Business'.

230 (1) ROBINSON, Rev. John. Modern history, for the use of schools: exhibiting a summary view of the rise, progress, revolutions, and present state, of the various nations of the world, from the fall of the Roman Empire, to the year 1807. By the Rev. John Robinson, of Christ's College, Cambridge; and Master of the Grammar-school at Ravenstonedale in Westmorland. London; printed for Richard Phillips, 6, Bridge-street, Blackfriars, by T. Gillet, Wild-court. 1807. [Price six shillings, bound and lettered.]

17×9.7 cm. Pp.[iv]+577 [578]. Folding map FP dated 1808.
[BL, rebound

The Advertisement, dated from Ravenstonedale, April 16, 1807, explains that the author has not included the history of England as that would require too much room, out of proportion to the space allotted to other countries, and he recommends the histories of Dr. Mavor, Mrs. Charlotte Smith and Dr. Goldsmith.

231 SMITH, Charlotte. A history of England. This title was often advertised by Phillips but in 1808 Tabart advertised it as his publication, with the title *The lady's history of England* from the earliest records to the peace of Amiens, 1802, with Views of the State of Society and Manners in each Age, in a Series of Letters, addressed to a young Lady at School. In three volumes, 12mo., price 15s. bound and lettered.

232 TALES OF FORMER TIMES; being a collection of old English metrical romances, formed upon acts of heroism, honour, and generosity. This title was advertised in 1810, price 9s., neatly bound and lettered.

233 TRIMMER, Sarah (Kirby). Little spelling book. This title was advertised in 1807, price 6d. J. Johnson and J. Hatchard published an edition in 1800.

234 WATKINS, Rev. John. Portable cyclopedia. This title was advertised in 1808 as 'published by Tabart and Co.', price 10s.6d. in boards or 12s. bound.

235 (1) WATKINS, Rev. John. Scripture biography.

An edition earlier than 1809 was probably published in 1804–5 but has not been traced. It was priced at 4s.6d. in boards or 5s. bound, and was advertised several times by Tabart, as well as by Richard Phillips. It was one of the 'very clever' religious books mentioned in E. Kilner's *A visit to London*, 1805 and 1808.

(2) Scripture biography: or Lives and characters of the principal personages recorded in the Old and New Testaments. The second edition, corrected and enlarged. By John Watkins, LL.D. [3 lines prose. St. Paul.] London: printed for Richard Phillips, No.6, Bridge-street, Blackfriars. 1809. Price 6s. bound. J. Adlard, Printer, Duke-street, Smithfield.

17.8×10.3 cm. Pp.x [xii]+592. No FP present in BL copy; 11 pls. Calf, black label, g, on sp.
[BL; Baldwin

Entered at Stationers' Hall by R. Phillips on 4.1.09. Puffed by E. Kilner in *A visit to London*, 1805 and 1808.

236 (1) WATKINS, Rev. John. A universal biographical and historical dictionary. Containing a faithful account of the lives, actions, and characters, of the most eminent persons of all ages and all countries; also the revolutions of states, and the succession of sovereign princes, ancient and modern. Collected from the best authorities, by John Watkins, A.M. LL.D. [One line Latin. Cicero.] London: printed by T. Davison and T. Gillet, Fleet-street, for R. Phillips, No.71, St. Paul's Church-yard; sold by T. Hurst and J. Wallis, Paternoster Row; ... Wilson and Spence, York; J. Archer and H. Colbert, Dublin; Brash and Reid, and J. Murdoch, Glagow; E. Balfour, J. Watson, and W. Mudie, Edinburgh. 1800. [Price 10s.6d. boards, or 12s. bound and lettered.]

21.5×11.9 cm. Pp. unnumbered. No illusns. Brown leather, g.
[BL

The Preface is dated April 7, 1800.

This book is included because Tabart often advertised it. There may have been a later edition with his imprint, not yet traced.

237 WINTER EVENINGS RATIONAL AMUSEMENTS. This title was advertised in 1810, 'being 14 pleasing and instructive games and forfeits'; new and improved edition, 1s.6d. It may = *Evening amusements*. 207 above.

The book of trades

Editions after 1805 of *The book of trades* have plates of various dates and the dates vary in different copies of one edition. The dates given in the bibliographical descriptions are not necessarily all found in one copy, but are representative of the changes as, presumably, the plates became worn.

16 (1) THE BOOK OF TRADES, or Library of the useful arts. Part I. Illustrated with eighteen copperplates. London: printed for Tabart and Co. No.157, New Bond-street: and to be had of all dealers in books. 1804. [Price three shillings for each of the three parts plain, or five shillings for each part with the plates beautifully coloured.]

13.7×8.5 cm. Pr by R. Taylor and Co. Black-Horse-court. Pp.[iv]+139 (p.[140] = bklist, 7 items). Most pls dated Aug. 11 1804 but 1 pl. dated Aug. 1 1804 and signed 'Deeres sc.' Marbled bds, red roan sp g.
[V & A; private coll.

(1A) Title as (1) except that the price is three shillings and sixpence for each of the three parts plain, or five shillings for each part ... coloured.

13.3×8.2 cm. Pr by R. Taylor & Co. Black-Horse-court. Pp. as (1). 18 pls pubd by R. Phillips dated July 2, 1804, or July 7th. Marbled bds, red roan sp g.
[BL, rebound; Exeter, with pls dated Aug. 11 1804; other locations for Part I, price unknown: Baldwin; S, many entries inc. 10.12.80/51

Part I was entered at Stationers' Hall by R. Phillips on 28.7.04. Three volumes were listed in MLA in Aug. 1805, supporting the suggestion that there was no third part in 1804 – see Part III below.

The prices of Part I are shown in advertisements variously as three shillings and three shillings and sixpence for plain plates; but always five shillings for coloured plates. Up to, and including, Part II, 1810, all other parts seem to have been three shillings plain; but the prices for coloured versions vary, as shown.

Part II, 1804. Illustrated with twenty-one copperplates, title otherwise as Part I.

13.1×7.7 cm. Pr by Taylor & Co. Black-Horse-court. Pp.[iv]+133+3pp. Tabart's bklist starting on v. of p.133. Pls in BL copy dated July 2 or 7 or Aug. 11 1804, by either Phillips or Tabart, but in Bod.'s copy all are by Tabart, dated Aug. 11 1804. Marbled bds, roan sp g.
[BL; Bod.; S 2.7.74/263, 5.6.80/51; private coll.

R. Phillips entered Part II at Stationers' Hall on 14.9.04.

Part III. No edition of Part II dated 1804 has been found and probably Part III, 1805, takes its place, especially as most of the plates are dated 1804.

All three parts were reprinted in America in 1807 by Jacob Johnson, Philadelphia and Richmond, Virginia (Welch 116).

The excellent plates in these volumes clearly illustrate the processes of every-day trades and professions. The text is simple and factual. Elizabeth Kilner puffed the book in her *A visit to London*, 94, and so did Mrs. Fenwick in *Visits to the Juvenile Library*, 43. It appears to have been one of Tabart's most successful publications.

Reviews: in The *Guardian of education*, vol. iv, p.304: 'This is a very amusing and instructive work, from which a general idea of a number of useful arts carried out in this and other Kingdoms, may be gained. Subjects of this kind are very proper for young minds to be occupied with in their hours of amusement, when they are not proposed in too scientific a way. ... The prints give a lively idea of what he [the manufacturer] is about. A few of the Prints relate to the employment of women, namely, the Straw-Hat Maker, the Lace-Maker; the Milliner; the Feather-Worker; the Laundress. These we think, in general, frivolous, excepting that the Prints are pretty. We recommend this Book as a valuable acquisition to the Juvenile Library. The Plates are uncommonly good.'

The juvenile review, 1817, quoted part of the above review and added: 'The Book of Trades is now published in one compact volume: we have seen a little book entitled, "Sequel to the Book of Trades," which is equally deserving the notice of our readers.' (This is, presumably, *The history of discoveries and inventions ... being a sequel to The Book of Trades*, 59.)

(2) THE BOOK OF TRADES, or Library of the useful arts. Part I. Illustrated with twenty-three copper-plates. The second edition. London: printed for Tabart and Co. No.157, New Bond-street: and to be had of all dealers in books. 1805. [Price three shillings for either of the three parts plain, or four shillings and sixpence for each part with the plates beautifully coloured.]

13×8 cm. Pr by R. Taylor & Co., 38, Shoe-lane. Pp.[iv]+170. FP n.d., most pls dated Aug. 11th 1804, the last three Oct. 4, 1805. Marbled bds, red roan sp.
[Private coll.

Part II, 1805. Illustrated with twenty-four copper-plates. Title otherwise as Part I, 1805.

13.4×8.6 cm. Pr by R. Taylor & Co., 38, Shoe-lane. Pp.[iv]+164. FP dated Sepr 1 1805, other pls same date or Aug. 1804. Marbled bds, red roan sp.
[Private coll.; S 2.6.75/205; NYCL

Part III, 1805. Illustrated with twenty copper-plates. [No edition shown.] [Price three shillings for either of the three parts plain, or four shillings for each part with the plates beautifully coloured.] Title otherwise as Part I, 1805.

13.4×8.2 cm. Pr by R. Taylor & Co., 38, Shoe-lane. Pp.[iv]+158+8 or 10pp. advts. FP dated Oct. 23 1804+19 other pls dated variously as FP, or Aug. 11 1804 or Jan. 1805. Marbled bds, red or black roan sp g. (See fig. 5)
[Baldwin; V & A; UCLA; private colls; S 2.6.75/205 &c. &c.; Liv U

This edition may have served also as Part III of the 1st edition.

(3) THE BOOK OF TRADES, or Library of the useful arts. Part I. Illustrated with twenty-three copper-plates. The third edtion. London: printed for Tabart and Co. No.157, New Bond-street: and to be had of all dealers in books. 1806. [Price three shillings for either of the three parts plain, or four shillings and sixpence for each part with the plates beautifully coloured.]

13.7×8.7 cm. Pr by R. Taylor and Co. 38, Shoe-lane. Pp.[iv]+152. FP dated Sepr 1 1805, other pls dated variously Aug. 1 or 11, 1804, Oct. 4 1805, Nov. 14th 1805, Jan. 1 1806 or as FP. Marbled bds, red roan sp g.
[BL; Osborne; Hockliffe; Opie; Baldwin; CUL; UCLA, h/c; Birm.; Renier; S 10.10.79/20, &c.

Part II, 1806. Illustrated with twenty-four copper-plates. Title otherwise as Part I, 1806.

13.7×8.4 cm. Pr by Barnard and Sultzer, Water Lane, Fleet Street. Pp.[iv]+163. FP dated Sepr 1 1805; other pls dated variously as FP or Aug. 11 1804, Nov. 14 1805, Oct. 4 1805 or 1806, some by R. Phillips. Marbled bds, red roan sp g.
[BL; Osborne; Opie; V & A; Baldwin; CUL; UCLA, h/c; S 10.10.79/20 &c; Hockliffe, h/c; private coll.; Renier, imp.; TCCU, imp.

Part III, 1807. Illustrated with twenty copper-plates. A new edition, corrected ... Title otherwise as Part I, 1806.

13.7×8.7 cm. Pr by C. Squire, Furnival's-Inn-court, Holborn. Pp.[iv]+158+16 or 18pp. bklist. FP dated Oct. 23 1804+19 pls dated variously as FP or Jan. 1805, Aug. 11 1804, Sep. 14 1806 or n.d. Marbled bds, green or red roan sp g.
[Osborne; Hockliffe, h/c; CUL; FCB pp.161–8; S 27.7.84/859 &c.; private coll.; Opie

(4) THE BOOK OF TRADES, or Library of the useful arts. Part I. Illustrated with twenty-three copper-plates. The fourth edition. London: printed for Tabart and Co. No.157, New Bond-street: and to be had of all dealers in books. 1810. [Price three shillings for either of the three parts plain, or four shillings and sixpence coloured.]

13.8×8.4 cm. Pr by W. Flint, Old Bailey. Pp.[iv]+210+2pp. bklist. Pls dated Aug. 1 or 11 1804, Oct. 4 1805, Jan. 1 1806 or n.d. Bds, red roan sp g.
[Hockliffe, h/c; Melb.; Miami; S 27.7.84/835

Part II, 1810. Title otherwise as Part I, 1810.

13.3×8.4 cm. Pr by W. Flint, Old Bailey. Pp.[iv]+188+12pp. bklist. FP and pls dated 1804–1808. Marbled bds, red roan sp.
[Norwich

Part III 1810 has not been located and may not have been published.

(5) THE BOOK OF TRADES, or Library of the useful arts. Part I. Illustrated with twenty-three copper plates. The fourth edition. London: printed for R. Phillips, No.7, Great Bridge-street, and to be had of all dealers in books. 1811. [Price three shillings and sixpence for either of the three parts, plain; or five shillings, coloured.]

13.5×8.2 cm. Pr by W. Flint, Old Bailey. Pp.[iv]+210+2pp. Tabart's bklist. FP dated Aug. 11 1804 or Sepr 1 1805, by Tabart & Co., other pls n.d. or Aug. 1 or 11 1804, Oct. 4 1805 or Jan. 1 1806. Brown paper-covered bds, red roan sp g.
[BL, rebound; S 5.2.68/22, 16.3.70/60 and 23.11.78/145; Baldwin; CUL has also 4pp. bklist of B. and R. Crosby; TCCU

Part II, 1811. Printed for Richard Phillips ... Otherwise as Part I, 1811.

13.5×8.2 cm. Pr by W. Flint, Old Bailey. Pp.[iv]+188+4pp. B. and R. Crosby's bklist in some copies. FP dated Aug. 11 1804 or Sepr 1 1805, by Tabart & Co., +22 pls dated variously Aug. 11 1804, Sepr 1 1805, Oct. 4 1805, Nov. 14 1805, Sep. 14 1808 or 1806, or n.d. Brown paper over bds, red roan sp g.
[V & A; CUL with Crosby's bklist; BL (rebound) and UCLA with 12pp. Phillips's bklist; Miami; S 27.7.84/835 &c.

Part III, 1811. Otherwise as Part I, 1811.

13.4×8.4 cm. Pr by W. Flint, Old Bailey. Pp.[iv]+158+18pp. bklist of Tabart's Juvenile Library. FP dated Oct. 23 1804, other pls same date or Aug. 11 1804, Jan. 1805 or Sep. 14 1806 (all by Tabart) or n.d.
[UCLA

(6) THE BOOK OF TRADES, or Library of the useful arts. Part III. Illustrated with twenty copper-plates. A new edition, corrected. London: printed for R. Phillips, No.7, Great Bridge-steet [*sic*]: and to be had of all dealers in books. 1811. [Price three shillings for either of the three parts plain, or four shillings and sixpence for each part with the plates beautifully coloured.]

13.5×8.1 cm. Pr by J. Adlard, Duke-street, Smithfield. Pp.[iv]+160+16pp. Phillips's bklist. FP dated Oct. 23 1804, other pls Aug. 11 1804, Jan. 1805 or n.d. Marbled bds, green roan sp g.
[CUL; Wandsworth; Baldwin; Melb.; Miami; S 27.7.84/835, h/c, &c.

(7) THE BOOK OF TRADES; or, Library of the useful arts. Part I. Illustrated with twenty-three copper-plates. The sixth edition. London: printed for R. Phillips, sold by J. Souter, No.1, Paternoster-row, and to be had of all booksellers. 1815. [Price three shillings and sixpence for either of the three parts, plain; or five shillings coloured.]

13.6×8.4 cm. Pr (on p.ii) by W. Lewis, St. John's Square, but on p.210 pr by W. Flint, Old Bailey. Pp.iv+210+2pp. Tabart's bklist. FP dated Aug. 11 1804, other pls dated as FP or Aug. 1 1804, Sepr 1 1805, Oct. 4 1805 or Jan 1 1806, all by Tabart. Marbled bds, red or green roan sp g.
[BL; CUL; UCLA; private coll.

A note on v. of TP reads: 'The Editor of this useful work will thankfully receive any hint for its improvement, from persons engaged in any of the trades or professions described.' The dated plates are very worn.

Part II, 1815. Title otherwise as Part I.

13.7×8.4 cm. Pr by W. Lewis, St. John's Square. Pp.[iv]+186+2pp. or 6pp. bklist; or 188pp. inc. 2pp. bklist (no pubr, but Phillips's titles), pr by J. Adlard, 23, Bartholomew Close. Pls in different copies various dates in 1804, 1805, 1806 or n.d. Plain brown bds, black roan sp g. or marbled bds, green roan sp g.
[BL; CUL; UCLA; private coll.

Part III, 1815. Illustrated with 20 copper-plates. Title otherwise as Part I, 1815.

13.9×7.8 cm. Pr by W. Lewis, St. John's Square. Pp.[iv]+160+(in some copies) 12pp. Souter's bklist dated 1815, inc. many of Phillips's and Tabart's titles. FP dated Oct. 23 1804, other pls dated as FP or Aug. 11 1804, Jan. 1805, Sep. 14 1806 or n.d., all by Tabart. Marbled bds, red roan sp g.
[BL; UCLA; CUL; Renier, imp.; S 27.2.67/131

(8) THE BOOK OF ENGLISH TRADES, or, Library of the useful arts. With plates. The three parts in one. London: printed by W. Lewis, St. John's-square for Richard Phillips; and sold by John Souter, No.1, Paternoster-row, and by all other booksellers. Price 8s. bound. 1816.

15 cm. Pp.[viii]+210 [212]; 185 [188]; 160. 68 engvd pls, some on wood, pubd by Tabart & Co. and dated 1804, 1805 or 1808. Some pls signed 'Tomanson sculpt'. Black sheep binding.
[PML

In spite of the printer's imprint on the title-page, p.210 carries 'W. Flint, Printer, Old Bailey, London' at its foot.

(9) THE BOOK OF ENGLISH TRADES, and Library of the useful arts. With seventy engravings. A new edition enlarged. London: stereotyped by G. Sidney, Northumberland-street, for Richard Phillips, published by J. Souter, at the Juvenile Library, 73, St. Paul's Church-yard, and to be had of all booksellers. 1818. (Price 9s. bound.)

15.9×9.3 cm. Pp.vi+442+2pp. bklist of Phillips and Souter. Pls, no impt, re-engvd from earlier edns. Preface dated July 27th, 1818.
[UCLA, with 71 engs, bound in black leather, sp g.; V & A; CUL

(10) THE BOOK OF TRADES, and Library of the useful arts. With seventy-four engravings. A new edition enlarged. London: stereotyped by G. Sidney, Northumberland-street, for Richard Phillips; published by J. Souter, at the Juvenile Library 73 St. Paul's Church-yard, and to be had of all booksellers. 1818. (Price 9s. bound.)

15.3×9.8 cm. Pp.vi+442+18 pp. containing 'Five hundred questions' +36pp. Phillips's bklist. Wood-engvd FP+69 full-p. wood-engs (V & A). Plain dark blue bds.
[V & A; S 23.5.83/9 with 74 illusns, 27 engvd from Tabart's edns, 6 others engvd, remainder wood-engvd.

In the two editions dated 1818 the number of plates sometimes differs from the number shown in the title.

C. & J. Rivington published another edition in 1827.

Imitations: The popularity of *The book of trades* encouraged other publishers to imitate it: for instance, Dean and Munday published, *c.*1830, *The book of trades: or, Familiar descriptions of the most useful trades, manufactures, and arts, practised in England* ...; and *The book of trades. With twenty-four coloured plates* was published by William Darton and Son at about the same time. Neither resembles the Tabart/Phillips production.

APPENDIX B

The Preface to William Godwin's Bible Stories

The following book is the production of a parent, who could not find, among the numerous works which for the last twenty years have been published for the use of children, one which he could with complete satisfaction put into the hands of his own.

The works lately written for the perusal of children are very different from those which they were accustomed to read twenty years ago; but are they better or worse? In the following respects they are worse.

1. They are much more incumbered with abstract and general propositions. The meanest narratives formerly written for the use of children, had at least the merit of going straight forward, and of stating in every sentence some fact to keep alive attention, or some picture to engage the imagination. They did not stop at every turn to moralize, in language which no child's understanding can comprehend, and no child's temper will relish.

2. The old books described the real tempers and passions of human beings. Their scenes were often supernatural and impossible, but their personages were of our own species. The modern books on the other hand abound in real scenes, but impossible personages. They would not for the world astonish the child's mind with a giant, a dragon or a fairy, but their young people are all so good, and their old people so sober, so demure, and so rational, that no genuine interest can be felt for their adventures. No two things can be more unlike, than the real inhabitants of the world, and these wonderful personages; their proceedings are destitute of the firmness and vigour of a healthful mind, and their records are artificial, repulsive and insipid.

3. These modern improvers have left out of their system that most essential branch of human nature the imagination. Our youth, according to the most approved recent systems of education, will be excellent geographers, natural historians and mechanics; they will be able to tell you from what part of the globe you receive every article of your furniture; and will explain the process in manufacturing a carpet, converting metals into the utensils of life, and clay into the cups of your tea-table, and the ornaments of your chimney: in a word, they are exactly informed about all those things, which if a man or woman were to live and die without knowing, neither man nor woman would be an atom the worse. Every thing is studied and attended to; except those things which open the heart, which insensibly initiate the learner in the relations and generous offices of society, and enable him to put himself in imagination into the place of his neighbour, to feel his feelings, and to wish his wishes.

Imagination is the ground-plot upon which the edifice of a sound morality must be erected. Without imagination we may have a certain cold and arid circle of principles, but we cannot have sentiments; we may learn by rote a catalogue of rules, and repeat our lesson with the exactness of a parrot, or play over our tricks with the docility of a monkey; but we can neither ourselves love, nor be fitted to excite the love of others.

Imagination is the characteristic of man. The dexterities of logic or of mathematical deduction belong rather to a well-regulated machine; they do not contain in them the living principle of our nature. It is the heart which most deserves to be cultivated: not the rules which may serve us in the nature of a compass to steer through the difficulties of life; but the pulses which beat with sympathy, and qualify us for the habits of charity, reverence and attachment. The intellectual faculty in the mind of youth is fully entitled to the attention of parents and instructors; but parents and instructors will perform their offices amiss, if they assign the first place to that which is only entitled to the second.

Many arguments can scarcely be necessary to recommend the object of the particular selection which is here submitted to the judgement of parents. The following narrations surpass in interest and simplicity any specimens of narration which can be found in the world. Scenes of pastoral life and patriarchal plainness are the fittest that can be imagined to form the first impressions which are to be made upon the memories of children. There is a style now in fashion, and which more or less infects every book for children which has been written for the last hundred years, stamped with the ultimate refinements of a high civilisation, and full of abstract terms and universal propositions. Why should we debauch the taste of our children by presenting this as the first object of their attention and admiration? Why should we confuse their little intellects and vex their little hearts with words, and phrases, and paragraphs, and chapters, which they cannot comprehend?

It has been a modern improvement in the art of education, to take the bibles from our children, and find out other books to put into their hands in their stead. There is some degree of good sense in this. The mysteries of religion, it may be, are not proper topics upon which to exercise the imperfect and infant understandings of children. There are many things dry and repulsive to the apprehensions of children to be found in the bible; and the rituals of the Mosaic system, as well as many other things which might be mentioned, are matters which it is not the part of a Christian parent early to put before his son: he would not wish to disgust him with the abstrusenesses of scripture, before his mind was ripe enough to feel its merits.

But it has not been immediately considered how much we lose for the cultivation of the youthful mind by laying aside the bible. Some of my readers may be old enough to have been educated under the exploded system, and to recollect the infinite delight they experienced in reading the stories of Isaac and Rebekah, of Jacob and Esau, of Joseph and his brethren, as well as many others variously dispersed through the sacred volume. There are no stories in the world so exquisitely fitted to interest the youthful imagination. There is no language in which stories can be told so simple, so dignified, so natural, and so impressive, as the language in which these stories are told.

The stories here selected are entirely detached from the greater mysteries of religion. I would advise that they should be read merely as historical, as tales of ancient times, and a selection made for the pleasure of children. I would reserve for a somewhat riper age the exquisite pleasure of the discovery, that they have a further importance beyond what the child originally apprehended, and belong to a system in which we are so many ways interested.

By following this plan we shall gain a point of the utmost value. The present volume will probably prove to the child a posy of sweet-smelling flowers, without one shrub of evil scent, or a single thorn, to detract from the pleasure it is able to afford. As the child grows up, he cannot fail to entertain a respect for the magazine from which he will ultimately learn that all these beauties are drawn. He will have none but pleasing recollections associated with the sacred volume. This foundation, if built upon by a skilful architect, is perhaps the happiest commencement which can be devised for a sincere and manly sentiment of religion.

One principal impression under which these little volumes have been compiled, has been the desirableness of preserving the exact phraseology which distinguishes our translation of the bible. To detail the histories here recited, in any other language than their own, strikes the ear of the compiler as having something in it of the nature of sacrilege. There are very obvious reasons why the phraseology of the original stories is greatly to be preferred.

1. The translation of the bible in ordinary use among us, is a literal translation, and therefore best preserves that enchanting simplicity and nature which characterise its original writers, and are so admirably in harmony with the manners and adventures which these writers record. 2. Our translation of the bible being now two hundred years old, and having been made precisely at that period when our language assumed a fixed and determinate form, the phraseology has an air of venerableness and antiquity about it, which gives it a peculiar charm. 3. Every interesting tale becomes associated in the memory of its hearer with its own appropriate dress, and will not bear to be clothed in a new and second dress, without giving to the mind a very painful and injurious sensation. I am therefore of opinion that the narratives of the bible should by all means be first conveyed to the youthful mind, in the very words which most strictly belong to them, and which must unavoidably be their clothing, at the period when the boy-student comes to put on the character of the man.

For these reasons it is upon very few occasions, and with extreme reluctance, that any single word has been exchanged in the course of these stories. Of what use then, an inattentive reader might ask, is this compilation? Of the greatest. No person has been accustomed to the intercourse of children, if he has at the same time been impressed with any sentiment of discrimination and scruple, without anxiously wishing that, even in the books best calculated for the use of children, he had the power, by the touch as it were of a fairy wand, of separating the substance of the book, from those accidental appendages which on various accounts, as too minute or too general, too dry or too elevated, he perceives to be entirely foreign to his object.

It is this separation which is attempted in the present compilation. The compiler recollected in the first place what were the stories which had seized most forcibly upon his youthful imagination. He was educated according to the old mode, and had read through every word of the Old and New

Testaments before he was seven years of age. The memory therefore of his early impressions served him as a guide in the sketch of his undertaking. Having drawn these stories together, he soon felt that with a little ingenuity and contrivance they might be made to form a sort of regular chain of the history of most of the more memorable events and revolutions of the Jewish affairs. This idea therefore he immediately incorporated into his plan. No attempt is here made to enter into that detail and subtlety of explanation which might be required in the genealogist or the chronologer; yet enough is given to enable the youthful reader of this compilation to recal his old impressions when he comes to peruse the history at large, and to say, With the grand incidents and outlines of this story I am already acquainted. The consequence will be, that, if he were to live to the age of the patriarchs themselves, he would never cease to recollect, and to recollect with delight, the great adventures of their lives.

One alteration which runs through the present volumes is the substitution of the word 'Jehovah,' in lieu of the English translation 'the LORD.' The most uninformed reader can scarcely need to be told that, wherever the word LORD in capital letters occurs in our received translation of the Old Testament, the word in the Hebrew is Jehovah. I shall therefore scarcely be censured for rendering our literal English translation of the bible, in this one point more literal than the translators themselves have left it. By this method I have put it in the power of the parents or instructors to explain the story in the manner which to their different modes of thinking shall appear most expedient. Those parents or instructors who are of opinion that we ought not to attempt to initiate the mind at a very early age in the higher mysteries of religion, will explain the word Jehovah as the individual designation of the God of the Jews. They can have no more reasonable objection to this term, than to the names of the Gods of the Greeks in Homer, or the Gods of the Latins in Ovid; and need unfold nothing more to the scholar, than that general idea of invisible agents and superior natures, which has existed in all ages and countries, unless a few of the most savage nations are to be excepted. The God of the Jews is the competitor and adversary of the Gods of the surrounding nations: in all contests between the parties, their opponents reposed their confidence in their national divinities, and the Jews in him who was regarded as the protector, and who had fixed the religious homage, of their earliest progenitors. Those parents and instructors on the other hand, who are of opinion that youth cannot be too early initiated in the sublimest doctrines of Christianity, and that we ought particularly to seize upon the tender minds of children to make upon them those profound impressions by which their eternal welfare may be decided, will of course expound the term Jehovah by the purest and most spiritualised definition of a first cause, and will inform their pupils that this is the awful and incommunicable name by which the first cause himself has thought proper to make himself known to the children of men.

APPENDIX C

Tabart's catalogue, 1801

Notes on the contents

CLASS THE FIRST

I. As soon as children are able distinctly to articulate the common sounds of speech, we should begin to make them acquainted with the LETTERS of the ALPHABET.

The following are the Books and Contrivances for this use, here on Sale:

Contrivances: The Letters of the Alphabet, comprising a wooden Frame, to be alternately dissected and put together.

Alphabetical Cards – Best set, 1.0.   Second Set, 0.9.

II. When they can read the Alphabet at sight, they proceed to spell and pronounce Monosyllables, &c. The best books for this use take, first, the easiest syllable sounds, – advancing from these to the most difficult; and begin as soon as possible to bring before the child monosyllables, dissyllables, &c. forming words in common use . . .

III. Another set of the books for this Age, are those commonly known as SPELLING-BOOKS. They comprehend Lessons and Tables of Syllables, from the simplest to the most complex. They should exhibit all the different species of the combinations of letters in the language: and the learner is to be taught to connect these readily, with all the corresponding sounds. They likewise join Grammar, which explains the species and relations of words, with reading and enunciation . . .

CLASS SECOND

Books for Children from Five to Eight Years of Age.

Between the Ages of Two Years and Five, Children, if tolerably docile, and in the hands of tender and judicious parents and teachers, may learn to read, at sight, almost all the common words and sentences in the English language. Grace, emphasis, the happy inflexions of voice, that significant expression in reading, which arises from habitual knowledge of passion, and from a feeling intelligence of what is read, – they cannot yet be expected to display. But of the dispositions of others around them, of the common utensils and transactions of life, of the appearances too of external nature, they have acquired some knowledge. Their curiosity is awakened. They are now, in some sort, qualified to adopt *our* notions, and to enter into *our* views. They begin to be capable of the distinctions of taste, of the perceptions of morality, of the sublime ideas of religion.

From the age of FIVE to that of EIGHT Years, they will be well employed in acquiring grace, ease, and emphatic propriety of enunciation in reading; in learning the principles of Grammar, and trying their first exercises in English Composition; in enlarging their acquaintance with the objects of material nature; in gaining a farther knowledge of moral duty from precept and historical example; and in having their minds opened to the truths of religion.

From the age of FIVE to that of EIGHT Years, they will be well employed in acquiring grace, ease, and emphatic propriety of enunciation in reading; in learning the principles of Grammar, and trying their first exercises in English Composition; in enlarging their acquaintance with the objects of material nature; in gaining a farther knowledge of moral duty from precept and historical example; and in having their minds opened to the truths of religion.

V. It is to be regretted, that we possess very few books, in which RELIGIOUS TRUTH is skilfully simplified to the Capacity of Children of between FIVE and EIGHT Years of Age. This circumstance has given rise to a very *erroneous* and *fatal*, though extensively prevalent opinion, – 'that young people are incapable of religion, till they attain considerable maturity of years.' – This opinion, persons of taste, piety, and literary ability, are called upon to refute, by producing suitable books for the early initiation of the young in the knowledge of their relations to a Divine Being . . .

CLASS THIRD
At the Age of EIGHT Years, well-educated Children may be expected to be capable of reading and speaking their native language with ease and propriety, – to possess some knowledge of the obligations of morality and religion, – and to have even a considerable acquaintance with the common practices of life, and with the appearances of external nature. Their understandings may have acquired no small vigour, correctness, and facility of reasoning. Their memories may have become not only quick and lively, but steadily tenacious. Imagination will be to them, in no small degree, vivid and expansive. They may know the grammatical laws, as well as the words and phrases of the English language; and may be therefore prepared to enter upon the study of such other languages as it shall be desirable for them to learn.

Between this age, then, and that of FIFTEEN Years, the Writing of *English Letters*, – the Keeping of *Books of Accounts*, – the *Classical Languages*, Antient and Modern, – the Elements of mixed and pure *Mathematics*, the higher branches of Natural and Civil *History*, – *Rhetorick, Logic, Moral Philosophy*, – *Natural Philosophy* and *Chemistry*, – with the applications of the Sciences to the Fine, the Mechanical, and the Chemical *Arts*, – and above all, the Elements and practical Power of *Religious Truth*, – are to be the subjects of the study of young persons. They are to learn, also, the *Art of Writing*, with those other arts, which, as either useful or elegant accomplishments, have been introduced into our system of education.

Different Destinations in Life require diversity of Study.

From the age of EIGHT also, if not earlier, it becomes necessary for the *different Sexes* to receive each an education in part peculiar, in its books, its instruments, and the modes in which it is conducted . . .

[The writer lists The *Monthly Preceptor* – apparently in course of production. Also] 'The Monthly Magazine, and other Monthly Publications . . . will be supplied by Mr. T. with the greatest care, and on the most reasonable terms.'

[In the list of recommended French books some lighter food for the mind is supplied by such titles as *Le Petit Grandison*, St. Pierre's *La Chaumière Indienne*, Le Nouveau Robinson, Marmontel's *Belisaire, Histoire de Gil Blas de Santillane*, by Le Sage.

[Among books on natural history, geography, etc. are Bewick's *History of Quadrupeds* and of *Birds*, Damberger's *Travels Through the Interior Regions of Africa* (an account of a series of the most extraordinary journies ever performed through the unknown interior parts of Africa, by a German Carpenter).

[Thereafter, the lists contain books more suited to adult, or young adult readers and students. Nearly 600 educational books are recommended. But at the end comes a list of much lighter literature for children: many Newbery and Marshall books, Robinson Crusoe, the Kilners, Darton's books, Goody Two Shoes, Fairy Tales, *The Pretty Pilgrim* (!), Watt's *Divine and Moral Songs*, Phillips's *British Plutarch*, an interesting list ('just published') of Marshall's titles, including Lady Fenn's (336 copperplates, douceurs), the *Doll's Library, Infant's Cabinet of Beasts and Birds, Infant's Library* and other little libraries, jig-saws, puzzles, colouring boxes, games, etc.

APPENDIX D

Some notes on the illustrations for the 'Silver Penny' and the 'Little Man and Little Maid'

Brian Alderson

I INTRODUCTION

Peculiarities in the engraved illustrations for early nineteenth-century picture books have been recognized for some time. In her *Check-List* of the publications of John Harris, 1976, Marjorie Moon tabulates the changes in two well-known examples: the wholesale substitution of new pictures in *The Butterfly's Ball* of 1808 (check-list 725 [7]) and the complicated tinkerings that went on with *Old Mother Hubbard* (559 [1]–[2]). Far from being isolated examples, however, these two little books may be seen as tokens of a widespread practice, the delineation of which is only hesitantly being incorporated into the catalogues of librarians, collectors and tradesmen.

The main reason for the slow growth of our understanding of this aspect of book-publishing is the scarcity of material. Not only are many of these picture books rare in any edition, they are also (by that fact) even more rarely found in locations which allow two or more copies to be placed side-by-side, compared, and – where necessary – differentiated. When such opportunities do arise, as here, a number of otherwise unnoticed characteristics may be brought to light which help to fill out our awareness of both the production and the reception of the book in question. Relationships between editions may be established, and steps may be taken towards determining such matters as priority of issue.

Much remains tentative however. In the following notes on two of Benjamin Tabart's more ambitious picture books some contrasts and comparisons are drawn which will, I hope, help to refine our bibliographical understanding of these productions. Nevertheless, by no means everything can be explained, and a fuller clarification of the circumstances surrounding this publishing movement must await first a closer study of the work of commercial intaglio printers at the start of the nineteenth century, and second, the building-up of more case-histories like these in order that a better insight into trade practice may be gained.

II A TRUE HISTORY OF A LITTLE OLD WOMAN, WHO FOUND A SILVER PENNY (1806)

As the first picture-book manifestation of the traditional story of 'The Old Woman and her Pig' *A True History* is an important children's book; and as an example of publishing ingenuity its panoramic conclusion is a notable *coup*. In terms of book-production, though, the book clearly gave Tabart some problems and these become apparent when three separate printings are compared. (By great good fortune, all three copies are in the Opie Collection and may therefore be examined together without recourse to laborious note-taking and the inevitable to-ing and fro-ing after material scattered across several collections.)

The first printing, (96A(1) in this bibliography) appears to be that by C. Squire, with a title-page dated 1806 and with the plate-paper watermarked 1805. There are twelve hand-coloured engraved plates, printed back to back on six leaves, and these are interspersed with ten leaves of text, fourteen of whose pages are printed and six are blank. This text-block is followed by the four-panel engraved panorama that completes the story. Advertising pages *ad lib.* may then be added.

Now that is a fairly complex production job, which must also have been tricky to cost, since it was designed to compete with its picture-book rivals at the standard 'hand-coloured' price of 1s.6d. Financial pressure may therefore be the chief explanation for shortcomings in the first printing – hastily put on the market to establish copyright and recoup capital outlay. The decision to print the engravings back-to-back may well have been taken in order to reduce the amount of plate-paper used, but it led to some rather messy backing-up. At the same time the engraving of at least four of the double-pages was extremely rough, with only the barest suggestion of such details as foliage and house-windows etc. – all patched over with hastily-applied water-colour.

Careless production, though, only becomes fully apparent when the book is compared to what is presumably a later 1806 issue, printed on paper without a watermark. Here the hand of the engraver and/or etcher* has clearly been at work on the plates and much more background detail has been added to the pictures. The colouring continues to be unreliable – the red of the Old Woman's cloak is often blotchy – but this second issue of the book would seem to come nearest to fulfilling the publisher's plans. A further edition in 1808, printed by W. Marchant (96A(2)) shows that the detail acquired by the plates in the second printing has not worn well. Moreover a thinner (cheaper) paper has been used for the printing and the colouring is still patchy.

III MEMOIRS OF THE LITTLE MAN AND THE LITTLE MAID (1807)

If Tabart made a rod for his own back out of the *Little Old Woman* it did not deter him from further experiments, and these attained a climax of complexity in the *Memoirs* (109). Here we are again fortunate in being able to bring much evidence together at a single table, but what might thus appear to aid our understanding of Tabart's publishing methods serves rather to increase

---

* Many of the plates in many of the children's books of this period were prepared by a mixture of engraving and etching, the two techniques being easily distinguished by the different qualities of line that are gained from graver and from needle. For brevity's sake 'engraving' here may also stand for 'engraving and etching'.

puzzlement and to require the construction of a highly conjectural scenario. The salient works to be considered are as follows:

(a) a preliminary printed text of the work, set below twelve original water-colour drawings on thin card, with dimensions c.180×130mm (private coll.);

(b) a copy of the presumed first edition printed by C. Squire, (109(1) above), dated 1807 on cover and title-page, with plates dated May, 1807, watermarked 1805, issued without music (Osborne Coll.);

(c) a copy of the same (109(2) above) with the text paper watermarked 1806, issued with text on pp.1–12 and with the plates interleaved by Dr Calcott's musical setting (private coll.);

(d) a copy of what the cover title calls 'a new edition', printed by C. Squire (109(3)) dated 1808 on cover and title-page. One issue (a) retains the May 1807 plates (not seen), but another issue (b) has entirely different plates, dated March 1, 1807 [sic]. One leaf of these is watermarked 1805. The six leaves following the title-page now consist of Calcott's music, and the plates are interleaved by six leaves (i.e. twelve pages) of text (private coll.).

[NB. Unfortunately the copy seen of this last item has had its Plate XI cut from the leaf at some time in the past, and the resultant large square gap has been filled by a plate from the May 1807 sequence, but re-dated 'London Published May 1816 by B. Tabart 85 Piccadilly', i.e. the edition at 109(4).]

After a prolonged examination of these four specimens I have attempted the following annotated chronology of events in the book's publishing history:

(i)   The book is conceived as a work of twelve leaves (perhaps accompanied by music) with a page size of approx. 170×95mm.

Precedent already existed for picture books in this format, for instance Wallis's two-volume *Picture Exhibition* (1801–2) and John Marshall's 32-page picture-book edition of *The history of a great many boys and girls* (1803) and *The wren* (1806). John Harris would later use it extensively for his large format 'cabinet' editions.

(ii)   As a first step in production, the text of the twelve stanzas is set-up and printed on the twelve sheets of card and a water-colour drawing is made above each stanza, with the stanza number added in ms.

The printing could well have been done by Squire (or Marchant who printed *A Silver Penny*). The type is a long-primer of 'modern-cut' such as both printers used in their advertisement leaves for these books. The artist responsible for the water-colours is not known, but he may well have worked on other books such as Harris's *Peter Prim's Pride* (1810) which has stylistic similarities.

(iii)   As work proceeds a new size is adopted (eventually to be 138×120mm.) which will allow for a letterpress text, engraved illustrations, and separately printed engraved music.

Although roughly square in shape this format is somewhat larger than the 'standard' size of square picture book that became popular with Harris's *Old*

Mother Hubbard of 1805. The decision to add music appears to be unprecedented and points again to Tabart's interest in experimentation. The Godwin firm was later to adapt the idea by putting a fold-out leaf of music into the picture-book edition of *Beauty and the Beast* (1811), which was to sell for no less than 5s.6d. coloured.

(iv)   A set of twelve engravings is cut with the date March 1, 1807. These feature the two figures of the ballad as they appear in the water-colour drawings and may well have been quickly traced from the drawings on to the copper. The cutting is hastily done with a raw vigour and various background details, not in the drawing, have been added in rough freehand: chairs, pictures, a mirror, etc. The most significant addition is the figure of a tradesman ('the butcher or the baker') making off through a doorway in Plate VIII, where the water-colour drawing only shows the fighting couple and a tipped-up chair and an overturned stool.

Lateral correspondence between these engravings and the water-colour originals is inconsistent. Plates I–IV are reversed; plates V–VIII are 'positive'; plate IX is reversed and plates X and XII are 'positive' [plate XI has been replaced by the later, 1816, version]. In so far as anything at all can be read from this it may be that the engravings were being done four to a plate (see section ix below) with the tracings being placed different ways round, but that does not explain the inconsistency in the final group – an inconsistency which precludes any watertight case for there to be a direct link between these two engravings and those dated May 1807 (Section vi).

(v)   Having been engraved, these plates are printed on heavy plate paper. Again, though, there seems to have been trouble over plates X and XI which have been printed on a thinner stock (visible for plate XI, even though the illustration has been excised). This thinner stock carries the watermark on Plate X: TURNER'S 05.

(vi)   Perhaps because of engraving problems, perhaps because the cutting was not felt to be elegant enough for a prestige picture-book, a new set of plates is commissioned, dated May 1807. These show a correspondence with the water-colour drawings which is much closer than that found in most of the March engravings. Not only has much of the extraneous detail been omitted but present-day tracings of the drawings tally almost exactly with the engraved pictures, and certain details (e.g. the floor-line) correspond where they did not do so in the March set. The engraving is now of much superior quality too, with the heavy line-work of the March set replaced by controlled and delicately-handled stipple engraving.

In the case of plate VIII, though, a strange thing has happened. As noted above, the water-colour drawing for this plate shows the tipped chair and the overturned stool but not the disappearing tradesman. In the finished engraving, however, the stool and chair have been omitted and the tradesman has been exactly copied from the March 1807 plate.

The two-way comparison between the drawings and the March engravings may at this point appear to be beyond all explanation, especially when it is observed that the May 1807 engravings do not regularly match the lateral organisation of the drawings. Plates I–IV are 'positive'; plates V–VIII are reversed; and plates IX–XII are again 'positive'. No immediate reason suggests itself for this, especially since the engravings remain closer to the drawings (except for the peculiar plate VIII). But as will be seen at section ix below, the difference may have been caused by the engravings having been done on different plates.

(vii)   These May 1807 plates are initially printed on paper with the watermark JOHN WISE 1805 and as such they appear in:

(viii)   The first edition of *Memoirs*, published in 1807, without music, but with the notice on the verso of the title-page that the ballad would be 'speedily' set to music.

(ix)   Later in the year the edition with music interleaved is published. The book's complex collation may have led to difficulties, however, and we find in at least one copy that plates V–VIII are printed on a thinner paper than the rest of the plates. Thanks to this peculiarity, it becomes possible to argue that the illustrations have been prepared four to a plate on three plates. (The alternative combination of two plates, one with four and one with eight engravings, cannot be entirely ruled out. What is significant is that the 'difficult' sequence of pictures, V–VIII, received separate treatment.)

Mr Iain Bain has suggested that the 'baffling varieties of paper' may have resulted from the practice of printing engraved work in small batches, on demand.

(x)   Perhaps because of demand for the *Memoirs*, perhaps because of problems over the wearing of the May engravings, the March set is called into service for the 'new edition' of 1808, with its somewhat simpler collation, although the May engravings also seem to have been called upon at this time with the regular make-up.

Since this article was written however a copy of the 1808 'new edition' has come to light, without music but with the May 1807 plates (109 3A). This gives rise to speculation that the March cuts may have been in use simultaneously for editions that were made up with music.

(xi)   Once this 'emergency edition' has sold out, production continues with the superior stippled plates of May 1807. These are redated when the book is published from the Piccadilly address in 1816, and they continue in use down to an edition issued by Souter (*c.*1826), who replaced Tabart's imprint on the plates with his own.

If any conclusion can be drawn from this rather opaque analysis it must surely be a trite *caveat lector*, or *caveat emptor*. The publishers of these little picture books were inconsistent in their designation of editions and were liable to mislead in their dating and re-dating of plates. A book, with all the appearance of being 'early', may be later than we think, and the discovery of its true place may only be finally established through the expansion of our knowledge of the number and location of copies. The often expensive business of comparison can then get under way.

Chronological index

The first-known editions of titles carrying Tabart's name. Undated books are placed as accurately as possible.

Perrault, C. *La barbe bleue*
———— *Blue Beard*
———— *Cendrillon*
———— *Cinderella*
———— *Hop o' my Thumb*
———— *Puss in Boots, and Diamonds and toads*
———— *Riquet with the Tuft*
———— *The sleeping beauty*
Proverbs
The renowned history of Valentine and Orson
[Rowse, E.] *Mythological amusement*
The story of Griselda
Tabart's collection of popular stories
A tour through England
A view of universal history
The wonders of the microscope

1805

Aladdin; or The wonderful lamp
Ali Baba; or, The forty thieves
The book of games
The book of the ranks and dignities ...
Defoe, D. *The life and adventures of Robinson Crusoe*
[Ella, A.] *Visits to the Leverian Museum*
[Fenwick, E.] *Presents for good boys*
[————] *Visits to the Juvenile Library*
Goldsmith, Rev. J. *Geography, on a popular plan*
Jauffret, L. F. *The little hermitage*
[Kilner, E.] *A visit to London*
Marmontel, J.-F. *Belisarius*
Mince pies for Christmas
Nourjahad
Perrin, J. B. *A new and easy method of learning ... French*
Richard Coeur de Lion
[Salignac de la Mothe Fénélon, F. de] *The adventures of Telemachus*
Songs for the nursery
[Swift, J.] *Gulliver's travels*
The voyages of Sinbad the sailor
The wonders of the telescope

1806

Blair, Rev. D. *Reading exercises*
[Fenwick, E.] *The class book*
Goldsmith, Rev. J. *The geographical copy-book*
[Jenner, I.] *Fortune's football*
Johnson, W. R. *The history of England, in easy verse*
[Kilner, D.?] *Jingles*

[Lewis, M. G.] *A true history of a little old woman ...*
Mavor, W. F. *Select lives of Plutarch*
[Semple, E.] *The magic lantern*
Somerville, E. *Leading strings to knowledge*

1807

Blair, Rev. D. *The first catechism for children*
Cockle, M. *The juvenile journal*
[Dorset, C. A.] *The lion's masquerade*
Entertaining instructions
The history of Jack and the bean-stalk
Johnson, W. R. *The history of Greece, in easy verse*
Memoirs of the little man and the little maid
Peacock, L. *Ambrose and Eleanor*
———— *A chronological abridgment of universal history*
———— *The Knight of the Rose*
[Perrault, C.] *The history of little Red Riding-Hood, in verse*
Taylor, J. *Ornithologia curioso*
[Wollstonecraft, M.] *Original stories from real life*
Woodland, M. *Tales for mothers and daughters*

1808

The adventures of Grimalkin
[Arnold, S. J.] *The tyger's theatre*
[Bertholet, G.] *Leçons choisies dans la morale ...*
Carey, J. *Learning better than house and land*
The child's true friend
Cockle, M. *The fishes grand gala*
The history of discoveries and inventions
Johnson, W. R. *The history of Rome. In easy verse*
Joyce, Rev. J. *A key to Joyce's Arithmetic*
———— *A system of practical arithmetic*
Lenoir, –. *The logographic-emblematical French spelling-book*
The lioness's ball
The lioness's rout
[Lynch, –]. *The nursery concert*
Natural history of the robin-red-breast
A numeration, addition and multiplication table
The school atlas
[Sharpe, R. S.] *The conjuror*

1809

Cockle, M. *The three gifts*
Defoe, D. *Robinson Crusoe*
 [harlequinade]
The dog of knowledge
The exile [harlequinade]
Hoole, B. *La fête de la rose*
Johnson, W. R. *Goldsmith's . . .*
 Geography rendered into easy verse
The juvenile miscellany
Mother Goose [harlequinade]
The pagan mythology
[Perrault, C.] *Blue Beard* (longer
 version)
Polish tyrant [harlequinade]
R. R. *The assembled alphabet*
———— *The invited alphabet*
Robin Hood [harlequinade]
Simple stories, in verse
Tabart's moral tales
*The true history of a little boy who cheated
 himself*
Woodland, M. *Bear and forbear*
———— *Matilda Mortimer*
———— *Rose and Agnes*

1810

Bertholet, G. *Soirées d'automne*
Fenwick, E. *Infantine stories*

The force of example
Hoole, B. *Tales, in verse*
[Kilner, E.] *Scenes at home*
Parnell's Hermit [harlequinade]
[Perrault, C.] *Hop o' my Thumb*
 [harlequinade]
R. R. *Infantile erudition*
Six stories, in English and French
[Taylor, A. and J.] *Signor Topsy-Turvy's
 wonderful magic lantern*
Woodland, M. *A tale of warning*

1812

[Dallaway, R. C.] *Observations on . . .
 education*
Sandham, E. *The perambulations of a bee
 and a butterfly*
Thornton, R. J. *School Virgil*

1817

Genlis, S. F. *The Palace of Truth*
The school magazine
Tabart, B. *Fairy tales*

1818

Tabart, B. *The national spelling-book*
———— *Popular fairy-tales*

Index